RAW TALENT

RAW TALENT

THE ADULT FILM INDUSTRY AS SEEN BY ITS MOST POPULAR MALE STAR

JERRY BUTLER

AS TOLD TO ROBERT RIMMER AND CATHERINE TAVEL

PROMETHEUS BOOKS

BUFFALO, NEW YORK

 Inquiries should be addressed to Prometheus Books, 700 East Amherst Street, Buffalo, New York 14215; 1-800-421-0351 (in New York State, 716-837-2475).

Library of Congress Card Catalog No. 89-42532
ISBN: 0-87975-530-X

Contents

CONTENTS

Foreword

All of us can create our own sexual fantasies. How? Simply by thinking about things that arouse us. Many of us, however, do even better with some outside assistance. This assistance can come in a number of ways: We can have someone whisper "dirty" words into our ear; we can examine an erotic work of art or observe a burlesque dancer; we can read a story, a novel, or even a comic strip; we can view a movie or videocassette. These are only some of the most prevalent ways. There are others. If a man fantasizes about being a woman, for example, he can dress up as a woman; that is, he can become a transvestite. And if this course is not open to him, he can read books or view movies about transvestites. Imagination is flexible.

In the not-too-distant past, those who sought assistance in creating sexual fantasies depended on the written or spoken word, or on personal involvement, either as a voyeur or as a willing participant with a partner. Recent technology has changed all this—first with the telephone (anonymous calls, dial-a-porn), then with radio, movies, television, and now video- and audiotapes.

A large segment of our society regards the kind of assistance I have described as *pornography.* The word comes from the Greek: *pornographos,* "the writing of or about prostitutes," which was one of the earliest forms of erotic fantasy. Pornography is certainly nothing new. Ancient Chinese, Hindu, and Greek cultures have all passed down to us examples of pornographic literature and art. Throughout history, such writings formed an important part of our literary tradition, although some pornographic works now seem quite chaste—in the sense that they avoid the use of explicit sexual language or those proverbial four-letter words. One of the most famous pornographic classics of the eighteenth century, John Cleland's *Fanny Hill,* is an example of this type of erotic writing. Other novels of that time were more explicit. Regardless of their sexual explicitness, however, *all* such pornography was usually officially banned during much of the late nineteenth and early twentieth centuries in this country.

But attitudes and standards change, and most of the erotic classics of the past are now legally available today, even if many have yet to be translated into English. The process of legalization has not been an even one, however. Motion pictures were slow to introduce overt sexuality. Indeed, for a long time movies shown in the United States had to pass through a censorship process that eliminated profanity and long kisses, let alone nudity and sexual contact. By 1940s movie standards, almost everything shown in cinemas today would be deemed pornographic. While today's television standards are not as harsh as that, network television lags behind other media when it comes to presenting erotic fantasy.

Despite this history of censorship, movies depicting overt sexuality have always circulated underground. Such movies were staples at stag parties held by otherwise "respectable" groups of men in such places as American Legion halls. Most of these films were very crudely filmed and edited—but that didn't diminish their popularity, which always rested on their sexual scenes. Eventually, one could purchase or rent such stag films for home-showing, which allowed women to view them as well.

As public standards evolved and official censorship gradually lessened, such movies came out into the open, first through theaters that specialized in showing such films. Then, as the standard movies became more open about sexuality, specialty sex films—those films depicting homosexuality, bisexuality, group sex, etc.—began to be made. Originally much of the audience for what came to be called "hard core" porno films was overwhelmingly male, usually young men who weren't married yet or who didn't have regular sexual partners, many of whom would be aroused by practically any overt portrayal of sex. A second group of male viewers was composed of older men who for some reason had difficulty becoming sexually aroused enough by their regular sexual partners to engage successfully in sexual intercourse. The fantasies they were able to create with the help of such "hard core" films aroused them as their regular companions could not.

The importance of fantasy has been recognized by a growing number of sex therapists, who have found the use of sexually explicit films helpful in dealing with the problems of many of their clients. In fact, specialty filmmakers have begun to make sexually explicit films specifically for use by therapists. And commercial filmmakers, realizing that there is even greater audience out there than they previously had thought, have also entered the field in larger numbers. The result: more competition among filmmakers, and better films. Pornographic movies now very often have engaging story lines, and professionals have replaced amateurs in every aspect of filming and production, from the acting to the directing and photography. As quality has improved and the audience has expanded, some of pornography's actors and actresses have achieved justifiable fame, as has Jerry Butler. No longer is triple-X fare populated by anonymous copulators. We see real people.

Inevitably, as our attachment to these movie characters has grown stronger, we have wanted to learn about the motivations, thoughts, and feelings of the actors and actresses who portrayed them. Why do they act in these films? Do they feel ashamed? Do they view themselves as prostitutes? Do they have families, children? And how do they get involved in this type of acting? Do they have problems getting (and staying) sexually aroused in front of a camera and crew?

These questions are almost never addressed in those fanzines that typically service the "adult-film" market. In *Raw Talent,* with uncommon frankness and clarity, they *are* addressed.

* * *

Jerry Butler's *Raw Talent* inaugurates a new series of "sexual autobiographies" that Prometheus Books is planning to publish. This series will tell the stories of others on the sexual margin of society, those whose fantasies are often stigmatized by words like "abnormal," "immoral," and "criminal." For the most part such individuals—transvestites, prostitutes, sexual surrogates, and transsexuals, for example—live both a public and a secret life, with their sexual identities hidden from most of those around them. (This is not quite true for Jerry Butler, as he reminds you here, because he is often recognized by those who've seen him on videos or film. Still, in most groups he can easily be anonymous.)

The important thing to emphasize is this: In many ways these people are not that different from you or me. What makes them different is that their sexual fantasies are not expressed in the same way many of ours are.

As a scholar, it is not my job to judge. My job is to understand. Jerry Butler's book will be elemental to anyone who wishes to understand the thinking, the emotions, and the very real work of the male porno star.

—Vern Bullough
State University of New York
Distinguished Professor
Dean, School of Natural and Social Sciences,
State University College of New York at Buffalo

Preface

My cousin Billy calls me a "porn virgin," and I suppose that title's pretty accurate. Here I am, active on the fringes of the erotic film industry, a woman who married the first man she ever made love to (two men and six years later). I've always been fascinated by the human body, but the nuns at St. Patrick's Grammar School taught me that sex was wicked. My red-faced parents evaded my questions with generalities, explaining that women had a "special opening." But I had no idea where this "special opening" was, and I kept hoping I would grow one soon. Imagine my disappointment when I discovered that it was the same old orifice!

Given my early curiosity about sexuality, it's not surprising that the first tape my husband Al and I popped into our VCR was an adult film. As a kid, I knew Dad sometimes went to the Deluxe Theater to see "dirty movies." Like my father, I became interested in adult films, but my absorption became more than just an occasional viewing. Renting them frequently, I became intrigued by the people who very kindly bared their behinds and shared their sexuality with me. Among them was a handsome actor who went by the name of "Jerry Butler." Not only did he have a very friendly penis, but he added a dimension to his roles that few people in pornos were able to do. There was a lot of eye contact, verbal communication, and laughter in his sex scenes. Jerry seemed like a guy you'd find on the stool next to you in the neighborhood bar.

Despite my self-taught adult-film awareness, it was still

hit-or-miss picking out movies of quality. My big toe was getting sore from pressing the fast-forward button on the VCR. Then I discovered Bob Rimmer's *X-Rated Videotape Guide.* At last, I had found intelligently written reviews of adult films, over 1,500 of them—and not one, but *two* photos of Richard Pacheco! Bob's critiques were comparable to Rex Reed's, Leonard Maltin's, or any other "legitimate" film reviewer's. Still, as I glanced through the book, I saw it was an innocent victim of a bad editor. My background in publishing wouldn't let me ignore incorrect photo credits and actors' names spelled three different ways in the same paragraph. There was a picture of Bob in the book, and he seemed to be a pleasant, distinguished-looking older man, definitely not a raincoat-toting lecher. So I thought it would be safe to write to him of my simultaneous joy and disappointment.

And, to my surprise, he wrote back! (Even Leonard Maltin didn't do that.) And a few weeks later, I received a call from the program coordinator for the "Ask Dr. Ruth" television show. Bob was scheduled to be a guest and thought I might like to be a participating member in the studio audience. Would I go? I said yes, but I was terrified.

The show was taped during one of the biggest snowstorms New York had had in years. Al and I practically skied crosstown from the subway. As we thawed out in the "green room" (which was beige), we met Bob very briefly. On camera, with my lower lip trembling, I admitted that I watched and rented adult films, and that I liked them, too! There was much confusion after the taping, so I didn't get the chance to speak to Bob again.

The show aired on Valentine's Day. Al convinced me to call Bob the next day to thank him for inviting us. Again, I was scared.

"His number's not on the letterhead," I said with a sigh of relief.

"Call information."

"It's probably not listed."

But it was. As it turned out, in the hurried "green room" introductions Bob hadn't realized I was "*that* Cathy." Impressed with my letters and my credentials, he asked whether I'd be interested in typing and editing his latest 250 reviews. Of course I would! This man had written eighteen books, including *The Harrad Experiment*, and he was asking me to work with him.

Typing the reviews was no easy task. I wrestled with Bob's chickenscratch and finally came out the victor. But it was a labor of love and fun. So began our unlikely partnership: a seventy-year-old retired businessman from Quincy, Massachusetts, and a twenty-seven-year-old secretary/aspiring writer from Brooklyn. But it worked. It worked beautifully—thanks to the postal service and the telephone company.

Nothing had prepared me for Bob's "You'll never guess who called me!" a few months later. He explained the proposition for Jerry Butler's book. I was ecstatic that he'd even consider me to collaborate with them. The next night, there was a message on my answering machine from Jerry. I called him the following day. He and Lisa, his wife, stopped by.

At first I was starstuck. I couldn't believe Jerry Butler was at my front door. After all, I had seen him naked. I even knew the kinds of faces he made when he climaxed. But Jerry made himself right at home, telling me how clean my apartment smelled but criticizing me for not taking the supermarket tags off the apples in the fruitbowl—all in the same breath. Jerry, Lisa, and I talked for hours. It was a full, overwhelming visit. When I walked them to the door, my knees were shaking. This was going to be an amazing project, but did he want me? A big hug from Jerry was my answer.

The two of them came back the following day with three blank cassette tapes. We sat down with cookies from an Italian bakery and a fresh pot of decaf (Jerry was so animated, he certainly didn't need caffeine!). What unraveled before me was more than I had ever imagined. It was like watching a flower bloom in time-lapse photography. Jerry talked and laughed and shouted. He paced the floor like a wounded lion. He took an orange from the fruitbowl (I had hastily removed the store tags before his arrival), tossed it from hand to hand, and squashed it in his fist when the words became painful. At one point, he was crying. I didn't know what to do. I wanted to hold him, comfort him, but the tape was rolling and I didn't want him to stop talking. I reached across the table and gently held his hand. He squeezed my fingers and continued.

To study his acting, I rented as many of Jerry's videotapes as I could find. Suddenly, the sex scenes became difficult to watch. In my mind, I had separated him into two people: Jerry Butler, who made porno movies, and Paul Siederman, who was my friend. It was Jerry who fucked the turkey carcass in *Raw Talent,* Paul who squeezed an orange in my kitchen. After Paul and Lisa returned to Los Angeles, an uneven patter of cassettes would come through the mail, despite earthquakes and moments of doubt. People told my husband they wouldn't allow *their* wives to work with a porno actor. Paul's parents were afraid of what he'd say about the family. But we still went on.

A standard ninety-minute cassette could take me as long as five hours to transcribe—depending on how fast Paul talked. And could he talk fast! Sometimes I had to slow down the machine until he sounded like the Jolly Green Giant on Valium, but doing that lost his intensity and emotion. Drawn to the work, I soon became obsessive. I couldn't wait to find out what was coming next. I typed in the stickiness of the summer, barefoot and naked. I typed in the winter, wearing long johns, sweaters, and fingerless gloves. Working for hours without a break, my fingers ached from stretching across the keyboard. My head throbbed from the uncomfortable headphones. Al often felt neglected, so I'd go into the living room and kiss him, then go back to the typewriter.

Following my notes, and asking him questions, Lisa was

at Paul's side in California as he dictated most of the tapes. Sometimes she was so quiet I hardly knew she was there until she uttered a word of assurance or encouragement. Sometimes Lisa had to stop the tape when her three-year-old daughter awoke with a nightmare and needed to be comforted. One minute Lisa was asking Paul whether Amber Lynn had orgasms, and the next she calmly listened as he described Nikki Randall's vagina. Lisa's superwoman illusion was shattered, however, when she told me that she occasionally swatted Paul when he admitted how thoroughly he had enjoyed a particular costar.

Some people think adult films have no heart or soul or reality. For many movies, that's sadly true. But I don't think you'll be able to say that about any of Jerry Butler's films, no matter how flimsy the script. Now, when you watch his work, you'll see the man behind the penis. You'll be able to pinpoint the ad-libs, the pieces of his life he offers for your examination, whether it be a word about hockey in *Divorce Court Exposé* or a reference to his childhood love, a hamster named Tammy, in *Raw Talent II.* In the book you're holding, Jerry shares more than his body; he goes beyond the flesh.

Before Paul approached Bob and me, he had tried working with a writer in Los Angeles. That project never quite got off the ground. But Paul and I speak the same language. Born only five months apart, we both grew up on Brooklyn's concrete streets, watching "Gumby" and "Gilligan's Island" on TV. I know what it's like to have french fries from Nathan's, to ride the D train. I, too, saw my first porno movie at "Cinema Kings Highway." Paul has become the brother I never had. His honesty has given me the courage to look more closely at myself and my life. Maybe he'll do that for you as well.

—Catherine Tavel

Introduction

In late 1979, when adult movies were among the first full-length features to appear on videotape, I thought it would be interesting to write a history of visual sex from 30,000 B.C. to the present. This was the premise: In Western countries at least, virtually *anything* could be written and published about sexuality. Words had passed beyond censorship. But *showing* actual human nudity—or, God forbid, showing female vulvas and males with their penises erect—in drawing, sculpture, painting, photography, printing, or moving pictures was still forbidden. *Playboy, Penthouse,* and the raunchier "skin magazines" were available for younger men, but in most countries actually seeing naked women and men making love was not only sinful but illegal as well. The men who made all the laws did not trust women or themselves.

The book never got published, but the editors who saw the manuscript discovered that in the process of covering every aspect of visual sex—from cave drawings made by our ancestors to Greek vases, famous paintings of the eighteenth and nineteenth centuries, French postcards, and stag movies—I had also reviewed many porno movies that were becoming available on videotape. The "sexvid" explosion was about to begin, and there was no guide to the three thousand or so movies that had been produced in the 1970s and were rapidly being transferred to tape.

My *X-Rated Videotape Guide* was first published in 1984 with 650 reviews of adult films. Now, though, I have reviewed close to 2,500 of them, or about one third of all the porno films that are available.

During this eight-year period, I met many of the actors and actresses who have appeared in sexvids. I realized that there had not yet appeared a true-to-life book about their careers, their personalities, their unique moral codes—a book written without the silly kind of hype you find in the various adult-film magazines. Such a book, written with honesty and dignity, would intrigue thousands of readers. Revealing how a particular person got into the business of fucking in front of a movie or video camera, the book might offer some fascinating insights into the whole area of sex, fidelity, and the family, as well as new approaches to premarital and postmarital relationships.

Since I had written many novels, including *The Harrad Experiment* and *Proposition 31*, which proposed freer but structured relationships, I was personally fascinated by the possibility of seeing such a book through to print. I told many of the actors and actresses I knew that if they ever wrote the story of their lives, I'd try to help them find a publisher. (Among them were Kay Parker and Richard Pacheco, both of whom told me that they had begun to write their autobiographies.) But the truth is, like many celebrities, porno stars freeze when they pick up a pen or sit in front of a typewriter. Actors and actresses can portray all kinds of people on stage and screen, but most of them (Shirley MacLaine is one exception) can't write two paragraphs in a row. Writing is not spontaneous enough, not "out loud" enough.

The only porno star to appear in print thus far, to my knowledge, is Jack Wrangler, whose autobiography was ghostwritten by Carl Johmes. But most of Wrangler's story concentrates on his homosexual activities (he was a top star in gay adult films) and his uneasy sexual relationship with Margaret Whiting, the famous 1940s pop singer. Reading his book, you get very little insight or background into the making of what Georgina Spelvin long ago labeled "fuck films."

I had never met Jerry Butler, but when he phoned me from Brooklyn, where he was visiting his parents, and told me that Chuck Vincent (producer of many quality X-rated films) had suggested I might be able to help him write the true story of his life, I listened in sheer amazement. Jerry talked to me nonstop for close to an hour! Here was a man who could sell refrigerators to the Eskimos! He was telling stories of his childhood, making jokes about himself, explaining how he was in love for the first time, telling why he was quitting the porno business, and continually flinging wild metaphors and similies at me to accentuate a point.

Listening, hypnotized and chuckling, a thought occurred to me. If Jerry could talk so easily to an unseen, unknown listener, could he do the same thing to a tape recorder, *without* an audience? I was intrigued. I doubted many collaborators had tried this approach. I knew that most ghostwriters used interviews and tape recorders as they worked with particular celebrities, questioning them and keeping them on track. But I had no interest in ghostwriting an autobiography. I feared that I would be too inclined to recreate a living person in *my* image of what he or she *should be.* Giving Jerry free reign to dictate tapes was a method that would, I hoped, reveal him much more completely. His autobiography would not be ghostwritten. His book would sound as if Jerry were talking directly to you and intimately revealing his triumphs, failures, and irritations. It would be the kind of "bed talk" that most people, even long married, are afraid to indulge in.

But there was one very critical missing link. I couldn't transcribe those tapes personally, and I knew that whoever did do the transcription would have to become totally mentally involved with Jerry and me in a unique three-way creative process. At this point, an angel of good fortune must have been smiling on Jerry Butler! I knew the woman who might do the transcription: Catherine Tavel. She had written me once, about a year before, and I had met her briefly when I was a guest on the "Ask Dr. Ruth" television show. Although we lived miles apart and I had never talked with her in person for more than a few minutes (except by phone), I knew that Cathy, at twenty-seven, was not only a published writer, but I was sure that within the next few years she'd be on the bestseller list with her own novel. In the meantime, because she was interested in the adult-film phenomenon, she had written several articles about sexvids and was typing and editing reviews for me. We were also working together on a screenplay called *Harrad Now!*, updating two of my novels. Cathy, an excellent writer, was also a good typist, and—*mirabile dictu!*—she lived in Brooklyn! When I told Jerry that Cathy might be interested in a three-way working arrangement, he was speechless for a moment: She lived only a few blocks from where Jerry was born, where he was calling me from!

So began the process, which took about a year. Traveling back and forth between Los Angeles, San Francisco, Brooklyn, and New York City, where he was making both R-and X-rated films, Jerry dictated the tapes, encouraged by his wife, Lisa. Occasionally meeting him in person, Cathy egged him on, coaxing him to stay in chronological order. She transcribed his tapes, lightly editing as she typed, tossing in punctuation and easing the thoughts into paragraphs. Then she'd send me thirty or forty double-spaced pages at a time.

When I received the first transcription, I knew I had been right. Jerry might never have been able to sit down at a typewriter to tell his story, but boy could he talk it! Not only did he have total recall of his life—giving you all the colorful, sometimes shocking details—but he could characterize his mother, father, sister, and his many friends so vividly that you would never forget them. On top of that, Jerry could take you into Pornoland and intimately describe its actors, actresses producers, and directors. Perhaps even more important, Jerry was able to reveal *himself*—as a warm, caring, antagonistic, sometimes even hateful person, whom you can't help liking.

So, this book is a triumph, with the emphasis on "tri." Three of us, coming together, did it. But Cathy and I are only on the periphery. This is Jerry's book all the way. My feeling is that Jerry has only begun as an author. For my money, he's a reincarnation of Henry Miller, a Brooklyn boy of another era. I'm sure Miller would have approved of Jerry.

—Robert Rimmer

One

Fish Out of Water

I am not Jerry Butler, not really.

My real name is Paul Siederman. I was born on Friday the thirteenth in May of 1959 in Brooklyn, New York. And from the very beginning, I have always been a highly sexual person. Ever since the age of three, I masturbated about fifteen times a day—no exaggeration. I'd just rub against the floor and do it. I didn't learn about hand-jobbing until I was nearly twelve. Before then, I was like a fish out of water, squirming on the floor.

Sexual pleasure always fascinated me. The sensation of climaxing with nothing coming out of my penis was much more intense than my orgasms are today. I don't know why, really, but maybe it was because my body was so small then, or because my life experience and opportunities for other pleasures were so limited. As adults, we become callous and let the outside world tell us how we should feel. So what do we do? We compare each orgasm to the one before it.

But as a child, here you are, a free little creature doing what feels good.

I'm happy to report that I never felt any sexual attraction toward my mother or my sister, Linda, even though I was *always* fantasizing about women—older women, especially: women I'd see in the streets or working in a store, teachers, women on television. I might start masturbating while watching Honey West on TV. Or Shari Lewis—but *never* Lamb Chop! My favorite was Ginger on "Gilligan's Island." When I was seven or eight, I was obsessed with Ginger. I was in love with that white dress, her tits, *everything*.

One day, my mom and dad went to a wedding and left my twelve-year-old sister to take care of me. I was in the living room, and Linda was probably off doing something that made her feel "grown up." (She used to like to snoop around the closets and try on my mom's clothes.) I remember watching the TV screen very closely. I was on my belly, squirming in ecstacy, because it was a major Ginger episode, and my titillating obsession was jiggling on camera most of the time. I was just about to come . . . I was coming . . . when, all of a sudden, the scene cut to the Professor. I had an orgasm coming to the fucking Professor! Do you know what that could do to a kid? Years later, I worked with Tina Louise (who played "Ginger") in a movie called *Evils of the Night*. I revealed my childhood crush, but she didn't know what to say.

Orgasms were very important, selective experiences to me. I'd walk down the street and choose unsuspecting women to star in my fantasies. Of course, they never knew their role in my life, but I secretly hoped some of them might tingle a little telepathically because of my intense sexual energy. I always had a tremendous thing for my teachers. I desired the shelter of an older, more mature woman. There was one teacher I fantasized about in particular: Miss Sowen (from kindergarten). If you look at the class photo, my elbow is digging into her tit.

To me, orgasms were like money. I'd invest my orgasms, saving them up for the right time. My dad taught me to be very conscious about money and spending. As a child, my finances were my orgasms. (As a porno actor, my climaxes have actually been transformed into dollars and cents.) Masturbation became my own creation, my privacy, my adored addiction. Later on in life, another addiction became my privacy, too: cocaine. Coke became the second stage in fantasizing about women in magazines or about women that I knew, but without the problems of live flesh. Many times I've climaxed on coke pretending I was a woman, trying to feel what a woman might feel. Snorting cocaine was my way of getting absorbed into a different dimension without having to make a commitment, without being caught. We all pretend to be cops and robbers, but we don't really rob a bank. It's just play.

As a kid, I was nervous about masturbating from the woman's point of view. I wondered whether that made me homosexual. When I was about eight, I told my friend Scott about it. He said that if I felt like a woman when I got off, it meant I was gay. So from that moment on, I strictly imagined myself (or another guy) fucking a woman. For a long time, I actually had a hang-up about it.

I don't want you to get the idea that I masturbated my childhood away. I also played stoopball and stickball. My dad was a big hockey buff who'd been going to the old Madison Square Garden since he was about eight, so it was he who brought me into the game of hockey, which soon became my real passion. One day, he took me to Thrifty's Toy Shop on Nostrand Avenue, which was right next to Whoops, a ladies' clothing store. The two O's in the sign were made to look like eyes, and they were topped with long, sexy lashes. Those big, bold eyes always seemed to be looking at me. In fact, the name alone used to get me aroused! At Thrifty's, my dad bought me a wooden hockey stick. I went to sleep with the stick that night, and I'm still picking the splinters out of my crotch. I wore off the paint on that stick in one night! Imagine what I would have done with a woman?

I remember going into supermarkets with my mother, and for some reason I would imagine myself tumbling and tumbling. Putting myself in a different dimension, I would actually *feel* myself tumbling. It was so intense that my whole body represented a penis and I would have an orgasm. In another tactile fantasy, I would imagine myself as a football player running for the goal line. A crowd of people would surround me—it didn't matter whether they were men or women. The important thing was to feel the pressure of bodies, *any* bodies. They'd grab me, touch me, clutch me, pull me, smack me, and hit me. I always managed to get away somehow and make that touchdown. It was the same feeling of total supremecy I achieved from having an orgasm. Later, I captured the same sensation making adult movies. Putting myself into the food processor, so to speak, I somehow always managed to escape before I was liquefied.

Two

Yankee Doodle Dandy

I never felt I could please my father. He painted beautiful outlines for me, but always forgot to dip the brush into the watercolors. That is, he gave me wonderful suggestions, but he never helped me follow through, nor did he focus on the positive things I did. For example, if I played forty minutes of great hockey, he'd dwell on the one minute I messed up. And I remember when Chuck Vincent's *Roommates* came out, in 1982. I played a very sensitive character, a guy named Eddie, who thought he was gay. Eddie was working as a waiter while trying to make it as an actor. Kind of like me, because I was still waiting tables at Nathan's in Coney Island. When my father saw the movie, all he did was point out my faults. We're so unalike in that way. I always look for the positive side of things, for the smallest bit of light in the tunnel—I have to . . . everything else is dark anyway. Things could be worse. For example: There's a lot of laziness in me, but I'm not as lazy as I could be. I'm not a fighter, but I could be. I'm not a "legit" actor, but I'm a damn good actor when I try to be.

Even when I was only thirteen, I had a goal. I wanted to be a professional hockey player, because that's what I thought my father wanted me to be. I wanted to be a "man." I regularly searched by chest for hair. My emphasis on achievement was always on being "macho." All I ever cared about in life was being tough, being manly, trying to get as big in every department of my body as I could. I resented the fact that my penis wasn't as big as some of the other guys on the hockey team. I used to come to the game fully dressed so they didn't have to see me. I tried not to shower with the guys. I'd take my protective cup off only when no one was looking.

And years later, here I am, fucking on film! But what you feel you lack is the force that makes you work harder. What we all want in life is what we don't have. I always wished I had a bigger penis. Maybe because I've often felt physically inferior, I had to compensate in other ways. I think it's made me a better person and a better lover. Today, I measure "big" by how much something is felt, not by how it looks.

I remember vividly the first time I saw my father cry. I was four, and John F. Kennedy had just been killed. The funeral was televised at night, and Dad was sitting in the lounge chair watching it. I remember seeing the American flag draped over the coffin, but I still didn't understand why everyone was so somber. I looked at the television, then I looked at my father crying. I learned a lot about life and death just by seeing his face. Dad was a tough guy from Coney Island. It was hot where he worked, and he'd always carry a white handkerchief to wipe the sweat from his face. It had a wonderful greasy french fry and hot dog aroma. That night, I took my father's handkerchief and wiped away his tears. Never have I felt closer to him, and he wasn't being a tough man, just being vulnerable and real. He was being my father.

Whenever my dad came home from work, I would run into the kitchen to greet him. I knew he had a special little blue bag with him. It was raggedy, like an old doll. This bag would move to any dimension, mold to any shape. I found the same things in it every day: a tire-pressure gauge and two packs of Yankee Doodles—you know, those cream-filled cupcakes. Sometimes there were coconut cookies or Ring Dings as well, but you couldn't mess with my Yankee Doodles!

One day I discovered something square and bulky in Dad's little blue bag, something so big the bag couldn't even zip shut. I opened the bag in anticipation of my Yankee Doodles, but I found another kind of treat.

Porno films.

John Holmes was on cover of one box. He had an arm around a brunette, who had a fancy 1960s hairstyle and wore piles of make-up. I couldn't believe it! Right next to my Yankee Doodles was a naked woman! Porno must be all right, I figured, because it was in the same bag as my snack.

My dad was a very sexual man, but what he did in bed with my mother was private. Once I happened to walk in on them by accident, though. My father's face was pressed between mom's legs. All I could think of was a cat licking the remains of a milk bowl. It actually bothered me when I heard them making love. My mom would be moaning—except it wasn't a pleasurable sound; it sounded almost painful. I wanted to run into their room, grab hold of Dad, and punch him.

I used to see my dad's "pee pee" a lot. If I called it a "dick," he'd correct me. "Call it a pecker," he'd tell me. What a wimpy word! You know something? If I stood my ground and called it a "dick," I'm sure I would have grown an eight-inch one. Since he made me call it a "pecker," it's still only seven.

Those porno films started coming in every night. My dad was selling them to the neighbors or fellow workers at Nathan's for eight to ten bucks a pop, while he was buying them for five. It was a money-making scheme with his brother Murray. Anyone named Murray Siederman has got to be a conniving guy. My sister and I made up a song about him. "Moishe had a candystore./ Business was so bad,/ he asked his wife what to do,/ and this is what she said:/ "Get a little kerosene,/ spill it on the floor./ Get a match, give a scratch/ Poof! No more candystore." That was Murray Siederman's national anthem.

Dad and Uncle Murray would take regular trips into Manhattan, bringing home about fifteen or twenty tapes. My father didn't seem to mind me looking at the pictures on the boxes. What he didn't know was that I was obsessed with the films inside.

At that time, Mom was working at Food Fair. I was a "latch key" kid. I'd come home from school and let myself in with my own key. Since I'd get home by three and Mom didn't arrive until four, I had roughly one hour to sneak into Dad's room and snoop through his dresser drawers, looking for the tapes. I knew he kept a movie projector under his desk. "Don't go near it," he warned me. "It doesn't work." But when I plugged it in, the gears spun like a top.

When I would hear my father coming, I'd get scared and try to put the tapes away real quickly. First I'd hear him getting out of his car. Then I'd hear the hood go up. I knew Dad opened the hood every time he parked his car, to disconnect the distributor wires so no one could steal the car. He even put a sign in the front window: "If you want the car, the wire is up in apartment 4-C." When I heard him slam the hood, I had about twenty-five seconds to a minute before he walked in the door. That was barely enough time to put everything away. And I'd always screw something up. I'd put the tapes in the wrong boxes, or I'd leave the lens cap out. Sometimes John Holmes would get a chocolate-chip-cookie stain on his face—he'd look like a black guy with a big white dick! Dad never found me masturbating, but he'd always know I was at the projector again. "I can tell you've been going through my stuff," he'd say. If you took a Number 2 pencil and replaced it with a Number 3, he'd know.

The first stag film I watched featured a woman being raped by five guys in an alley. I don't remember who she was, but she had a beautiful sluttiness about her. This woman's face was matted with make-up—blue was smudged around her eyes and red smeared her lips. She wore a miniskirt, white boots, and a red top. The guys really fucked her over. At first she didn't like it, but then she got into it. Of course, there was no sound on these films, but you could tell when she was cooperating.

When I'd string a film through the projector, it would often snap apart. I couldn't handle the film too well—after all, I wasn't even seven yet. By the time my father watched a movie, there was nothing left but the credits! Everything else was on my cutting room floor. You could say that I was learning editing and masturbating at the same time. Sometimes I'd have to stick a pencil here or there to get the projector going again. It was a machine that serviced my pleasure.

My dad even had pornographic playing cards. I remember that one of the pictures looked like Susan Dey, another like Adrienne Barbeau. At eight, I used to steal Dad's porno cards and sell them individually to kids in the neighborhood. When my father caught me, he couldn't scold me without first scolding himself. *He* was the pornbroker. It was *his* money-making scheme that turned me into a sexual fanatic.

Looking back, I have to say that I wish I didn't get into the whole porno thing as a child. I would have had a lot more time to play with G. I. Joe, that's for sure. But I raced to a level of sexual maturity. Watching the movies gave me the justification for being in an adult group, but what happened was I became more private, more alone. And that little film projector became kind of like a computer: I could tap into all the sexuality there was to be imagined, all different men, all different women, everything I needed.

Three

Family Affair

A bit of Siederman family history. My grandfather Sam was the half-brother of Leon Trotsky. He and Leon had the same mother, but they certainly went in different directions. While Leon was off deposing the Russian czar and tangling with a guy named Stalin, Sam was a singing waiter on the Boardwalk of Coney Island, working alongside Jimmy Durante and Eddie Cantor.

As you might have already guessed, my father is Jewish. My mother is 50 percent Jewish . . . by injection. Actually, she had a German-Irish mother and a Cherokee Indian dad. But Mom recently turned fifty, and I believe that any woman over the age of fifty automatically *becomes* part-Jewish. There's no question about that. With the make-up on, Mom's Christian. But take the make-up off, put her in a housecoat, and she's screaming, "Where's the bagels? Leave me alone already!" She's always looking for a sale or is worried that there won't be milk left for coffee in the morning.

I know my mom loves me. But for some crazy reason, every time we have a big argument she says things that devastate me. Well, like all families, we sometimes say terrible things to each other. Don't get me wrong, I love my mom very much. There's a harmless, sensitive love that I have for her. Dad's more educated, more worldy. He started at Nathan's when he was about twenty and worked his way up to manager. He's been there almost forty years. But Mom' s pretty sheltered. She's not aware of much outside of her family. She dropped out of school at fourteen, was married at fifteen, had my sister at sixteen. My dad is eight or nine years older, and Mom has always depended on him. "Please lead me," she always seems to say.

As a young woman, my mother was extremely beautiful, the stunning blonde in any group. Now she's getting older, and she's starting to show a little wear. I think she's giving up, giving in to life. Although she's never actually told me, my guess is that mom doesn't like what I've been doing for a living. I'm not sure whether she's ever seen any of my films. She's very modest and quiet about things like that. I know my mother loves me, but damn, she just loves me the wrong way. The love I need is communication, not emotion.

When I think of my Mom's dog, Sandy, I see myself as a child. Sandy was so overprotected. At ten years old, that dog didn't even know how to sit. He was a cute dog, a loving dog. He was soft and harmless, but he didn't *know* anything. Sandy was fed, taken care of, provided for, but he couldn't even go outside alone. Growing up, I was lacking the kind of leadership I really needed. What good is polishing the car when you don't service the engine? Instead of explaining things, my parents usually scolded. I had to try to find out everything for myself. We didn't communicate.

Despite that, I managed to have a childhood I wouldn't trade for anyone's. The friends, the memories, the feelings, the historic places, the monuments. It only started to get ridiculous as I grew older.

Underneath it all, I'm a very soft person, and I never believed I had to cover that vulnerable part of myself. In fact, I've always enjoyed a good cry. Showing emotions is important, and that's how I weigh out what a "man" is. Obviously, you know you're a man from your physical structure. Your prick is there when you drop your pants. But I think a real man isn't afraid to be honest and reveal his true feelings.

This definition of a man is totally different than my father's. In the Jewish religion, you become a man when you're bar mitzvahed, and I wasn't. I think my dad was pretty upset that I never took up the Jewish faith. Even though Dad was Jewish, he never was religious. The only reason I might have favored the Jewish religion as a kid was because there were more holidays. Christians really suffer. They have about twenty fewer holidays than the Jews.

The truth is, I was embarrassed to be Jewish. Except for a few Jewish kids, the neighborhood I was brought up in was basically black and Italian. The Jews were the ones to get all the racial jokes. I never looked Jewish and was always trying to hide my heritage. I had this little snappy nose like a popstick and looked German, like my mom. When I first played hockey, I put two *n*s at the end of my name to make it seem German. I remember an incident at a game at New Hyde Park. When they put my name in the scorer's box, they spelled it with two *n*s. When the game was over, someone pointed to the box score and said, "You're German, right?" And I said, "Yeah." Consonants are great. Just add another one and you become someone else. I learned that long before I became "Jerry Butler."

You can probably guess that dressing up for Halloween was a special thrill for me. I remember my first costume. All of the kids dressed up like Batman or other superheroes. When you put on a Batman mask, you automatically become fearless, crime-fighting, bold, and aggressive. Eventually I put on various kinds of masks to aquire their qualities—but, that first time, I was a cat, a soft, sensitive, vulnerable, warmth-seeking, love-seeking animal. And you couldn't tell whether I was a boy or a girl—*it didn't matter.* That night, I was just a person who elected to wear a particular costume. I automatically felt very petite, tight, trim, and slimly muscular. At the same time, I had this smooth manner about me—like a zoot suit dressed as a cat.

The kids were trick-or-treating all around Bragg Street. They had their candy bags and were swinging smashed-up chalk pieces in socks, which they used to mark up buildings. I wasn't interested in throwing eggs or being destructive—not while I was wearing a cat outfit, because that would be out of character. Everyone went up to one particular lady's door. We all smiled and shouted, "Trick or Treat!"

With a sad look on her face, the lady told us, "All I have is raisins."

Trick-or-treaters hope for things like wrapped candy bars and pennies. Raisins are loose and sticky. How could you eat raisins out of a bag filled with toys and goodies? Everyone went, "Nah," and they walked away. When I looked back, the lady had the most helpless expression on her face. I ran back so she could give me a scoop of raisins. Why? I felt sorry and embarrassed for her—she was only trying to be good and generous.

The rest of my childhood is a puzzle of memories. I always found myself building things, creating spaces that were big enough so I could squeeze in. I loved to squish my body under beds, between bushes, or slide myself into warm, sheltered situations. I was sealing myself in because I never got that necessary seal at home. My dad never really held me, at least not the way I wanted him to. When he came home from work, I'd scream, "Daddy!" and jump into his arms. He'd hold me a little, but then he'd go right upstairs. He rarely played with me.

My mom held me, but very sparingly, so I looked for affection elsewhere. I found myself knocking on women's doors and asking for a glass of water, even if I wasn't thirsty.

Now, when I hold my wife, Lisa, in my arms, my life feels full and complete. There's a feeling of reaching out, of stretching and caring. I couldn't get that close to my mom or dad.

Working on this book is difficult for me: I know I'm going to hurt people I care about—like my parents and Lisa—but I also hope we'll become closer. I'm an addict to the way things are. I feel very insecure about life right now. I've got less than ten bucks in my wallet. And every time I get a cold or sneeze, I'm sure I have AIDS. (I took tests and they came back negative, but who knows how accurate they are?)

My biggest insecurity is Lisa. God, I'm so damned in love with her. But one question never leaves my mind: Why did this beautiful woman, who could have any man she wants, choose me?

Four

Roy, Bonzoli, and Tammy

Before Lisa, there were other people in my life, other things that meant a lot to me. At home I had a beloved rocking horse, a yellow one. I rode it so hard, the thing would tip over. Operating something I could straddle and work to the point of exhaustion was exhilarating. I remember the feeling of being in my pajamas, with the attached feeties, wearing those smooth cotton-nylon bottoms. The feeling of rubbing myself against the saddle of that horse was just incredible. Roy Rogers was my idol then. I was a macho little gunslinger singing "Happy Trails" along with him. Rocking the hell out of my nuts, I'd try to come while I was doing it. The bottom half of me was Dale Evans and the top half was Roy. It was wild. Ride 'em, cowboy!

My mother collected Green Stamps and she used to buy me something with them. I always wanted "Bobo the Clown." Bobo was a punching-bag toy that was even bigger than me. It had a red nose that squeaked when you popped it one, but

I was never into beating him. I used to turn him over and fuck the hell out of him! No, I couldn't bear to look at his face. I couldn't get off on something that was smiling at me. I'd roll on Bobo, bounce all around the house with him. I'd pretend he was dominating me, then I was dominating him. I would squirm and squeal, then I would make those sounds for Bobo, although he was usually a very quiet lover. I must have gone through at least four Bobo dolls, and I was circumcised, too.

In my neverending quest for pleasure, I also used to climb poles. I'd go up and down all afternoon. After a while, those signposts sagged into forty-five degree angles! I was also into sucking my fingers, and I nursed on the middle two until I calloused the hell out of them. When I couldn't play with my penis, this was an orgasm for my mouth: I'd actually reach a sensation of climaxing. One finger would touch my cheek and one would touch my upper lip. My thumb would go underneath and play with my bottom lip. It was like I was playing billiards with my mouth, setting up shots.

Then there was this granite turtle in the schoolyard. (It's still there.) I used to climb on that turtle and rub against it. Wearing shorts in the summer, my penis would feel very loose, as though it could go anywhere it wanted. I enjoyed that feeling of sexual roaming and freedom. It was almost primal. I made love to barrels, to the granite turtle, to street signs. I couldn't just rub against something and then step down. I had to reach some kind of resolution, achieve some type of intense relationship with that object.

I had another park playmate, which the kids called "The Shower Pole." It looked like a mushroom with holes in the top, through which water shot. I would stand over it so that a stream of water would go right up into my bathing suit, tickling my penis and asshole. Kids were all around, but no one could see that I was having this bursting, throbbing orgasm.

The sensation of water on your belly was great, but the

best thing was sitting on the shower pole. Water would spray between my legs and sprinkle everyone else within a certain distance. From the mist the water created, there were rainbows shining in the sun. It was a total sensual delight.

There was a kid in the neighborhood named Bonzoli. He was no bigger than a chocolate doll—but back then he seemed like a giant. Bonzoli was the first person to touch my penis. It happened when we were both about five. I was wearing my little green bathing suit, standing with my beach pail in hand, waiting for my parents. Bonzoli and some other kid came over to me. I probably had just a smidge or a smudge of a penis. Bonzoli gave me the funniest, most encouraging, somewhat embarrassed, ridiculous face. Without a word, he reached out and touched my "pee-pee." Imagine how you'd feel if the first person who ever fondled you was named Bonzoli?

Oh, did I love kindergarten! That first day, Miss Sowen asked us to name some songs we'd like to hear. When I broke in and told her that Rudolph the Red-Nosed Reindeer had actually visited my house, she spun around and played it on the piano. I knew what I told her wasn't true—but at that age, I thought anything I said or wished for would magically come true.

But school wasn't always fun and games. I'll never forget the day that Joseph, Eddie, and I pulled the fire alarm. We tried to run away, but they still caught us. I was sitting in the principal's office, hoping to disappear. They let Eddie go, but I was left sitting there with Joseph because he actually pulled the alarm and I boosted him up. The principal's office was like a funeral parlor. There was an announcement on the school's P.A. system. Then the firemen arrived. The principal asked why I did it. I told him, "I thought I was boosting Joseph up a tree. I wasn't looking up. I was looking down."

With my eyes on the floor, I waited for Mrs. Snyder, my first grade teacher, to show up and save me. I didn't even care whether she scolded me. I just wanted to *see* her. But when Mrs. Snyder walked in to get her mail, she could barely stand to look at me. "That's a very bad thing you did," she said, walking away angrily. I really thought I was going to jail at six years old, that I'd never see my parents again. Today, there's not that much commotion when somebody robs a bank.

My friends and I used to fill shoeboxes with coins, checkers, baseball cards, little dolls, and jacks—and we'd walk around shouting, "Selling! Selling! For Sale!" This is how we got spare change. One day, I fell in love with a little white hamster at the Congo Aquarium. She cost $1.20, and I was dying to buy her, but all I had was eighty cents from my shoe-box sales. After selling some more, all I needed was two cents. The store owner wouldn't even let that slide, so I went home and sold a discarded camera for two cents. Luckily, my parents never found out.

I named the hamster "Tammy." She was my little precious animal, and she meant everything to me. Tammy nipped me a few times, but I loved her anyway. I had had her about a year and a half when I found her dead in the tiny house I had bought for her. When my parents came home, I was crying. Dad tried to console me, but he didn't say the right things. "It's okay," he kept telling me, "I'll buy you another one." But I didn't want "another one." I just wanted to live through the experience that something I loved had died. I did finally give in, though, and let my dad buy "Tammy the Second." (For some reason, I named all my hamsters Tammy. I think I got as far as "Tammy the Third.")

One day, Tammy the Second wasn't feeling well. She seemed very somber and wasn't moving much. I didn't know what to do, so I looked up a veterinarian in the phone book. On my Royce Union "stingray" bike, I rode the eight miles down Coney Island Avenue to a vet near Prospect Park. It took me quite a while to pour out all of my feelings for poor Tammy. "It's getting dark and my bike's outside and the lock ain't good," I told him. "What am I going to do?"

Puffing on his pipe, he just shrugged. "Give the hamster an aspirin."

So, I went home, crushed an aspirin, and put it in Tammy's water just like he told me. She died two days later.

Five

Young Dinosaur

Hockey. My dad is the one who put the stick in my hand. Hockey came to symbolize value and self-worth to me—it was a *man's* sport. Other guys were technically better than me, but I had this tremendous emotion when I played the game. I adopted the sport. I claimed and proclaimed it.

First, we played hockey on foot. We were always looking for big snowstorms, the kind that don't happen too often back home anymore. Sometimes there'd be a snowstorm during the night and the next morning there'd be a homemade ice-skating rink on Brigham Street around the corner. Playing hockey in the snow, I felt like a fawn in a forest. I didn't have to hit anybody, it was just delight: the hat on my head, my frosty cheeks, my belly that was hungry, my lips that were frozen.

I didn't ease into the sport, I jumped. I went from Gumby to hockey. Perhaps there should have been something in between.

Once I put on wheels, I had speed, *thrust.* I was moving faster physically than I ever had before. I had the cheap kind of rollerskates that you slipped on over your shoes, but no one ever made fun of me. I was too good a hockey player. There I was, speeding down in a breakaway and ready to shoot, when my skate would fall off my sneaker! Still attached to my ankle, I had to drag it behind as I tried to score a goal.

By the time the roller hockey league started, I was a damn good skater. Although I could go backwards and make screeching turns, I still didn't have that crazed toughness. My favorite hockey player was Rod Gilbert. He was a very good-looking guy, and I was emotionally affected by his appearance; he looked a lot like my father. (Funny—I never realized that until just now.) Maybe that's why I was so drawn to Gilbert. What I couldn't get from my dad, I idolized in someone else. The uniform, the face, and the structure . . . I could fill all of that in. I took my own emotional crayons and colored in what was missing.

Gilbert wasn't a very aggressive man. He was a flashy right winger for the New York Rangers. Very swift and flamboyant, he was admired for his looks by both men and women. Emulating him, I played right wing for the newly formed Kings Bay Boys' Club Roller Hockey League. I was flashy and shifty, too. I was the first one ever to score a goal in the brand-new league. In fact, I scored two goals in the first game. I looked so much like my mother that people called me a "little Shirley Siederman on skates."

I think I still have my old jersey at home. I couldn't afford to buy numbers, so I made my "12" out of tape. I had these big pants, too. I remember going to grammar school wearing my uniform. Kids would wear their baseball uniforms or basketball uniforms, so why couldn't I? There I was, going to math and science class wearing my shoulderpads. Sitting through hours and hours of school like that. All because I wanted to feel like a big guy.

My dad found out about an ice-hockey program that was coming into the area. I had been going to games watching the older guys, the Brooklyn Stars, and was mightily impressed with them. To really feel like Rod Gilbert, I'd have to wear the kind of skates they wore. I'd have to play on the same surface.

At the ice-hockey clinic, I went down to the rink early in the morning and got on the ice with about 150 kids three times a week. I was one of the Peewees, in the twelve-to-thirteen-year-old age group. It cost twenty dollars for the whole summer. They gave you a little tank-top shirt that said "GNYCIHL"—Greater New York City Ice Hockey League. The night before, I'd have to sleep with my dad so I'd hear his Westinghouse alarm clock go off. I hated that thing.

Before I started the clinic, I needed ice skates. My dad took me down to E.J. Korvettes. Anyone in hockey would laugh if you told them you bought your skates there. We found Franklin ice skates on sale for sixteen bucks. A decent pair of hockey skates costs fifty to sixty; a *great* pair went for a hundred. You also had to buy them at least three sizes too small—so they'd be tight enough. My dad didn't go for that idea—he figured I was going to grow, so he got me the "correct" size. So, down at the clinic, I had to wear several pairs of socks, and my feet looked like they had casts on them. I even had to pad the skates with sponge. To make up for my terrible skates, I had to play much harder just to get by.

They divided the rink in two: one side for the new guys, the other for the experienced players. Every time you skated you were reminded that the guys on the other side were better than you were. One day, I took the puck and skated all the way down the ice and put the puck into the net on the other side. Frank—a husky, little Italian guy on the Brooklyn Stars—was watching me. He was my idol, and I wanted to impress him. Frank looked at me and said, "You belong on the other side."

A guy named Angelo coached the Peewee Brooklyn Stars. They were the New York Yankees of hockey in the tri-state area. I would have been ecstatic just to make the crummy "House League." I couldn't believe that Angelo wanted me on the Stars. But at twelve, I had the slapshot of a seventeen year old. Next, Angelo told me, "You be a defenseman."

I didn't want to be a defenseman. Defensemen get hit a lot because they have to block the puck with their bodies. But the Brooklyn Stars . . . I'd do anything to be on that team. They played sixty-five games a year, went to Canada and Washington D.C., and got letters from the President. They were first-class. I became a defenseman.

Being with the older guys gave me a tremendous boost in self-confidence. I started getting cocky. Sometimes I shot the puck too high and hard and almost rearranged someone's face. At least I was being recognized and praised. Soon I earned the nickname "Hot Shot." (Rod Gilbert's nickname was "Hot Rod.") I wasn't afraid of anyone—except for Angelo, who was terrifying. When you looked up at him, you looked further than up because you were scared to look him straight in the face. This man could condemn, degrade, and destroy anything in his path.

Angelo used to call me "Ziedie." He would brag to everybody, "I got the Ziederman kid." (He thought my name was "Ziederman," and I was too afraid to correct him.) Angelo never stopped drilling us. The wingman would pass the puck and Angelo would stand there screaming, "Slap that puck! Slap that fucking thing!" The scariest man alive was shouting his appreciation for me. I had crossed the line. I became a warrior on ice.

He was really tough on the new kids and cursed out twelve-year-olds like they were Army recruits. Some kids even quit the clinic because of him. "You motherfuckers! You piece of shit motherfuck! Scum-bag motherfucker! You don't use your head, you fucking cocksucker!" he'd yell at the top of his lungs.

Angelo helped me perfect cursing as an art form.

After every drill practice, we'd have skating races. I had the sloppiest skates in the world. Angelo was indignant, screaming, "Get those fucking things off your fucking feet! You deserve a better pair of skates." He actually embarrassed my father into getting me hundred-dollar skates. After that, I never lost a race. In a dash, I could beat anybody. Angelo used to say to me, "If you want to make this God-damned team, skate hard, and skate harder, Ziederman!"

Making the Brooklyn Stars was one of the most gratifying moments of my life. It was the first thing I had ever achieved on my own. My father beamed. He told me, "You don't really have to be a Brooklyn Star. The team is too tough." My mother was proud, too. She treated my uniform as if it were another child.

Hockey was a game with no responsibilities, no blame. If I played badly and lost, everyone lost—from the team to the fans in the stands. If my friend got hurt on the ice, I was hurt, too, because I didn't do my job to protect him. The way you play this game is by hitting people, hurting people. If you attack someone on the street, you could get a few years in jail. Slash someone in the rink and you get two minutes. I was mixed up. When I put on my hockey equipment, I became a young dinosaur. At home, I was treated like a plush animal. It was a difficult adjustment.

Because of hockey, I finally discovered masturbating with my hand. It was during my first summer at the J.C. Trembley Hockey Camp. Back at the Holiday Inn in Ontario, a bunch of guys tried to fill up a cup with come. Everyone passed the glass around, jerking off with their fists. After we all came in it, we left the cup in the elevator. That was the greatest orgasm of my life. I fell in love with my right hand after that. My damn dick stayed swollen for a day and a half. I thought I'd discovered a great new way to make it grow, but it eventually went back to normal size.

Around that time, I met Big Mike, who had a son on the team. Mike was married to a pretty woman named Lucille, who looked like *Entertainment Tonight*'s Mary Hart, except she had platinum blond hair and big round tits. I never told Little Mike, but when I slept at his house, I used to masturbate to thoughts of his mother.

But Big Mike was impressive, too, intense and strong. A husky guy, he wore a cowboy hat and had a five o'clock shadow even after he shaved. Big Mike was bald, but he never let you see him as Mr. Clean. And when Big Mike put on his toupee, he looked like something that belonged in the Bronx Zoo with the lights out. His chest hair was always flowing out of the front of his fringed shirt. Big Mike was always joking around. He'd grab a kid's dick in the rink, pretend to pull it off, and embarrass the hell out of him. Or he'd get a guy in a headlock and bite his face.

When I made the team, Big Mike took me under his wing. "Hey, big guy," he'd say to me, "we got to get you some new gloves, some new pads." I could see my father bristling. Big Mike would buy me anything under the sun. Maybe I was the kind of kid he wanted his son to be, but I *know* that Big Mike was the father I wished I had. My dad was very protective, but with Big Mike I was an adventurer, an explorer. Before I even turned thirteen, he had me driving his Buick. I had to raise myself high on the seat so I could see over the dashboard. Then I'd go home to my father. If I didn't brush my teeth at night, he'd make me wear my toothbrush around my neck the next day. My dad gave me fifty cents allowance while Big Mike was shoving twenty-dollar bills into my pocket.

Big Mike also gave me his son's hand-me-down hockey equipment, which was worth more than anything my father had ever bought. When I tried to thank him, he'd tell me, "Hey, big guy, I'm putting you on salary." At an away game in Washington D.C. once, Big Mike was thrown out of the rink because he was promising his team five bucks for a goal, four for an assist, and two if you beat someone up!

I always believed that Big Mike was in love with my mother. He probably would have tried for her, but had too much respect for my dad. He eventually went out with my sister, Linda, probably because she was the next best thing. Big Mike's wife eventually left him because of Linda. That's why Little Mike grew to hate anyone with the Siederman name. That, plus Big Mike always slighted his son because of me.

One day, we were at Skyrink when Big Mike came back from Dallas. He was a cameraman and had been shooting a golf classic there. He had a horoscope necklace for me and another for himself. Little Mike realized his father had forgotten him. I felt terrible when I saw the look on his face. Big Mike tried to cover it up and took off his own necklace. "Dad, I'm not a Sagittarius," Little Mike told him sadly.

I guess you could say that Big Mike broke my cherry to life. The first time I flew on an airplane was with him. He was shooting a Mets game in St. Louis, and he took Little Mike and me along. We stayed in the same hotel as the Mets. When Big Mike saw that there was a tennis court out back, he ran down to the sports shop and bought us two eighty-dollar Wilson racquets—black ones, sleek . . . something you'd imagine a female tennis star using for a dildo.

That night he brought a gorgeous brunette up to our room. (He thought Little Mike and I were sleeping, but I only pretended to be.) I was fascinated watching both of them in the adjoining room. Big Mike had the first uncircumcised dick I had ever seen—not including John Holmes in the stag movies. I thought he'd forgotten to take the cap off or something.

He told the girl, "Just climb on this hammer here." Watching her fuck Big Mike, I was at last being brought into the real world of sex. It would still be a few years before I would experience it myself, but I was seeing it right before my eyes for the first time.

Six

Fallen Dinosaur

Hockey doesn't come without its share of bumps, bruises, and broken bones. At an exhibition game in Cantiague Park, I was chewing on a lump of bubble gum. I got hit and fell to the ice, choking and gasping for air. Everyone just thought I had the wind knocked out of me. Finally, Angelo ran out to the ice. He shoved his hand down my throat and ripped out the blob of gum. As I came to, he started cursing me out in from of about 150 people. "You son of a bitch piece of scum. Don't you *ever* chew gum on the ice again!"

We played all of our home games at the Abe Stark Rink in Coney Island. It was my favorite place, because the boards seemed soft—at least it didn't hurt so much getting smashed against them. I remember playing a team from Framingham, Massachusetts. We were getting slaughtered 4 to 0 in the first period. It was six in the morning, a crazy time to have a game, but we played whenever the ice was available. The janitor was cleaning out the bathroom, using massive amounts of ammonia. Angelo was so angry after the first period that he threw the janitor out of the bathroom and brought the entire team in, making us breathe in the ammonia. "Maybe this will wake you up, you Goddamned motherfuckers," he shouted at us. He made us stay in there fifteen minutes. We came out and won the game 12 to 4.

The first time I broke my leg was at Skyrink. We were playing a Bantam team in a tune-up game. Most of the players were at least two years older than us Peewees. A kid took a slapshot and hit me in the ankle. It hurt like a son of a bitch, but I was able to resume the game. When went home, my leg started stiffening up on me. I woke up at three in the morning, screaming in pain. I often complained of pain, so my father thought I was crying wolf. "Don't be such a baby," he told me. I went back to bed.

The next morning I couldn't move my foot. My sister took me to the emergency room of Coney Island Hospital. They put a walking cast on my ankle. Linda and I took a cab home and I ran up the steps with the cast on my foot, eager to show my father that he was wrong. When I saw him, I started crying, "When will you ever believe me?"

Luckily, I didn't lose my spot on the team. The next season, I was a Bantam. During a preseason game, we were playing a team called the LIAC Flyers in Hicksville, Long Island. It was a very cold rink. In fact, after games you had to use a hair dryer to thaw out your nuts. LIAC wasn't a contending team, but they were very big and played rough. We were winning the game 1 to 0 in the first period. With six seconds left on the clock, the puck went into the corner in my defensive end. I hit this kid as hard as I could. Bang! I body-checked him, but I got the worst of it. While I was lying helplessly on the ice, he deliberately jumped on my foot with the blade of his skate. The pain was excruciating. I had to wait twenty minutes for an ambulance. My mother was a total wreck. She has a beautiful face, but when she gets nervous, it wrinkles like tissue paper, and that's what she looked like then. As I lay on the ice, Little Mike tried to avenge me—and show off for his dad—by leaping on the guy who had broken my leg. Poor Mike got his ass kicked.

At the hospital, they had to cut my skate with scissors. It was a beautiful, clean break. They told me I'd have to wear a cast that went up to my crotch for two and a half months. It would be nothing like the walking cast I had the year before, and I'd have to use crutches. I was feeling very sorry for myself.

All I wanted to do was go to bed and cry, but we were stuck in a massive traffic jam on the Long Island Expressway. As we slowly moved along, we discovered there had been a terrible car accident involving more than twenty cars. A number of people had died. It turned out that the accident occurred just about the time I would have left the game, if I hadn't gone to the hospital. So, if I had played the whole game, who knows? I do believe in predestination—the idea that things happen for reasons—but I don't get too caught up in it like someone like Shirley MacLaine does. If you think about fate too much, the coffee'll get cold and you'll miss dessert.

The next day, I went to an orthopedic specialist, who told me, very bluntly, that there was a chance my leg wouldn't grow properly, that it might be three inches shorter than the left! If that happened, they'd have to break it again. *No way,* I thought. I refused to be handicapped or deformed. I realized for the first time in my life that I was mortal. Something awful could actually happen to me.

The two and a half months I spent in my room were incredibly lousy. My crutches became my door lock. I'd prop them under the knob while I'd masturbate constantly, looking at girlie magazines. I was in pain, but I still felt terribly sexy. Many times I had an erection because the cast made me feel submissive and in the power of the beautiful women in the magazines. Feeling helpless, I'd rub my cock against any soft material I could find and shower it with my come.

My hockey uniform was the only thing that kept me sane in that little, dreary room. Hanging up behind the door, I thought it was the only thing that gave me value as a person. I'll never forget the day I had to give it up. I could understand that the team needed someone to fill in their roster. They said it was only temporary, but I didn't want to part with my uniform. Another kid's father came to pick it up. I was crushed, and he saw it in my face. He looked at me and told my mom, "I'm very sorry to have to do this, Shirley." When he took the uniform, he took a piece of me. I felt empty inside. Now I was nothing.

I still went down to the rink and watched my teammates play. They'd tell me that I was still part of them, but I never believed them or felt it. When I went into the locker room, another kid was wearing my uniform.

I couldn't go to school, so I had a tutor at home. One day, he asked me to write a story. In a very cool, precise style, I wrote a sexy story about a young boy who was into fucking lots of women. The kid took drugs and masturbated constantly. Women would go down on him and suck him off. Then a bunch of women would tie him up. The kid was helpless, totally submissive to them, just as I was helpless and submissive wearing my cast. Finally, the young boy went to sleep under the wheel of a bus and died. Needless to say, the tutor was shocked.

Years later, when I started doing porno movies, I'd snort cocaine, trying to reach the *ultimate* submissive high. I'd take some coke and do it up the nose first. Then I'd put a bit of powder in my mouth, and then up my anus. The high was tremendous. Three of my orifices were numb and submissive at the same time, as I'd try to reach the ultimate orgasm. I'd sometimes get close, but the synchronization was tough.

Cocaine is white. It comes in a neat little package, sort of like a bar of soap. I guess I was trying to clean and purify myself. I'd try to get back into the secrecy, the privacy of what sex used to be before porno. I'd put the cocaine on a mirror and take out a fashion magazine like *Cosmopolitan.* I'd flip through and try to find the woman I really wanted. I challenged myself with an idealized woman I couldn't have in reality. Maybe I was trying to punish myself, but I don't think it was for doing porno films per se. It was for losing my romantic conception of lovemaking. I actually lost my prick to the movies. Wearing that cast, I felt the innocent submissiveness I would later lose.

When they finally took off the cast, my foot looked like a skeleton. I still needed crutches. The next day, I knew my team was leaving for a game at Syracuse. More than anything, I wanted to be there when they left. Big Mike took me down to the rink. I was in a lot of pain, but I limped over to the van, smiling, without my crutches, just to show them how tough I was. Getting back into playing the game was a very slow process. About four months later, the team allowed me to join them during intermission and skate around on the ice. They gave me a new number and I came back for the last portion of the season.

Here I was, I had broken my leg two years in a row. I never believed anything like that could happen to me. Death was my ultimate fright. I remember driving home from Rangers games down Ocean Parkway. We'd pass Washington Cemetery near Avenue M. I'd feel very frightened looking at the tombstones. How could I tell my father why I was crying? How could I tell him I knew I was going to die some day and I wasn't going to have him or play hockey forever? One time I *did* tell him and Dad said, "Forget it. You're not going to die." But I knew the truth, even young dinosaurs die.

The second year after my injury, I played much better. A fourteen-year-old Bantam, the team relied on me even more. That's when I met Vinnie, who's still a close friend. A little bull of an Italian, he's now going bald and worries about it every day of his life. He's a tough guy, but he opens up in front of me. In fact, he's told me that I'm the only person he's cried in front of. I always saw an interesting softness and gentleness underneath this very un-soft exterior.

When we were in our teens, Vinnie and I would drive around in his old Le Mans and pick up girls. I'll never forget one day: We were cruising around Coney Island Avenue, talking to these two girls, when, all of a sudden, we heard a screech. A car hit us in the rear as it was going maybe 55-60 miles an hour. The back of Vinnie's car was smashed all the way up to our seats, but we didn't get a scratch. We looked at each other, thankful we were safe, and we hugged each other. It was the first time we expressed our feelings.

Now, when I see Vinnie after many years and we reminisce or hear certain songs on the radio, we cry together. I love him very much. He's got a wife and a baby now, and he doesn't have much time for me, so we are not as close as we once were. When I'm in town, I'm always on the run, but he's the land even after the building is torn down. You couldn't find a stronger bond of friendship anywhere.

Even though Vinnie was always acting like some kind of nut, he thought *I* was the bigger psychopath. At a game in Philadelphia, when we played for the New York Americans, I fought three guys in a row. Vinnie was on the sidelines yelling "psycho" at me, goading me on.

In hockey, you were taught to fight. I have kept that lesson. I remember one game where a total free-for-all broke out. The benches emptied, but I was very cautious. Then, *bang!* Some guy hit me across the temple and gave me a big welt. My mother pulled me off the ice. She yelled at me, "If you ever let somebody hit you like that again, I'm going to hit you!" You'd expect your coach to say that, but not your mother! After that, I never gave anyone the opportunity to hit me. I always threw the first punch. Now, I fight to kill.

Seven

Onward and Upward

I'm sure you're curious about my teenage years. When did I first have sex? And how did I get involved in acting?

The first girl I *could* have fucked was in the seventh grade. Vickie had the biggest chest in the whole school. She liked me, and I was crazy about her. The night before I had a date with her, I'd take a pack of cigarettes and put one of the filtered ends as far as I could into my penis hole. Then I'd put it back into the pack. When she'd smoke it, I practically had an orgasm watching her. I used to tell myself, "She's sucking my cock, because the cigarette was in my pee-hole." One day, Vickie and I went back to my house while my parents were at work. We both got a little drunk, and she started to touch me. I knew I could have gotten laid, but I was too scared.

I started hanging around with a guy named Kenny. He had terrible acne and was kind of homely, so I got all the girls. Soon, I was seeing Misty, a beautiful, tall, big-busted twelve-and-a-half-year-old. Misty and I went out on dates and got into some heavy-duty tongue kissing. Since Kenny's parents were away in Europe for a month, we took advantage of the situation. We invited Misty and another girl to come up to the apartment. Misty and I hugged and kissed, but never made love. She did, however, give me something to remember her by: mononucleosis.

Then, in junior high school, I met Angela. At home, I'd take a ruler and measure my dick when I had an erection. It was close to six inches in those days. I put a little line on the ruler to mark it off and showed the ruler to Angela in class—except she had no idea what the line symbolized. Little did she know, I used to look at that ruler and imagine fucking the hell out of her.

One of the first porno movies my friends and I ever went to see was at the Cinema Kings Highway. I guess we looked older than we were, because they let us in without a question. We walked in on the middle of *Long Jeanne Silver,* during the scene where her leg is deep in some guy's asshole. I couldn't believe it! In amazement, I said, "Jesus Christ, where's the sneaker?" I liked porno, but this was ridiculous. "How the hell am I going to jerk off to *this?*" I asked out loud, which made everyone in the place laugh. When Jeanne finally pulled out, I was even more astounded. She had left her foot inside! I didn't learn until I worked with her many years later that Long Jeanne Silver was an amputee. Her left leg had been removed at the age of two because she was missing a bone.

I was sixteen the first time I got laid. Vinnie told me about a place called "Episodes." It was a whorehouse on Remsen Street in Brooklyn, opposite St. Francis College, and it was open twenty-four hours a day. You'd get there, park your car, go to the second floor, get beeped in, and pay the Madame ten bucks (plus forty cents tax). I was nervous as a motherfucker. It was a cold, wintery day near Christmas. I was wearing a pink shirt that said "Number One" on it. I guess I needed the ego artillery. I chose this very pretty Puerto Rican woman and gave her a card that said "Alcohol and mitt rub." She took me to her room and told me to get undressed. When she came back, the first thing she asked me was how big of a tip I was going to leave. Keep in mind I didn't have a job and had been saving up for this for a week. I said, "Honey, I don't have a tip."

She sighed, "Okay, baby. I'll just have to give you the usual."

As she washed my dick, I held a basin under it. Putting a little Phisoderm into the water, she mixed it with her hand. Then she gripped my penis and squeezed it hard. Checking for V.D., I guess, but nothing came out. Except anxiety.

I crawled on top of her. She didn't have to get me hard, because I already had an erection in anticipation. I knew exactly how my dick was going to feel in her pussy. I knew how my hips and the muscles of my ass were going to move. I wanted to go on forever, but I came in about twenty-two seconds. Then she hit me on the back and said, "Come on, baby. That's it." She didn't even wash me, just walked out of the room.

I went to "Episodes" at least twenty-five times after that. Soon, I fell in love with a hooker named April. I was about seventeen, and she was probably twenty-five. I had a part-time job in a bagel store and helped myself to a few bucks from the cash register just so I could be with her. I paid to make love to April for about two months. Then all of a sudden, she wasn't there anymore.

After that, I met Joanne in high school. I was in the eleventh grade and she was in twelfth. Now I was in love with a big-titted, bleached-blonde Italian girl who smoked cigarettes and wore a leather jacket. Joanne was cool, and she always gave me the hottest looks. I'd stare back at her, totally taken by her charisma. Sometimes we'd have lunch together, but she was dating another guy. Because Joanne couldn't go out with me, I started to see Michelle.

Michelle worked at Martin's Restaurant with my sister. We never did anything but dry hump. After I drove her home in my beat-up Ford Fairlane, I'd come home with a tremendous stain on my pants. Michelle's parents hated my guts. Her mother looked like a fat Joan Rivers and her father looked like Ernest Borgnine. I'd dry hump Michelle on the living room sofa until we both came.

One time, Michelle was just about to suck me off when her father walked in. I quickly pulled my shirt over my dick. Thank God he wasn't wearing his glasses, but I swear he knew what was going on. He was a retired detective, and I was afraid he'd kill me.

Michelle and I bickered all the time, and I still had a crush on Joanne, but I didn't know where she lived. One day, as I made a right turn on Avenue Z, I saw Joanne crossing the street. I stopped the car. She looked beautiful, her hair all blonded-out like Barry Manilow and combed back in a D.A. I said, "Hi, remember me?"

And she smiled, "Sure I do."

When Joanne stepped into my car, it was like I was suddenly a woman being penetrated by a guy for the first time. She had discovered an extra orifice and was deep inside me. With the car door closed, I felt total security. I was so surrounded, cradled. I thought I had it all. This was a girl I didn't have to pay. This was *my* girl. And she only lived five blocks away.

Joanne and I began seeing each other. Within two weeks, we were in love. I couldn't wait to make love to her, but she didn't want to do it in my room. We went to the Manhattan Beach Hotel. There were roaches crawling around, but I didn't care. I was going to get laid.

Two strokes and it was over! "You came?" she asked. I

wanted to die. My life was over. I wished my mother had never met my father. But Joanne was nice about it. "It's all right," she said, holding me. Of course, my dick soon came back to life. We did it again. And again.

From that time on, Joanne and I would screw anytime, everywhere. In the back seat of my car. In the front seat of my car. In the morning, before my mom woke up. In Joanne's house, when her parents went out. We used to fight like cats and dogs, but boy did we fuck. Joanne loved to be on top, and I loved to watch her come. In sex, I've always been the giver more than the receiver.

Sadly, my first love ended on a very sour note after seven months. Joanne was very neurotic and was always getting sick. After a lot of feuding, I just had to leave her. A few years later, she married a very jealous Cuban guy. We tried to keep in touch, but her husband wanted to bust my head open.

After Joanne, I went back to doing what I always did the best—whacking the hell out of my dick.

I still loved hockey, but I knew I had no future in it. I did, however, make it as far as semi-pro, on the New Haven Nighthawks (a New York Rangers farm team), and I played three exhibition games. I was being conditioned to develop only one ray in the spectrum of life: violence. It was the only survival tactic on the ice. I made the mistake of taking that violence home with me.

That kind of attitude was getting the best of me. I was only happy when I hurt someone or instilled fear—but I wanted people to respect me for the person I was, not because I scared the shit out of them.

So, I was ready to leave hockey. I really didn't know what to do with my life. Outside of the rink, I had always relied on my good looks. I thought that was all I needed. I was the wrapper, the bow, *and* the box. All I knew was that I had feelings and looks, but the big question was, "Is there anything *inside?*" I hoped I had some other talent besides beating up guys on the ice and looking cute.

I had a scholarhip to Winona College, but I didn't take it. I guess I didn't feel I was ready for college. It's funny, I lived the life of a tough guy from Brooklyn, a real callous specimen, but I had the insecurities of not wanting to leave home. I wanted to stay pretty close to my family. While I might have played hockey up in Canada here and there, I would always come home. I didn't want to be far from my family or my friends or my girlfriends.

Eventually I commuted to Kingsborough Community College. I didn't really know what I was doing at the time. I was about to give up hockey, and I was taking courses in accounting—and doing pretty well. But I just knew it wasn't my life to sit behind a desk and spend hours figuring out worksheets. I was a radical, gung-ho guy, always taking the lead, and I couldn't get used to following the leader, which was what college was pretty much all about. I wanted to go my own way.

In any case, my college career didn't last long. I got suspended for belting a teacher, and I quit soon after that.

I wanted to be a "somebody." One day I was going through the *TV Guide* and spotted an ad for "The Barbizon School of Acting." It was a route that might give me a future, but I needed $564 to attend. My mom had just cashed in some stocks and had a little extra money. Without a second thought, she gave me the tuition on the spot. She would give you her last dime if you needed it.

On a warm summer afternoon, my friend Scott drove me down to Barbizon. A very nice lady interviewed me. I could have wiped my ass right in front of her and she would have smiled, "Great job!" She enrolled me in a class with twenty students. The teacher's name was James Beard, and he'd appeared in many "soaps." I liked him. He was friendly and really wanted to help us succeed.

The class had a typical New York City variety of people: black, white, Hispanic, Indonesian—a frightened but hopeful slice of the United Nations. We all wanted to get somewhere. We all looked at each other, thinking, "Hey, maybe I'm the one." At Barbizon, they pumped up our egos and made us feel like big stars, but we were really tiny lugnuts that needed a lot of oiling.

When I told my Dad how well I was doing in acting class, he only shrugged, "When are they going to get you a job?" Finally, they did send me out on an audition. It was a commerical for some kind of hair product, but I didn't get the job.

Next, I tried out for a part at Manhattan Lambda Productions. It was at a dark, grimy theater. You had to walk up a flight of stairs to get there, past a bum and two puddles of urine. Little did I know that this was a gay theater and I was the only non-gay person there. I read for the part of Adam Oakheart in a play called *Dirty Work at the Crossroads.* How the hell was I supposed to know that this play was going to be in drag? Or that guys were going to be playing the roles of women? So there I was, reading opposite this guy who's playing the part of Mom. He's starting to hold me, his son, very affectionately. I nearly peed in my pants. Twice.

I didn't think I gave a good reading, but the next day they called and said they wanted me to play "Adam." I was overjoyed. I fell in love with the role—but I didn't want my friends to see me in it, because the character was such a soft, gentle guy, and they'd probably laugh. Growing up in Brooklyn, you have to be tough. I had to bite harder than I really wanted to. Now I was playing this soft character and working with homosexuals. But there was no sexual pressure. Not yet.

Eight

Among the Wolves

One of the actors from *Dirty Work at the Crossroads* took a terrific liking to me. Frank told me that he had a "girlfriend," but I never saw her. He often used to come to our house—and one night he even asked if he could stay over. We wrestled, fooling around in my bedroom. I could tell by the way he was holding me that there was something more to it, because he wasn't rough. After a tough man's sport like hockey, suddenly I'm playing macho games with a guy who really wanted to be cuddly.

Backstage at *Dirty Work,* I met Charles, one of the producers. A little Polish guy in black-rimmed glasses, he was in his early fifties. Charlie was a homosexual, but I figured there was no harm in being his friend. I was naive enough to think that, as long as I kept my zipper up, there would be no problem. Besides, he wanted to "help" my "acting career," and he seemed lonely, and I felt sorry for him. Then he started getting personal, touching me, laying his hand on my shoulder. He kept trying to get me to kiss him.

At that time, I weighed about 210 and was into bodybuilding. We'd walk around the Village, and he was proud to be seen with me. Charlie kept saying how me loved me, how he wanted to make love to me. Of course I felt uncomfortable, but I continued the relationship for what he could do for my career. I kept hoping he'd see me for the person I was, but he never did. Instead, he told me he wanted to marry me in a gay church. He started to criticize the girls I went out with. Then he started harassing me, calling me at three in the morning. If I wasn't in, he'd grill me the next day about where I'd been.

After *Dirty Work* closed, the next thing I did was *Phaedo,* in which I played the lead. *Phaedo* is about an Athenian who is forced into sexual submission by the Romans. He goes on the auction block—naked, of course. The nudity didn't bother me, but there were a couple of other things I didn't like. For example, I had to be fist-fucked every night (only simulated, of course). I did it, though; if I didn't, I'd lose the part. For some reason, I invited my grandmother to see the play. She sat in the front row. What did she think? She never said, though I do know she had to go to the bathroom five times.

In *Phaedo,* there was a scene where the Romans beat me up. It's dark and there are thunderous noises. Then the lights come up and I'm chained and half-naked. My friend takes off the chains and wipes the blood from my leg. A guy named Ken played the role. He had the hots for me. While I was still chained, he would wipe off the blood and play with my cock. At one performance, I got so pissed off at him that I slammed my elbow into his face. The next night, I gave him lines from a play I had done the year before. Bewildered, he didn't know where the lines were coming from.

While I was appearing in *Phaedo,* I was also auditioning for work with ABC. I did a few walk-ons for the soap "One Life to Live." The casting director was really harassing me. He even offered me the part of "Brad" if I would go to bed with him. He tried anything and everything to get me alone in his office. Then another actor invited me into his dressing room. He told me that one day very soon we were going to smoke pot in the nude and get it on together. He even phoned me at home, and my mom was really impressed that it was the guy who played Brad's father on "One Life To Live." Little did she know what he wanted from me. He and another actor in the series were taking bets on who was going to get me first.

On top of that, Charlie from *Dirty Work at the Crossroads* was still pressuring me to be his lover. Mom couldn't understand why I was so aloof when Charlie was doing so much for my career and didn't ask for a penny. If the man was being so nice, then why wasn't I nice back? I just couldn't tell her. This was my mother, who used to come down and watch me beat the hell out of other guys at hockey. She saw me come home with blood on my hands. How could I tell her that a homosexual wanted me, that he wanted to marry me in a gay church?

The next time Charlie called, I told my mother that I didn't want to talk to him. "Why not?" she asked.

"I just don't want to talk to him."

Mom kept asking why. She covered the receiver and talked to me through gritted teeth, afraid that he could hear her. "You know something? I can't take the way you treat Charlie, the way you treat the family."

That's when it all came out. I told her, "Listen, the reason I don't want to see Charlie is because he wants to *fuck me in the ass!*"

She couldn't believe it. "What?"

"This man on the phone wants to *fuck your son in the ass!* Now do you understand? This man wants to marry me. *Is that what you want?"*

After *Phaedo* closed down, I sent out my photos and resumes to every agent I could find. I was surprised to hear from a big agent named Michael. Before I knew it, he invited me to his posh apartment at the Revere on 57th Street. Michael gave me the best advice I had ever got from any guy trying to get down my pants. He told me, "I don't give a damn if you have to rob a bank, but go to the Neighborhood Playhouse." And I did. I saved all the money I could and finally got to the Playhouse. I worked with Bill Alderson and Sandy Meisner. It was the best move I could have made for my acting career.

The night Carlos Palomino was fighting Aaron Pryor, Michael and I went to a neighborhood bar to watch it. He didn't give a fuck about boxing, and he spent the night trying to get me drunk on Harvey's Bristol Cream. I was petrified that he was going to make his move on me. I had four Valiums in my pocket and started feeding them to him, pretending I was taking them too. I hoped maybe they'd calm him down and make him sleepy. Nothing worked: Michael was still horny. He told me he'd send me out on auditions and manage my career if I'd be "nice" to him. What the hell could I do? I went to bed with him that night, and I sucked his damned cock. It was ridiculous, and it was terrible. When he went down on me, I had to fantasize that he was a woman.

The pressure on me from gays was often unbearable. Not all of the agents were gay, but those who were always wanted sex from me, even the agent of one of America's most revered comedians. This guy looked like a skinny Winston Churchill and was probably eighty years old. I remember going to lunch with him. As I'm taking a bite of out of my hamburger, he tells me how much he loves to suck cock. There goes the frilly toothpick down my throat!

Somehow, I had to keep my sanity and save my asshole for the toilet. Although I manage to do this, I still wasn't happy with my life. I began lifting weights and working out more heavily. One day, I caught a glimpse of myself in a mirror. I saw a good-looking guy, but I was petrified. I stopped and teared in the eye. "There's something wrong," I thought, "I'm worried more about the outside of this body than the inside."

Around that time, I was doing a show at the Actors' Playhouse, called *The Gay Dracula.* I played one of Dracula's disciples: Hank Halloway, a country bumpkin. Again, I had to undress every night in front of an audience. And again, I only took the role because I thought it was going to get me somewhere. When I undressed, some people were offended, but the gays loved it. I grew to feel that I wasn't the naked one, *they* were. I found freedom in nudity.

About two days before the show was about to open, I was walking through the Village. My name was on the marquee across the street, but I wasn't feeling very good about myself. I had no real career. Although I had done a few walk-ons and a radio commercial, it didn't amount to much. I was doing Monday night sketches at the Actors' Playhouse, recreating scenes from *Orpheus Descending* and *P.S. Your Cat Is Dead.* I was well-known in the Village, and people liked my work. I was getting applause, but I had to dig deep for seventy-five cents to get home on the subway. No, I wasn't where I really wanted to be.

Walking down the street, I spotted an ancient-looking black man shining shoes. Maybe I'd feel better if I had my shoes shined. (It always worked for Fred Astaire.) As the little shoeshine guy's working on me, he's singing, laughing, and feeling good. I just couldn't take it anymore. Finally, I demanded to know, "What the fuck are you so happy about?"

He stopped and looked up at me as though he'd heard

it a million times. Putting the rag aside, he even shut the lid on the polish. I felt so small, and *he* was the one on his knees. "You know something, youngblood? You're a good-looking guy. You probably got a lot going for you, but there's one thing wrong. You're not happy."

He was right, but I still asked him, "What about you? You're a goddamned shoeshiner."

He grinned at me, "Yeah, but I got my soul. I got the sun shining. I got my feeling."

I couldn't be as happy as the shoeshiner, but I kept trying to make myself into something I'd be proud of, as a person and as an actor. Like every other performer, I always bought the latest issue of *Backstage Magazine,* searching for that big break. Not long after I met the shoeshiner, I found it, sort of. The ad read: "Extras needed for porno film."

I went to the East 23rd Street address and walked through a big set of black double doors. About fifteen X-rated posters were plastered all over the walls. It looked like the Taj Mahal of smut. Carter Stevens, the guy I was there to see, looked like the King Tut character right out of "Batman." Carter was one of the early makers of "fuck-films." Like the others, he had been making movies since the early 1970s, and for one reason: to make a buck.

I told him I was answering his ad about the extras. Carter took one look at me and said, "Why don't you just be in the movie?" It only took about eight seconds for me to say, "Sure." From that moment, I opened the door to heaven—or hell—I'm still not sure which. My cock was already stirring at the thought that I was going to fuck one of those monstrous ten-foot-tall porno women I had jerked off to all of my life. Here was a chance to get away from all the harrassment I was getting from the gays in legitimate acting and to put some money in my pocket.

The director was Jim Clark, and the movie was called *Wet, Wild, and Wonderful.* I worked with Kandi Barbour and one other woman whose name I can't recall. Forgive me for forgetting, but there are a lot of women like that in porno, women who do just one film—for the hell of it, I guess. They stop cold as soon as they get scared that a guy they really love, or their parents, might see them fucking on screen. The consequences become too great. They're not like the Georgina Spelvins, Marilyn Chamberses, Tracey Adamses, and Amber Lynns, who are the foundations of the business, who keep fucking until their bellies are too round and their tits sag.

The film—probably 16mm—was shot in a house right near Union Square. In my first scene, a woman gave me head. She wasn't very good looking, and I thought I was going to have trouble. Down on her knees, she started sucking my cock in the most unbelievable way. I couldn't hold back and I came all over her face. Afterwards, I discovered that she was a drug addict. Maybe my cock represented her next fix and that's why she was sucking it with such desperation.

That was my first sex scene in porno. There was no buildup, no gradual excitement, no fear. I just pulled my pants down and got a blow job. It gives me chills to think that was more than ten years ago. I was only eighteen. The same day, we did another scene, during which I fucked the luscious Kandi Barbour. At last, I wasn't acting with homosexuals! This was something I really knew about: fucking pretty women. We did it in a classroom, and neither of us enjoyed it too much. That part didn't matter, because I was paid $150 for the sex-scene days and seventy-five dollars for the non-sex days. The whole thing took about three days. With a wad of money in my pocket, I swore I'd never do another porno.

I've said that many times in my life, but making porno movies is like burning your hand in an oven. If you're like me, a few days later you'll get careless and do the same thing all over again.

After completing one of my first movies, I went to an office to pick up my check. I had to decide on a name to appear on the credits. Jerry Butler was singing "Only the Strong Survive" on the radio. I always liked him and the music of the '50s. The lyrics of that song meant a lot to me: "Only the strong survive,/ You've got to be a man,/ You've got to take a stand. . . ." Luckily, Doris Day wasn't singing, because then I might have done gay movies! I decided to use "Jerry Butler" as my porno name. Well, as one of them.

I went from being "Arthur West" to various German names made up from haphazard bunches of letters stuck together. The reason, of course, was that I knew I was committing professional suicide.

In *Manhattan Mistress,* the director used my real name on the credits. I freaked out because I was so afraid of getting caught. I was afraid to admit to myself what I did for a living. If I kept changing my name, my career wouldn't catch up to me. With every switch, it allowed that person to die and get away with what he did. I became a new person because I was taking the responsibility away from myself and hiding behind these mythical identities. I kept mixing and matching names like a shifty card dealer. If you shuffle them fast enough, no one can see what you're doing.

I finally realized that I couldn't pretend any longer. I realized I'd rather dislike the person I'm *not* lying about than dislike the person I am lying about.

When I first started doing pornos, I was sitting in a diner called Del Rio's with Vinnie. He was always praising me, but I was always trying to ignore him. Because I was doing the films, he was convinced that I was a celebrity. How could I tell him I wasn't really happy with what I did? I only did it for the money. Vinnie was shocked when I told him I was thinking of quitting. He said, "What's so wrong with what you're doing? You can make a beautiful living. Accept it. Stop fighting it." From that day on, I stayed with the name "Jerry Butler" and continued in my career.

Vinnie has a very pretty wife, Maria. Her father loves me, but if I ever went out with one of his daughters, forget it. You see, there's a difference. People like "Jerry Butler," and they're amused by "Jerry Butler." But if "Jerry Butler" goes out with your daughter, all of a sudden it's, "Hey, I'll break your fucking head." On one hand, I'm allowed to go, go, go, and then all of a sudden, a cloud comes by.

Porno to me has always been like putting kids in a crib. You touch each other, you smack each other, and there's no real consequence. It's not mature. Porno's just a very immature business. It becomes complicated when you start *getting* mature, about feelings, emotions . . . and about health. But in the early days anyway, to take your clothes off, to hold a woman, to feel a little embarrassed, and have a little fun, and get a bit sloppy and dirty—it was the excitement of the playpen. It can never stay that way, especially when you leave the set. And ten years later, I still haven't made the transition. It's very tough being identified and represented by the name "Jerry Butler." The other day, I asked Lisa if I could do another film. How do you ask your wife such a thing? Doing porno, I have lost all concept of sex. Getting my penis up and shoving it into some woman so I could preserve my longevity in this business became as simple as getting a grease job. But when I have Lisa in my arms, I wonder how I could ever be so casual about sex. You've got to understand what it's like. Sex on the set isn't as emotionally involving as it is in real life, so I'd never consider I was "cheating" on Lisa. It's nothing like the special times she and I share. In porno, sex became a job that had to be done.

Lisa worked for one of the biggest porno producers and distributors, Caballero Control Corporation. Although she's an actress, she's never appeared in a porno film and never will. On the other hand, as Regional Sales Manager she was paid to endorse what I get paid to do. When Lisa used to bring home the latest releases, she insisted we watch them together, "because of the book." I told her, "You're as much a part of this as I am. You're really driving the getaway car. You're an accessory, too."

I'm completely involved when I make love with Lisa—but sometimes, if it's too constructed or choreographed, I get panicky. A lot of women in this business don't really want to fuck or suck cock, but they do it to get done and get paid. The other day, I was making love with Lisa and I suddenly felt she was touching me just to get the job done. For my benefit. I couldn't accept that. I protested and got crazy with her. Sometimes I'm worse than Al Pacino in *Dog Day Afternoon.* I am energy with a heartbeat and blonde hair.

I know one thing. I'm addicted to sex! I'm sure that a lot of guys don't want to come six or seven times a day, but I can—and do. Maybe sex is my security blanket. When we make love, I'm keeping some of Lisa inside of me. But I'm still so insecure about losing her. I just have to remember that you don't have to put a safe in a safe if the first safe is strong enough.

Nine

Iris and Other Flowers

Soon after making *Wet, Wild and Wonderful,* I met Iris. I still remember her phone number: 996-3706. But she's no longer there.

I met her at the restaurant my dad managed. If you've ever been to Coney Island, you've probably seen Nathan's. It's a landmark, and, as their sign says, they've been there "since 1919." There's a self-service counter on the street, but there's also a small dining room with ten small tables. (In all his forty years of working there, my father tells me I'm one of the two waiters he ever had to fire.) One day I saw a sexy Puerto Rican Barbie Doll sitting at Table Ten. A little Spandex top stretched across the roundest tits I've ever seen. They were like proud little apples. A look at her gave me the impression that, at any given moment, she might lie herself down on the table and offer herself to me. It wasn't even my station, but I walked over to the other waiter and said, "I want to work that table."

Little did I know what I was getting myself into. All I felt was the warmth of that dark skin. I *knew* I was going to make love with her. My family was very opinionated about blacks and Puerto Ricans. Maybe that's why I found them so attractive. I took down Iris's phone number and picked her up at Jet Foods, a grocery store near Sea Gate. In the car, she gave me a fantastic blow job. Saliva dripped down her hand and bathed my cock. She wore a million rings. And even before I came, there was saliva dripping from one ring to the next. That and her long red fingernails were enough to make me explode. The only problem was that she had stale marijuana breath.

The first time I made love to Iris in her apartment was horrendous. She didn't really enjoy me as a lover at first, thinking I was very cold. But the truth was that I was nervous about doing it in a place where her boyfriend was paying the rent. The bedroom was awful, with fake fish and lobsters all over the place and with a big net hanging on the wall. I couldn't help but think that the net would entrap me and her boyfriend would come home and find me there. So Iris and I began meeting in hotels, and I started to find my sexual roots. Sometimes we'd screw to an orgasm five or six times a night. Sometimes Iris's pussy lips would swell up to the thickness of my middle fingers. She'd have to put ice on them to relieve the swelling.

Eventually, I moved in with Iris. By this time, we were fucking almost continually. The kids who lived downstairs would tease us and make noises like squeaky bedsprings whenever they saw us. It was pure sex. My cock was in love with Iris. But we didn't get along mentally, socially, or emotionally. Most of the time, life with Iris was fight and fuck, or fuck and fight.

One time, she sprayed aerosol in my face. I hate to hit a woman, but controlling my temper isn't easy. After all, I played hockey for years, and beating the shit out of someone who annoys you is fine when you're in the rink. When Iris bombed me with aerosol, I was afraid to open my eyes and kept throwing overhand rights. With my eyes closed, I felt my fist slam into her skull and heard her hit the floor. As she fell, she bumped her head on the metal radiator. There she was with a hole in her head the size of a golf ball—a slutty Puerto Rican, lying half naked with her perfect little tits popping out, nipples hard, wearing short shorts cleaving to her crotch and high-heeled shoes showing her painted toenails. The sight of her gave me a massive erection.

But blood was shooting out of her head. My brain was in a whirl. How could I make this up to her in five minutes? First, I had to patch up the gash. That would take about three minutes. Only two minutes left to get my dick in her.

On the bathroom floor, I put some peroxide into the cap and poured a capful into the gouge. The stuff bubbled like a hot tub filled with bath salts. I took a needle, some black thread and some ice. I knew what I was doing, because I did the same thing to myself when I played hockey. Freezing Iris's head with the ice, I sewed up the wound and held it together with a butterfly stitch. Iris watched me intently. I knew she was into pain, and she was probably just as turned on as I was. (Sometimes when we fucked, she'd give me a knife, ask me to slit my thumb and drip blood all over her face as I was pumping away. She kept a mirror handy so she could look at herself. Iris would come, screaming like a banshee.) After I stitched up her head, I kept my hand clamped over it for about two hours, lapping her nipples all the while.

Sea Gate, where I lived with Iris, is a private community closed off from Coney Island. They have their own security police, who always gave me a hard time. They knew that, even though I only had a guest pass, I really lived there. One day I came home from work and I saw a cruising car parked outside of our building. As I walked up the steps, I heard voices coming from our apartment. I walked into the kitchen. There was Iris, wearing nothing more than a nightgown, sitting at the table, entertaining two cops. If their hats had been on, I might have been a nicer guy, but their hats were lying upside-down on the kitchen table. One guy was a fat sergeant, the other, a good-looking rookie.

"What the fuck are you doing here?" I yelled at them. They gave some lame excuses. "Get you asses out of my house right now." I shoved Iris into the bedroom. "And take your fucking hats with you," I growled at them. They didn't say a thing, just left in a hurry. I opened the window and started shouting, "The next time you want to fuck my woman, come to the door and ask me." I was especially upset because I had been desperately trying to get Iris pregnant. I thought that was the only way to keep her. Despite our constant arguments, I really believed I was in love with her. I bought her a golden butterfly charm because she was a beautiful, fleeing creature I knew I would lose someday. You just couldn't tie her down.

While I was living with Iris, I got a small part in *Manhattan Mistress,* which was filmed out in the Hamptons in Long Island. I had one sex scene with Merle Michaels, and I couldn't get my dick up. This had never happened to me before (but it would happen many times after). Very sheepishly, I asked her to finger my asshole. Iris and I often did some crazy things together. We'd tie each other up. I'd stick cucumbers inside her. I'd ass-fuck her at least once a night. I could stick my whole hand (up to the wrist) in her vagina. She'd tie me up with a jump rope and then stick the plastic handle up my ass and I'd come. But with Merle, there were so many people watching that I was distracted. Obediently, she stuck her finger up my ass and my dick immediately got hard. Luckily, the cameras focused on my dick, not her finger.

I loved Iris's three-year-old daughter, Danielle, but I was so jealous of her. I was jealous of anyone who had Iris's affection. I did some terrible things to try to get Iris to love me more than she did her daughter. Once I went into the bathroom and pissed all over Danielle's potty and onto the floor. Then I scribbled all over the walls of Danielle's room with her crayons. When Iris got angry at her, she paid more attention to me. I tried to make it up to the kid and took Danielle everywhere. She really liked me, but I could see some hostility in her eyes. She knew we were both rivals for her mother's affections.

When Iris's old boyfriend came around in his van to pick up Danielle, Iris would go downstairs and talk with him. Whenever she spent a moment with a man she used to screw, it killed me. I was always afraid she'd go back with him. Eventually, she did. The guy owned a furniture warehouse and could support her better than I could.

I began doing more and more porno. One of my next films was *Angel Buns.* I played an angel who was into anal sex. I admit, the plot was kind of dumb, but it made Chuck Vincent, one of the best X-directors around, notice me, and it turned my career around. Chuck didn't like the movie, but he was impressed with my performance. He had me in mind for a role in *Roommates.* Chuck was always straight out with me. He's a homosexual, but he never made an overt pass at me. He's such a sweet man that at times I almost wished I *could* give him something sexually. He seemed like such a lonely guy and was so good to me. But I'm a heterosexual. I might have acted in gay productions, but I wasn't gay. I've never done gay porn. I had absolutely no desire to be with a man, no matter how much it paid.

Recently, Chuck's traded in making high-class pornos for

B-movies like *Deranged* and *New York's Finest.* In the early 80s, Chuck was one of the first people to give adult films class and charisma. He shaved the ugly corners off pornography. As I mentioned earlier, *Roommates* was a big breakthrough film. Only my fifth or sixth movie, I was working with some of the greatest porno talents in New York: Samantha Fox, Veronica Hart, Kelly Nichols, Jamie Gillis, Jack Wrangler.

Roommates was about the trials and tribulations of three female roommates. Shot openly in the streets of Manhattan and Queens, there was none of this sneaking around shit like there is today on the West Coast. When I did *Angel Buns,* I swam in sleaze, but this was different. It took about five days to shoot, an eternity for an adult movie. Chuck even rented an entire theater on West 14th Street to shoot some non-sex scenes.

While we were filming it, I met a beautiful woman with long, brown braided hair. She was an actress in the soap "The Guiding Light." We had lunch and she invited me home that night. She knew I was doing a sex film, and she didn't want to fuck me. Instead, she gave me a blow job. Maybe what she really wanted was a statue, a symbol of porno dirtiness, but not the real thing. I was whatever she wanted me to be.

Roommates opened at the 8th Street Playhouse, which runs general-release movies, not porn. I couldn't believe the audiences's response; they loved it. Judith Crist gave *Roommates* a good review and singled out my performance. She stressed that it was an adult movie, but most people wouldn't be offended. People in the sex business didn't take it seriously, though. Jealous, I guess. Somebody who's looking to get off would rather see five barrels of come on some girl's face than emotion and drama. There was scene after scene of no sex and a lot of *internal* ejaculations. It wasn't all prettiness; it was life being captured by a camera.

Veronica Hart and I had a lot of fun together. Later, she said our sex scene was the only one in porno that ever "felt like love" to her, and her husband still teases her about it. We even shot some exteriors in the Village, where, months earlier, Charlie strolled proudly by my side, showing me off. There I was, doing a movie, singing and dancing down Cherry Lane.

After *Roommates,* I met Camille. She will always be a very sweet flower in my memory: a rose with a few thorns hiding on the stem. Camille worked in a health spa and had beautiful, strong thighs. She was a typical Italian girl from Bensonhurst. For some reason, her folks never liked me, even though they didn't know about my porno life. I always meant to send her old man some hard-core movie stills, but I never got around to it.

Camille and I got pretty serious. I was making a few movies on the side, but she knew it. Soon, I bought her a pretty, little engagement ring for $250. It was all I could afford. I gave it to her on Christmas at my sister Linda's apartment. Camille trembled and cried. Elated, we went back to tell her parents. When her mother looked at the ring, she said, "That's it?" I was so embarrassed. The next week, Camille took some of her own money and we traded in the ring for a bigger one. She still has it today.

Although she'll deny it, Camille was bulimic. She also thought her chest was too small and her nose was too big, but I was happy with her shape as it was. Finally, though, she got her nose job and then wanted a tit job and a hip job. She was constantly at war with herself. Camille also had the smelliest vagina I ever encountered off-screen. When I was fucking to eat, I didn't care, but when I was making love, it was different. She trimmed her pussy hairs so that they stood up like the top of Dennis the Menace's head, when she knew I liked a lush, natural bush.

Despite all of that, I really did have a lot of love for Camille. Of all the women I've been with, she still goes to my parents' apartment to visit them. Even though I knew Camille was holding me back, I tried to convince myself that whatever she gave me was enough.

During this time, I was still acting in legit theater, and I had the part of "Donald" in *American Buffalo* in an off-off-Broadway production. It was written by David Mamet, who has since become very well-known. I'll never forget the night Camille and I parked outside of the Marlboro Housing Projects on Stillwell Avenue after one performance. While we were kissing in the car, a big shot gun came in through the window. "Get down on your knees, motherfucker," a voice yelled. I thought it was a cop, but it was five black kids. They held a gun to my temple for about an hour, ransacked the car, went through my pockets, and molested Camille. At that time, I hadn't even touched her yet. Horrified, I saw them playing with her tits and fingering her crotch. She started crying that she was pregnant. I caught on quickly.

"That's right," I lied, with tears pouring down my cheeks. "It's my baby. Please don't hurt her."

They told Camille, "We're not going to kill you. We're just going to kill this motherfucker."

I was sure my life was over. I prepared myself to die. Waiting to hear the gunshot, I put myself into a numb state. After they had their fun tormenting us, they threw the keys under the car and left. I could have gone chasing after them, but I just wanted to go home. I just wanted to see my father.

"Dad," I cried, as soon as I walked in, "thank God 'I'm alive! Come here and hold me. Just hold me."

"What's the matter?" he asked.

"Hold me. Just tell me you love me. Just hold me."

He kept asking, "What happened?"

I kept trying to tell him, but couldn't. I had been so close to death that I still wasn't sure I was alive. I just wanted this man to hold me. I just wanted this man to love me. He held me, but not like I needed him to. Then I got mad and yelled, "Hold me! Will you really *hold* me?"

But he just couldn't do it."It's all right," he said.

"It's *not* all right."

"It's over. Nothing happened. It's okay.

But I sobbed, "It's *not* okay. Don't you understand?"

I'm not sure I understood it myself.

Ten

Bi-Coastal

Soon, I found an escape-hatch from my stifling relationship with Camille. Dave Marsh, from Collector's Video, saw me in a movie and asked me to shoot a film out in California, but Camille had just made me promise to stop doing porno. To make a living, I was working at Nathan's. Again.

Dave's offer was tempting. He even sent me plane tickets. I finally decided *to hell with it. Why not?* I packed up and taxied to the airport (where I got drunk, because I hate to fly). Five hours later, I was in California. A chauffeur picked me up and brought me to the Highland Hotel. The next day, I met Richard Pacheco and Jamie Gillis, two of porn's great male leads. I was in Hollywood! Totally overwhelmed, I was swallowed up by that town. My only sex scene in that film was simulated. (It's the only way Camille would let me do it.) Dave's wife Svetlana *had* to have me for that movie, but it was on my terms.

Richard and I played Jamie's manager. He had to fuck 5,000

women in a month. We shot the film all over town, and I met everyone under the California sun. I even went down to the "General Hospital" set for auditions.

"Monique" was also in the movie. I'd seen her as a *Penthouse* centerfold. Now she's a "B" actress, always popping up in those *Danger Zone* movies. At that time, she had the most gorgeous tits and the ultimate, perfect body. I took Monique back to my room at the Highland. Ron Jeremy wanted her too—but then, Ron wants *everybody*. I managed to get rid of him and spend some time alone with her. Monique made these purring sounds when I screwed her. It got on my nerves. I hate when women purr. You can be an animal when it comes to sex, but you don't have to *sound* like one.

After we wrapped up *Nice Girls Do*, I came back to New York. I was uneasy because I really didn't want to see Camille again. Although I didn't screw on camera, I had fucked a few women out West. The shoot was only six days, but I stayed about eleven. I knew Camille was going to be waiting for me at the airport, but it was over. I put on a happy face and tried to give her a "hello" hug. In California, I had seen the ocean. I just couldn't live by the creek any longer.

It isn't easy to break up, even when your feelings of love are gone. I thought up an elaborate scheme to let Camille down easy. I had hurt my back. A doctor gave me a prescription, some big red painkillers. To make Camille lose interest, I told her I was now a drug addict. When that didn't work, I told her I was turning gay. Finally, I told her the truth. I felt terrible, but I just didn't want her anymore.

After Camille and I broke up, I almost abandoned the business. I was studying acting at the Neighborhood Playhouse and was terrified of being labeled as a porno person. Two things in life scared me then—death and holding back my acting career by doing pornography. One night, I was sitting at Table Two in Nathan's, not feeling very good. My dad said, "Why don't you do another movie?" To him, it was like taking an aspirin for a headache. Although my mom and sister were embarrassed, my dad found nothing wrong with me working in porno. "Call Chuck Vincent," my dad urged. I did, and Chuck told me he was shooting a movie the next week.

"I've been trying to reach you," he said. But *everyone* says that. In porno, if you don't keep in touch, they just find someone else to plug up the holes. Kevin James had my part in *In Love.* Chuck fired Kevin and gave the role to me. Kevin's resented me ever since, and I don't blame him.

In Love was like another *Roommates,* but it had an even bigger budget. We rehearsed in New York, and then we shot three or four days in Florida, before wrapping it up in New York again. I was quickly fitted for wardrobe. (Yes, you do need a wardrobe in porno!) I told the Neighborhood Playhouse I was taking a brief leave of absense.

In Love is a very pretty movie. Some even regard it as one of porno's most artistic moments. It chronicles a twenty-year unrequited love affair between my character and one played by Kelly Nichols. I never really enjoyed working with Kelly, and I found her to be very tedious. What saved me was the fact that most of the sex scenes were very stylized. (We had one long sex scene in a rowboat!) Because you couldn't see a lot of ins and outs, you couldn't tell that I wasn't totally erect. With Larry Revene's high quality camerawork, *In Love* is a visually pleasant film to watch.

Back in New York, we had a couple of days off before finishing the rest of the movie at Adventureland Studios in Corona, Queens. By that time, I had already taken a week and a half off from the Neighborhood Playhouse. I called Bill Alderson, the manager there. He was very cold to me, and I knew right away I was out of the Workshop. When I told Bill I'd come by to pay him some money I owed him, he said, "Don't bother." He had found out that I'd done pornography and was terrified that his esteemed company's reputation had been blackened. (Sanford Meisner's Neighborhood Playhouse is almost as well-known as Lee Strasberg's Actors' Studio.) I wrote a note to Bill, telling him I knew why they didn't want me; but I still wouldn't give up. I had learned a lot from the Playhouse and nobody could ever take that away from me. If I went back there today, I think I'd find many of the same students sitting in the same seats, too afraid to test their talent.

Dave Marsh called me again. He and Svetlana *had* to have me for another movie they were shooting—this time in Hawaii. At first, Hawaii looked like Florida to me. I couldn't understand what the big deal was until we took a little prop plane to a more desolate island, which had only one airstrip. *This* place impressed me. I felt proud of where porno had taken me. All because I fucked on film! My dick was like a winning lottery ticket. Looking around at the changing colors and greenery, I wished my mom were there to see it. Maybe then she wouldn't be so embarrassed by me.

That first time in Hawaii is a maze of memories. I stepped on a centipede and I still have the mark on my foot. I was in Stacey Donovan's first sex scene ever, and she was crying. The sound man had a run-in with Dave, and Svetlana and hid the audio tapes. We also shot another film, *A Little Bit of Hanky Panky.* Before I could catch my flight, I had to "rape" Ginger Lynn on the beach. The sun was setting, but I managed to fuck the hell out of her and just make my plane back to the main island to shoot another movie in California, *Taboo III.*

Kirdy Stevens picked me up at the L.A. Airport. To this day, he tells me how stunning I looked with a deep tan and my hair bleached by the sun. "I was even falling in love with you, and I'm an old man," he joked. After *Taboo III,* I had $4,000 in my pocket. Back in New York, I put that money in the bank. I settled into my old life: working at Nathan's and studying acting.

In California, I had met up with Alexis, a makeup girl. Her dad was a *Penthouse* photographer. The first time I did cocaine was when I found a vial of it in Alexis's sock. It was my first time, but not my last. In New York, the $4,000 I had banked quickly dwindled. I made a lot of money in porno, and when people ask me where it is, I tell them that I blew it. Literally. I spent most of it on cocaine. When you make a dirty dollar, you spend it fast.

Before I went to Los Angeles the first time, there weren't too many pornos being shot in New York. But in L.A., everyone and his brother were making "adult films," as they liked to call them. I was soon making an average of two a week, doing one-day movies, three-day movies. People must think I've made a million dollars in porno. Far from it! If I worked two days a week at five hundred bucks a day, that's a thousand bucks. If I made four movies a month, that's only two thousand. Not bad, but not a hell of a lot either. A lot of my roles were one-day "pop shots." Top female stars make double or triple of what the guys do. Standard for a woman in a lead role is $750 a day, and they don't even have to give a "cum shot"! For guys, it's somewhere between $350 and $700, usually paid in cash at the end of the shoot. John Leslie claims he gets a thousand a day. Guys on the street always ask me how they can get into the movies. Money: *damn.* I normally don't like to tally up the money I've made in this business—it makes me feel worse about what I've done, and what I didn't do.

I certainly haven't made a lot of money. You might make a movie once or twice every couple of weeks and make a thousand bucks or so . . . but then you might not work for two weeks . . . or you can do five films straight. I would guess that the average porno actor makes no less than $20,000 a year. A guy can pull in up to $65,000 if he pushes his fanny. Women, of course, can get astronomical bucks—up to $150,000, because they got the mail-order business, the private parties, etc. People like Marylin Chambers and Seka can get between

$10,000 and $20,000 a movie . . . but they might not work as much.

Sixty-five thousand is like a million to me. The problem is, when a porno actor gets paid, it's usually in hundred-dollar bills. And they become like one-dollar bills because you make them so fast. If we were paid in smaller denominations—or change!—we wouldn't spend it so fast. The sheer bigness of the lump sum would jolt us back to our senses.

Porno is not easy work. It's not glamorous. And there are lots of consequences.

But I wasn't thinking of the consequences when I left New York. On the East Coast, I was only making about two movies a month and I was going bananas living with my parents. If I was going to continue in porno, I had to go to California, because that's where most of the work was. When I first arrived in L.A., in 1983, I stayed with a photographer named Joel. I met him doing *Pink Lagoon* that first trip to Hawaii. I moved into his loft apartment in the heart of sleazy downtown L.A. When I wasn't working, I used to sit with the bums and order pizzas for them.

I had heard talk about a porno casting agent named Jim South, who ran a place called "World Modeling Agency," so I phoned him. Jim knew who I was, but he told me to come down to a "cattle call." I had already done a lot of movies and was nominated for "Best Actor" awards. I wasn't going to any "cattle call." Jim wanted me to come down and let him "see" me. Shit, if he wanted to "see" me, he could watch one of my movies. This wasn't real Hollywood. And what did he want to check out? The size of my dick?

When I met Jim, I didn't like his appearance. He was too immaculate and articulate for porn. One thing I didn't want was "properness." I had to find reality, a family. I decided not to get involved with Jim South.

Fortunately, there was another big agent in town, Reb Sawitz. His operation was called "Pretty Girl International." Even though I was "Jerry Butler," I was hesitant to phone him. Reb was so grateful when I did call, though. He was almost in awe. "Jerry Butler!" he said enthusiastically. "I want you to come down here right now." I finally felt wanted. Of course there were dollar signs involved, but I didn't hear that in Reb's voice.

Reb was not like Jim South. He was a big, comfortable-looking guy with a sloppy belly. When he talked to you, he put his legs up on the desk. He was so warm and accommodating, like your favorite uncle. And that's what I needed to survive in porno, not to mention life.

Reb invited me to live in his house. What a place! It was like a corral of smut, a farm to breed porno actors. At any given time, there could be fifteen porno people sleeping on his living-room floor. We made lots of money, but most of us spent it on drugs.

Reb got me a lot of work. Porno casting agencies like his operate on a commission basis. At the time, the video companies gave him fifty dollars for every actor he supplied for a job. If the work was out of town, the plane ticket and the script would be waiting at Reb's office. I guess he makes a lot of money. He runs ads in local newspapers like the *Hollywood Press*, the *Daily News*, even in the *Los Angeles Times*. The ads call for "nude modeling." Reb leads the women in with the whole nude-modeling bit. When they get comfortable, he tells them he has a good feeling about their talent. Then he says, "You could also make five hundred to a thousand dollars a day doing movies." The dollar signs light up in their eyes.

There's always been a lot of conflict between modeling/porno agencies like Reb's and Jim's. If they just collaborated, they'd end the tension. Actually, they create most of the tension themselves. The agents consider themselves to be right there in the war with you, but they really aren't. While the bullets are flying at you on the battlefield, they're in the kitchen peeling potatoes. Then they go home to their nice little lives in their nice little houses. No one sees their faces. Nobody knows who they are.

Watching "Hunter" on TV the other day, I caught a glimpse of the Hollywood Inn on Highland Avenue, which was where I used to live before I moved in with a guy named Lee in Palm Springs. Lee had been casting director for 20th Century Fox and supposedly cast *The Sound of Music.* Even though he was a homosexual, I thought he might really want to help my career, like he promised. I took a Greyhound out to Palm Springs. At his place, Lee threw a fifteen-page management contract at me. True, I was looking for some sort of leadership, but not the kind he proposed. He wanted to change my acting name to "Stud Butler" and said he would put me into the prime-time TV series "Three's Company." I'd have to play "Stud Butler, porno guy." I didn't do it; I didn't want to make fun of the industry or be a stereotype.

From the minute I walked in Lee's front door, he put the make on me. "I just want to take care of you," he told me. "I want you to live here. I want to feed you, bathe you. You don't have to do anything." Lee scared me, but I was impressed with who he was, so I stayed with him for a while.

I finally left Lee on bad terms. I just walked out one day and kept the car he had rented for me. I actually lived in the car for two weeks with a puppy named Bandit. Reb wouldn't let me stay with him, so I parked outside of his house.

Lee was searching all over the place for me. Finally, a friend drove with me out to Palm Springs. I left the car outside his house and split after running up a $1,300 rental bill. I figured he owed me at least that much for the weeks of sexual harassment I'd suffered, but Lee saw it differently. He kept calling Reb looking for me, claiming that he was going to take me to court. I knew too much information about the sleazeball to let him get away with that.

Collector's Video called again. This time Dave and Svetlana wanted me to do *Pink Lagoon* (the sequel to *Surrender in Paradise*) and *Panty Raid* in Hawaii. Dave, Svetlana, Eugene (the cameraman), and myself went out there three days before everyone else. Cocaine wasn't plentiful on the island, but the marijuana was world-famous. Ginger didn't fall for me the second time around, but a woman named Raven did. She came from an extremely wealthy family in South Carolina, and she wanted to set me up in daddy's business and marry me. Raven was cute, but I declined the offer.

By the time I got back from Hawaii, I had worn out my welcome with Joel, so I went to Reb's again. Then I met Claudia, who worked for a men's magazine. She gave me an open invitation to move in with her. When I took one look at Reb's trailer, I knew I couldn't stay there. On to Claudia in Culver City! She had the most charming little house.

There was only one bedroom, so we slept together, but Claudia really didn't like sex. She'd say "ouch" with each thrust. It felt like I was making love to a pin-cushion with feelings. At first, I thought she was sore, so I waited a few days before trying again. The next time I was kissing her, sucking her nipples—she had beautiful breasts—I saw that look on her face again. It was as though she were thinking, "Damn, are we going to have sex again?" I took it slow and spread her legs so I could see her pretty little black-haired pussy. Easing the head of my cock in, she moaned, "Ouch." What could I do? I pulled out, came on her leg, and went to sleep.

Except for sex, Claudia and I got along well. She'd work, and when I wasn't making movies, I'd sit home and watch cable TV. My friend Buck Adams—whom I'd met at Reb's—would come by and we'd have Pioneer Chicken, Pepsi, and we'd party. When I wasn't watching TV or eating chicken, I'd jerk off. Claudia would come home and find baby oil stains on her beautiful powder-blue sofa pillows. I kept turning them over, trying to hide the stains. But how long can you do that?

I went to a lot of parties where Claudia worked. At one of them I met two girls, named Cathy and Laurie. We all came back from the party drunk. I had the balls to ask Claudia if she minded me screwing them, since we weren't really lovers. To my surprise, she said it was fine. In fact, she lay on the sofabed and watched us. With one eye closed, she reminded me of the "one-eyed cat peeking through the seafood store" from the rock-n-roll song "Shake, Rattle and Roll."

Cathy, Laurie, and I became pretty close after that, and I eventually moved in with Laurie in Venice. Cathy would stop by and we'd screw together in the afternoon. But it wasn't a threesome fantasy from a porno movie. When I kissed one pal, I had to kiss the other—or else fur would fly! There was too much pressure on having the only cock in the relationship, so I broke it off. (The relationship, I mean. Not my cock.)

As I talk right now, I'm sitting here looking at a skull I made a long time ago. I remember picking up the kit at a toy store at the Corte Madera Shopping Center. We were making *One Night In Bancock* and I had the day off in the middle of a four-day shoot. I went to the nearby toy store and bought some things to keep me occupied. Directors hated when I brought toys to the set, but at least they kept me out of trouble. Sort of. Once I picked up sticks of brown clay to make fake dog shit. I'd put them all over the set and in front of people's doors at the hotel. I also bought little toys and gifts for everyone: Mr. Potatoheads, Slinkys. During breaks the cast and crew had so much fun that they told me to be sure to bring my Cowboys and Indians the next day.

The day I got the skull, a little boy followed me through the entire store. It seemed as though he were looking for a substitute father. He looked lonely, so I bought him something. Then he told me a little about himself. His parents were divorced, he said, and his mother was at work. She'd drop him off at the shopping center every day and pick him up after work. I felt sorry for the kid. Since he was all alone, I asked him to have dinner with me.

People knew me at the Peppermill Restaurant because I had been there before while making other movies. There I was, sitting happily in the booth with a ten-year-old kid. The waitress started acting strange, telling me that the kid came there all the time with his mother. It was as if she were telling me, "Don't pull any sharp moves, Jerry Butler, because I'm a witness."

I grabbed the waitress by the arm and said I knew what she was up to. Although I didn't owe her any explanations, I told her how I had met the boy. "I'll slap you down if you have any other ideas. I'd end my life before I'd look to fuck up a little kid," I added. Everyone was looking at us, and the manager rushed over. I was so upset that I started crying. The poor kid didn't understand what was going on. He was just sitting there confused, playing with the Gumby figure I had bought him. He admitted to everyone there was nothing sexual between us. The manager apologized, and I think they fired the waitress.

That situation really made me feel dirty. I was being judged by what I did for a living, not for what I really was. We finished dinner, but it wasn't the same. I admitted to the boy that I made movies with women. "Maybe this will teach you not to trust anybody," I told him. "I thought you might need a pal for the day. I'm not ashamed of what I am, but it hurts."

I felt terrible that night. I needed someone to understand me. Maybe I *was* a slimy bastard. I began to feel like one. So, I went home with my skull, and I took some clay and started building a face on it. At least I wouldn't be alone, because I had this inhuman companion. The face needed eyes, so I put Mr. Potatohead's eyes on it. It was beginning to look devilish—which I liked—so I finished by putting two horns on top of the head, fake teeth in the mouth. It's so hideous that Lisa can't bear to look at the creepy thing. But that's me: a devil with an idea.

Eleven

Santa-X

Talking about Danielle, Iris, and Camille brought back some bittersweet memories. When I was with Iris, I felt terrible about what our constant bickering was doing to Danielle. Somehow, I wanted to make it up to her. Christmas came around, and I thought of the perfect thing. I took out an old Santa Claus suit and decided to surprise her. When Danielle opened the door, there I was, her own personal Santa Claus. The poor kid was really starting to suffer a whole lot from the relationship her mother and I had, but that night I took the sadness out of her eyes.

Christmas time is the most special time of the year for me. I'm not religious, Christian, Catholic, or even Jewish. Beads, crosses, and menorahs don't mean much to me. I can't tell you about the birth of Jesus, but I can tell you how I feel. I go out of my way when it comes to Christmas.

Many years ago, my mother bought a Santa Claus suit at Red's. My sister wore it the first time, but I knew that suit really belonged to me. After all, Linda made a strange-looking, cigarette-smoking Santa! When I wore it the next year, there were nicotine stains all around the whiskers. I put a picture of Vanessa Del Rio on my sack and called her "Mrs. Santa Claus." I gave out presents and "Ho-ho-ed" all over the place.

The next year, I added to the costume. At the time, I was driving a truck for Nathan's, delivering catered goods for parties. My dad and I stopped off at a fabric store so I could buy a better hat and acrylic for a beard. The year after, a costume designer named Jeffrey reworked my Santa Claus outfit, making it look fantastic. I decided to start visiting the Children's Ward at Coney Island Hospital.

My Uncle Paulie (whom I was named after) was dying up on the ninth floor of the hospital. I wasn't in such a festive mood, but I bought a bagful of toys from Smith's department store on Flatlands Avenue anyway. (They gave me discounted toys in exchange for porno gossip and promo photos.) My dad thought I was crazy. He couldn't understand how I spent hundreds of dollars on stuffed animals for kids I didn't even know.

Camille drove me to the hospital, all dressed up as Santa's helper. There I was, handing out toys and secretly drinking Johnny Walker Red from a pint bottle. Camille was cute in her elf costume, very delighted. But it was much more than a delight for me. There was one darling little girl who was really scared of me, but the other kids were grinning, "Hi, Santa." Finally, the little girl started coming closer, warming up to me. If she hadn't, I think it would have ruined the whole night.

As I was giving out the presents, a little Puerto Rican man approached me. I could tell he was wearing his only suit. The rest of the year, he probably wore a dirty T-shirt and sneakers, like me. Very quietly, he said, "Santa, will you do me a favor? My wife's dying of cancer. She's up on the seventh floor. Could you go up there and wish her a Merry Christmas?"

The little man was waiting outside of his wife's room. I walked in to see this frail, weak soul. There was more bone on her body than flesh. The woman reached out and grabbed me. Here I was, a big ox of a man, being handled by a dying woman. Her grip was stronger than you could imagine. There was the smell of cancer, of decay in the air. I felt repulsed, sick, and so scared that I wanted to run away. All of a sudden, though, a tremendous strength surged through me. I held the woman against my chest, stroking her softly, comforting her.

As I was leaving, the man stopped me outside of her room. "I don't know who you are," he said, "but I love you."

The last time I dressed up as Santa, I had flown in from the West Coast. It was freezing. I was sick and worried that I might have AIDS. That year, there weren't many kids at the Pediatrics Ward, but three cops had been shot, one critically. I asked the nurse if I could go in to see them.

There was a fruitcake pantomine clown pulling fake flowers out of his pants when I arrived. I patiently waited for him to finish and then handed out stuffed animals, telling all the cop jokes I know. One policeman was laughing so hard, the nurse told me to cool it. "Look, he has internal stitches and he's going to bust them," she warned. At least I left them feeling good.

I used to wear that Santa costume for three days, even sleep with the pillow in my pants. If a beautiful woman came on to me, I wouldn't go out with her—after all, Santa wouldn't cheat on Mrs. Claus! It's been two Christmases since I've put on that outfit. I had just met Lisa in December, 1986, and I was so head over heels in love that I spent the holidays in California with her. Maybe I'll dig out my suit next Christmas. But it won't be the same in a place where it doesn't snow.

Twelve

Thirty-One Flavors

In my long, lonely search for a special lady like Lisa, I had sex with scores of other women—on and off the screen. For many of you, I'm sure this is what you hope the "meat and potatoes" of this book will be. But let me warn you: One thing you *won't* find here is the kind of hype you usually see in the video magazines. I'm sure I'll burst a few bubbles, but I've just written what I've heard and seen and felt.

Some of the following sketches are more complete than others. You will find actresses who'll tell you their life stories at the drop of a hat; others are shy and keep pretty much to themselves off-camera. I guess that makes sense. When you have sex on screen, maybe you have to keep a tiny part of "you" private.

There isn't one particular kind of woman in the business whom I most enjoy working with. Sure, there are sexy women. Some turn me on, but some don't. It's a highly personal thing. Watching pornos, you don't see the reality, you just see a pretty picture. A lot of starlets are very plain-looking without their makeup, fake nails, and hairspray.

It's always better for me not to know who I'm going to work with. The mystery, the big question mark is exciting. The more I know, the more debilitating it is. The more you ponder, the more resistance you build. And a porno actor has to be totally free and uninhibited.

Most good porno scenes progress *rhythmically*. People may think my screen sex is wild and uncontained, but that's not so. I get going like a train. The engine is running even before it leaves the station. Once I get my dick going, it's like the coal burning in the train's furnace. The locomotive has no choice but to go. I put my hips in automatic.

Other times, I feel like a matador facing an unpredictable bull. The woman prepares for the moment, grooming herself, perfuming, douching. Every little kink must be worked out. Same thing goes for the males. True, some guys just jump out of their pants and fuck, dirty socks and all—but for the most part, an actor will refresh himself, shower, or go through some little good-luck ritual. Like a pornographic Felix the Cat, I always carried my little bag of tricks. Irish Spring soap is my favorite. When it isn't available on the set, I'll send someone out to get it. Also, I *must* have Edge shaving cream, plus a Gilette Good News razor. If I use a razor with a pivoting head, forget it; my scene is *doomed*.

Finally, the matador faces the bull. There's always an inkling of fear that maybe this will be the bull that will gore you and possibly end your career. Just as the matador controls the bull, the male is the leader in the dance of the sex scene. If someone gets out of step, then you stumble all over each other, and that makes for a sloppy show. The matador tries to seduce and tease and control. He doesn't want to kill the bull until the last moment. Similarly, the porno actor tries to keep his dick up as long as he possibly can. The longer he does, the more he's praised and appreciated. But, sometimes, the bull is too ugly or too rough. Then the matador puts an end to the performance as fast as he can and hopes he lives to fight another day.

Guys always ask me what it's like to work with Vanessa Del Rio or Traci Lords. Jokingly, I usually tell them to smell my fingers and find out. By this time, you're probably anxious to learn some of the nitty-gritty details and mechanics of the porno industry. What's behind the surface? I'll tell you what I know. A lot of people might get upset by my honesty. But I hope that, by now, you know I don't want to hurt anybody. I'm just an addict to the truth.

So, in no particular order, I'll tell your about the performers and directors I've been associated with during the past ten years, and I'll give recollections about making particular movies. To show you that I really am a gentleman, it's "ladies first." I'll start with the actresses: their personalities, their fears, what they're like in sex scenes, what they feel and taste like. More flavors than Baskin-Robbins!

I always wanted to like Amber Lynn. I felt very brotherly toward her. But, like brothers and sisters, sometimes we don't get along. Amber's a demanding person. Why? If I wanted to psychoanalyze her, I could guess that she's insecure, that she feels she wasn't given enough love as a child.

I've viewed our relationship like a grueling tennis match, "Played to the death," so to speak. She *seems* to want affection, entertainment, and companionship. But when she gets some, she doesn't want it anymore, so I've always had this slight bit of hostility toward Amber. I think it might be because I know there is a loving woman hiding somewhere beneath the bitchiness. Like a mechanic, I always try to find the problem and fix it. Amber and I do get along very well when we don't discuss the business and we allow ourselves to become people.

Before doing *The Four-X Feeling* with Amber in New York, we were staying at the Edison Hotel. I was doing some cocaine. Maybe the coke made me more intense, but Amber and I got into a pretty heavy conversation. I had never made love to her off-screen. It was sort of a self-imposed policy. That night, though, she let me stay in her room. We talked and talked, and she told me things about her childhood that I'd never known. Her mom died at an early age, and her dad ran away. We started crying to each other about the fact that we didn't have love, and we tried to comfort each other. I was very open with her, asking her to do something that I felt very shy about. I let her take a hairbrush and stick the handle up my behind. (To this day, she always smiles about it.) We made love and woke up the next morning a little late, but still giggling. It was almost a romance, but not quite.

Once we were on the set, however, she became Amber Lynn again. I could almost see the hard shell forming around her. Maybe she felt naked because she had bared so much of herself. Our sex scene was very hot, because we were still horny from the night before—but there was no *intimacy.* I think Amber resents me because I force out what she's trying to hide. But I'll always have a very warm feeling for her.

As far as Amber's acting is concerned, she's a professional—clean, and prompt. She puts her heart into her work. I try to bring out the special qualities her acting has, qualities she'd normally not evoke. I trick her to play better. Our sex scenes are usually intense, and I always get a hard-on *beforehand,* which is rare.

Many women in the business are scared about what comes next. Porno people in general don't live for tomorrow. They live their lives as though it could end five minutes from now. That's why they live so freely, so loosely, so abruptly, so carelessly. Like so many other porno starlets, Amber's searching for recognition as a person and as a woman. But starlets will almost never get that respect. How the hell *could* they? People use Amber Lynn as *masturbation material.* They don't take her seriously. She's little more than a magazine cover with pretty tits to be spattered with come. But I think she wants to be more than that. And she *is* more. I know she is.

Danielle is another type of blonde bombshell, but she looks softer than Amber. I found her to be very pretty in magazine layouts, but when I met her, I was a little discouraged. A small-breasted woman with an attractive husky, raspy voice, she has an unusual magnetism. But she isn't too appealing without her makeup.

Don't get me wrong, Danielle's a very hot lady, but I always felt she enjoyed women more than men, and that tends to dampen my drive. A lot of women in porno seem to feel that way. Women have to find the easiest way to make the same amount of money—and girl-girl is simply less strenuous physically. I've had good sex with Danielle only because she's a very professional porno actress, but sometimes she's *too* professional. In a lazy mood, for example, she might turn on the "oh baby, oh baby" too much. Then again, sometimes she'll start touching her pussy and doing things just for my pleasure; it's like a show within a show. And when I'm having trouble, Danielle knows just what to do. My nipples are the most sensitive part of my body: more than my penis, more than my anus. And Danielle knows exactly how to touch them and how to get me off.

Danielle and I did a lot of movies together in San Francisco. There, we became *people.* We did everyday things, like shopping together. We even slept together, but we've never had sex off-camera. We slept together for *companionship.* I've got to find the person underneath. I just can't fuck and forget.

The relationship Danielle and I have is similar to the one Amber and I have. But it's almost impossible to have something serious going with a porno actress. You meet them because of the job. You screw them because of the job. But because of natural male/female attraction, you can't help your feelings of affection. Despite what others may think, porno people are not mechanical robots.

Everyone wants to know about Taija Rae. Let me tell you about her . . . then and now. It's almost as though there are *two* Taijas, because she has gone through quite a transformation. Waiting to rehearse for my role in *Naked Scents* (I played a tennis pro), I was standing next to this chubby young girl who had squeezed herself into tight Spandex pants. I had no idea who she was. Meet Taija Rae.

Taija and I started reading our scene, and I was pretty impressed. She had studied acting and worked in legitimate stage plays. But Taija still didn't appeal to me sexually. She didn't pay too much attention to her body back then. I was nervous, thinking, "How can I get my dick up for this one?"

I still don't know how Taija got started in the business. She's quiet, very much a loner, but she usually complains a lot about the work and the long hours. I like to make her laugh, and I always do, even though she tries to keep a very firm grip on herself I think her curt manner is a defense mechanism.

These day, Taija's lost a lot of weight, almost to the point of looking anorexic. Maybe the old Taija felt insecure because she was a little too plump—one critic who loved her look called her a "sexy sugar doughnut"—but the change in her is too drastic. She's lost weight in all the important places. Her face is drawn, and her once voluptuous breasts are now nothing.

Sometimes Taija seemed unclean, and she always "creamed" a lot. In *Moonlusting,* she did a fuck-and-suck with me and immediately went into a girl-girl with Tracey Adams, without even washing. *Yeachh!* That shocked me. I always make damned sure I'm clean. My biggest hang-up in a sex scene is worrying whether my behind is clean. In fact, I always put perfume in my crack, even though it stings. In dire situations, hairspray does the job, but it gives me the stickiest butt in the jizz-biz

Taija keeps telling everybody that she's going to quit the business. Any time a porno actress continually says this and never follows through, it's only because she's supplying herself with a lot of false hope. Most actresses come back. "Just one more film," they almost apologize. Either the rent is due or the credit-card bill is out of control. Just one more movie to make it right. Porno becomes a type of drug, a fix. Oh, it's not just for the money. When you create a new image with a new name, you have to supply it with ego-gratification as well as life. After a while, the sex becomes secondary.

Taija and I have always talked on a very businesslike level—never any person-to-person nitty-gritty. I always take her phone number and she always takes mine, but we never call each other. On the set, we have those downbeat, almost glum conversations. We gossip about who's bad and who's not, who sucks and who's okay. She's always looking at the worst side of the business. I am, too, but I'm able to laugh at it. Poor Taija is always brooding on the set, cut off from everyone, wearing headphones or reading a book. That's the way she patiently waits for a scene, before she finally gets involved. Sometimes Taija gives the impression that she's standing at a bus stop. When the bus arrives, she climbs aboard and simply gets off at her destination. The trip's over and forgotten.

Have you seen *She Comes In Colors?* I worked with Elle Rio for the first time in that one. She was brand-new to the business then. In Elle, I visualized a symbolic, lusty, Latin fuck-mate, a Brazilian sex goddess built to please the American libido. In a sex scene, it seemed as though she were trying to satisfy everyone on the set.

When I knew I was going to work with her, I had an erection as I drove out to the Malibu location. Any time a porno actor gets a natural hard-on, it's a treat. For once there's no "work" involved! Elle doesn't speak English too well, so verbally she might appear reserved during sex scenes. Her voice-box may not be in action, but her tongue and the rest of her sure is!

Our famous body-painting scene was in incredible experience. The crew had spread a big canvas on the floor and placed vials of body paint next to it. With any other girl, I would have told the director, "Bullshit. I'm not getting this crap all over me." But with Elle I didn't care. The paint was on my cock when I was going in and out of her. The color stained the soles my feet for a month and a half afterwards. This woman was changing colors right before my eyes. Elle had paint in her mouth, on her face, in her long, brown hair, in her vagina. Everywhere. I was a little cautious about getting it in my own mouth, but then she took her finger and shoved it between my lips. That did it! I let go totally. I enjoyed the most free, unconscious, uninhibited fuck scene of my life. My cock felt as if it were going to jump out of its skin. I could have fucked Elle on a chandelier, or on the wing of an airplane. At the end of the scene, I took her from behind, grabbed her by the hair, and said something that wasn't in the script: "Sickness is creativity." That's exactly what I felt at that moment.

Elle and I worked together again, but we never captured that same wildness. From the location in Malibu, we went back to Hollywood to do another scene with Elle and Sharon Mitchell. I was exhausted and wondered how I was going to get it up. To help myself out, I flipped through pictures of Brigitte Nielsen in *Playboy* and *Penthouse.* Then I went upstairs to watch Elle and Sharon's scene. As soon as F. J. Lincoln (the director) let the two of them go at it, Elle went down on Sharon. In case you're not familiar with Sharon, she's been making fuck-films for almost fifteen years and is *always* in control. But Elle devastated her. Sharon's eyes rolled back in her head. It was like watching the heavyweight champ get knocked out by the underdog. I always thought Sharon was invincible. She could take any size dick. She could do anything, but Elle made her numb. When I entered the scene, I was ready for the both of them.

As my character in the story, I thought I loved Elle. She had promised me she'd never go to bed with anyone else. When I see the both of them together, I'm supposed to sob in shock. I had to cry and then become aroused a few seconds later. I've always had trouble maintaining an erection in dramatic scenes. I find that it's almost a contradiction. Although I was watching the girls off-camera with an erection, I couldn't actually walk in aroused. It was difficult to adjust emotionally.

Later I discovered that Elle didn't really understand how to choreograph a sex scene. She had absolutely no sense of rhythm. Like a trotter who breaks step, she was all over the place. Porno actors have to maintain a certain pace, but Elle could get out of control. She might actually leave teeth marks when she took your finger and put it into her mouth, or she would pull your hair too hard. Once, she stuck her fingernail up my asshole without any lubricant. She might personally enjoy that kind of pain, but I don't. With the language barrier, I couldn't communicate these problems to her, and I wound up getting very irritated. Watching Elle perform is exciting, but to work with her again, no thanks!

I first heard about Nikki Charm at Reb's office. There was a lot of talk going around about this cute little blonde. Nikki's name held true—she had a charming innocence. At the same time, some girls with dirty blonde hair give the impression that they're really dirty—slutty with an earthy sensuality. Nikki was one of those ladies.

Nikki's probably in her early twenties now, but she seemed really young when we first worked together. It was in Malibu, a crummy Carlos Tobalinas film, but the best sex scenes are usually with people you've just met. It offers something fresh in a very stale industry. We did it in the living room, and Nikki was getting very turned on. All of a sudden, I felt her holding me back, as if to warn me something was going to happen. She kept pushing me back, holding herself back, and then she let out an unbelievable scream. I felt as though someone had shot my penis with a grease gun. The scene stopped. Poor Nikki was so embarrassed that she apologized to me. Carlos told her, "That was great!" Even the crew had never seen anything like it. After the shock, we continued the scene. I was bathed in her hot, sticky juices, completely aroused because I *knew* I had gotten her off. The evidence was all over me.

You see, when Nikki comes, she acutally *spurts,* almost like a man does. She splattered my dick, drenched my balls, and soaked the couch. She has those G-spot orgasms you hear so much about. If you don't believe me, check out *Talk Dirty to Me One More Time, Part IV.* Nikki's ejaculation is unbelievable. It's a very clear shot showing her spurting a fluid. John Leslie was so amazed, he took his mouth off her pussy and watched. I'm surprised the industry didn't capitalize on it.

After that, Nikki became very inhibited. She didn't want to climax on film anymore. She only let it happen once or twice again—because I imagine orgasms like that are very private things. But I *was* able to tickle her privacy once, when she climaxed on camera with me.

It's always cracked me up how people in the industry walk around so businesslike, with their attache cases and appointment books. Can't you just see a woman flipping pages and saying, "Hmmm. Who's the next guy who'll fuck me in the ass? Jerry Butler on the sixteenth? I'll pencil it in." Women like Tracey Adams, Colleen Brennan, and Taija Rae try to keep things so neat and folded. But with people like Nikki, you have a wild puppy on your hands. If you can keep her away from her bad habits, you'll have a sweet little product. Otherwise, she'll crumble a worksheet in her back pocket and search for it like crazy later.

Thirteen

Vanessa and Friends

I'm sure you've seen *Miss* Sharon Mitchell, as she's now called in films. (After you've been in the business as long as she has, they automatically call you "Miss.") Sharon's even expanded her horizons. I heard she has a record out in Europe and that she sings very well. People tell me she funded her recording career with the proceeds from the movie *Dick of Death,* which she produced and directed. I appeared in it as "James Blonde," but I never got paid. She still owes me $1,300.

I met Sharon many, many years ago. She started making movies in the early 1970s, when porn was very raunchy and sleazy. Sharon's not conventionally beautiful, and she has such a dominant feel about her that's almost frightening. I have discovered her unique prettiness, though. Sex with Sharon is always fulfilling. I was never wildly turned on by her, but I have very good sex with her. I guess our chemistry works. Sharon and I kid around and tell jokes when we make love.

I could run into her twenty-five years from now, and we could talk forever, but we'd never get down to the scrambled eggs. Native New Yorkers have a kind of armor around them.

Sharon has tremendous muscle, and she takes her acting seriously. While sometimes she might overact—using her eyes or her hands too much—she *does* try to forget herself and get wholly involved in a character, especially when she's working with a good director or when she finds the script challenging. When Sharon and I are doing a scene together, she always seems to be touching me with a sense of true pleasure. She knows how to release me from any macho image I might have of myself. I remember being in Long Island, doing a Henri Pachard movie called *She's So Fine* (which I'll discuss in more depth later on). Our sex scene was wildness personified. She played an abusive punk rocker and was in total control. I was like Silly Putty in her hands. Almost telepathically, she understood what needed to be done. "Miss" Mitchell, you will always be a cherished "old soul" for me . . . in a business where souls can get lost.

The first and only movie I ever did with "Angel" was *Star Angel*, and I'll never forget it. The day before we began shooting, I partied all night. Then I drank from five to seven in the morning to come down from the coke. I felt petrified going to the set stoned. The producers drove me to the location in New Jersey. The mansion we worked in was right across the street from where President Nixon was living at the time.

As soon as I arrived, Cecil Howard (the director) shoved me into a scene. I literally had to jump into my outfit, and I hadn't even read the script. So Anne Randall, Cecil's scriptwriter, gave me a quick synopsis of the plot as I dressed.

The scene with Angel took place in a diner. In her, I saw

a beautiful and fresh creature. She looked as perfect and unspoiled as a freshly picked apple from the produce section of Waldbaum's. Angel looked like a virgin come to life, yet you could see the desire in her eyes. I was so moved by her, I couldn't even get my lines straight. Angel and I fell into this tremendous passion. (I ended up winning an Erotica Award for my performance.)

That night, the cast and crew slept in the fifteen-room mansion. Angel and I were with each other all night and soon we were kissing and touching. There were people all over the place. We couldn't find a private spot, so we set up two mattresses behind a bar and made love there. Euphoric from coke, my defenses were down. We could hear a fight going on somewhere in the house with knives and fists, so we huddled together.

Angel told me she was involved with an older man who was very wealthy but who was not good-looking. She said he used to chain her up to keep her in the house, and he often beat her. Angel's parents had died when she was very young, and this man took her in when she was fifteen. Soon after that, he had her doing awful things for him. We talked about love, and I was giving her advice—but who was I to talk about love? I didn't even know what it was myself.

Still, I felt sorry for Angel. She was far gone and probably needed professional help. Angel knew she had to leave this guy, but I doubted that she ever could. When I told her that she had to start living for herself, she started to cry. This guy had given her tons of jewelry. I was shocked when she took off her ruby bracelet and diamond ring and threw them out the window. I told her to sell the things, but she didn't want any ties to this man at all. It was a dramatic moment, a cocaine moment, and our resolve didn't last. When we woke up the next morning, we were sure that we had nothing in common. Angel was already in tears thinking about that old guy again.

Over the years, I've worried a lot about Angel. I've heard a few times that she's making a comeback. But I haven't run into her yet. I hope she's doing all right.

There are a lot of Angels out there. They sell what they've been told is a private, beautiful thing. There are times when I, too, have felt I've exploited myself so much that I don't know whom I belong to. And then I think I have learned too much about life, and that's why I can't live comfortably. I have allowed myself to be in the raw of society—I've been in every sexual situation, done movies on every controversial subject, lived such an extreme existence that I've hopelessly complicated basic, simple things. I'm like a race-car driver who's gone around the track at 200 m.p.h., who's won Indy, who has celebrated victory, who's come close to death. How can he find pleasure getting into a normal car and going out to get the newspaper?

Well, at least Angel was treated fairly by Cecil, but a lot of other people took advantage of her, producers and directors who pressure you to say yes when you want to say no. It's up to the director to understand *why* an actor refuses to do something, but they usually don't. Their main concern is the product, not the people. But without the people, there *is* no product.

Did you watch the hour-long PBS Frontline documentary "Death of a Porn Queen?" It was all about Colleen Applegate, the small-town girl from Minnesota who became "Shauna Grant." Many people thought she was a beautiful, innocent young lady who was led astray by the nasty guys in the business—and that's partly true.

I never saw Shauna laugh. I never saw the corners of her mouth reach each earlobe. I saw her smirk. I saw her giggle. But when I did see her giggle, she would always look around for assurance, as though she didn't have enough confidence to decide for herself what was funny.

I hate to give a negative description of a dead person, but to me Shauna was very plain-looking. She wore fake fingernails, which always came off during a sex scene. Then you would see the crud on the real nail underneath.

I was angry that Shauna allowed herself to get into a business that was swallowing her up. It didn't leave any room for her to breathe. She fought against sex, never relaxed or enjoyed her own needs. Working with Shauna was always strained: stop . . . proceed . . . halt. I had to really concentrate to get firm enough to enter her. And once inside, I couldn't pull out too far because I wasn't fully erect.

I had only one favorite position with Shauna: "Come real fast." Actually, doggie-style or simple missionary got the job done most quickly. At least gravity was on my side then. I could *never* do a Cowgirl with Shauna. ("Cowgirl" is when the woman gets on top.) In order to do a Cowgirl, she needed about fifteen camera cuts in between. The best time working with Shauna was when I could tell the director, "Okay, I'm ready for the come shot."

Everybody made a big fuss about Shauna. As you probably know, Shauna was only in the business about two years before she put a shotgun to her head. Shauna had tried to commit suicide with pills back home, before she even started to do porno. Shauna was another person who wanted to be loved, to be found. She was temporarily found, but in a business that has no love.

Shauna tried to cover up her unhappiness with cocaine. Sometimes she came to the set with her nose bleeding and dripping. Then she got herself mixed up with a drug dealer. A few days before she died, Shauna told her friend Richard Pacheco that her life was in danger. I asked the interviewer from the "Frontline" crew what the inside story was, and he told me that Shauna's mom thinks she was murdered. Maybe we'll never know the truth.

I did only about eight or ten movies with Shauna. To me, she was a pillowy mannequin who looked prettier wearing clothes, so non-sex scenes were fine. But if I had to make love to her, she was so unwilling that I felt almost as though I were raping her. Unbearable as it was, I had no choice but to work with Shauna—once you refuse to work with an actress, word gets around that you're "difficult," and you're not hired.

When I heard Shauna had committed suicide, I was living with Honey Wilder. Shauna's best friend, actress Laurie Smith, called Honey and broke the news. Honey was shocked, but I wasn't. Shauna was the fragile kind of girl you expected suicide from sooner or later. She was a victim: of sex, of the industry, of herself. She wanted to be proclaimed, but what she didn't give us was what we demanded more of. Just like when you go to a strip joint and the woman takes off everything but one glove. She's naked, but what you really, really want to see is that glove come off her hand. Shauna Grant was that glove. People wanted to see what Shauna really couldn't give. She couldn't even give it to herself.

After she died, I kept questioning myself, wondering what was wrong with me. Why wasn't I crying? Her death didn't faze me until a year later. I was walking down Bragg Street in Brooklyn, toward the Foursome Diner, late at night. Crossing the street, the light shone in a diagonal line. I followed the beam of brightness. It was the same path I'd follow every night when I'd go for my cup of coffee. Passing under a big tree, I just stopped cold. The wind started gusting. My body felt chillled. Suddenly, I thought of Shuana, and I fell down to my knees and started crying. Maybe time and distance helped me see the pure sadness of it all. Whatever anybody in this business goes through, whether it be suicide, AIDS, or drugs, we *all* go through.

Boarding the airplane to do *Surrender in Paradise* in Hawaii, I noticed a pretty blonde wearing little red shoes. One look at Ginger Lynn, and I told myself, "This is the girl you're going to be with for the rest of your life." She had done only one film before this, a short "loop" for Suze Randall. Ginger was so nervous and shy, she sat on her hands through practically the whole flight.

At our hotel on the beach, Ginger and I became inseparable. I couldn't believe this beautiful, raw gem of a woman. There she was, ready to be cut into something even more beautiful.

Ginger was worried; she had never done any acting before. We went over a scene that especially bothered her: our "rape" scene from *A Little Bit of Hanky Panky.* (A few films were being shot at the same time, one after the other, *Surrender in Paradise* included.) In the story, I'm on a motorcycle and I chase Ginger across the sand. When we read the script, she couldn't muster up the proper emotions. I tried a sneaky "method acting" technique on her. I told her to put the script down. Earlier, Ginger had told me that her grandfather had been the most important person in her life, but he'd recently died. With that in mind, I told her how I felt about old people—they should be left to die when they reached a certain age. Of course I really didn't feel that way, but I was trying to reach her most sensitive buttons. Ginger couldn't believe what I was saying. Suddenly her prince was turning into a warlock. I had shattered her dreams. Ginger was so angry, she started trembling and ran for the door. I stopped her, slapped the script into her hand and said, "Okay, *now* do the scene."

Ginger and I made love after that. She screamed louder than any girl I've ever been with and came three times in fifteen minutes. It was pure heaven. I didn't even wash until the next day because I wanted to feel her on me. If the lights had gone out, I could have kept the room lit with my smile.

Later, we went down to the beach with Ron Jeremy and

a few other people. Ron, lech that he is, went right for Ginger. Swimming way out in the water, I turned around and saw her sucking Ron's cock on the beach. Porno was one thing, but there were no cameras in sight! Although I joined them for a threesome, I was still hurt. Afterwards, I told Ginger to stay the hell away from me. She was so upset that she complained to Dave and Svetlana. They were angry as hell—with *me*! "What are you doing? This is Ginger's first movie. Be nice to her."

Ginger finally apologized, and we became friendly again, but only in a distant way. When I saw her falling for a member of the crew, I knew she'd be trouble in the long run, but still I couldn't stay away. I left the island early to do *Taboo III* in California. When Ginger arrived back in L.A., we were even planning to move in together. This was all from knowing each other for six days! Back in California, I bought her a little pre-engagement ring, wrapped it in a seven-foot box, and then went to pick her up at the airport. She wasn't even on the plane.

When Ginger and I worked together years later in *Beverly Hills Cox,* I was contemplating quitting the business. I just wasn't functioning well sexually. On top of that, I was working for Caballero, and for some reason I could never reach my full erection capacity when I was working for them. There was always a lot of tension on their shoots.

Prior to my scene, I warned myself, "If you don't do well, that's it. You're quitting."

If you've seen *Beverly Hills Cox,* you know that I did do well. Playing a grubby, dirty car mechanic, I screwed Ginger on top of a red Porsche. My face was streaked with grease, while she looked gorgeous in a white T-shirt and a tight pair of jeans. For the first time in a sex scene, I was able to use an object and not a woman to get me excited. I was glistening in the shiny glow of this gorgeous automobile. It was almost as easy as doing an outdoor sex scene. (I can fuck anybody outside, when the sun is beating down on my body, sweating it up and making it hot.) In that smoky garage, I was making love not only to Ginger, but to the car as well. With her spread-eagled on the hood, I was fucking this expensive piece of metal. My penis felt so long that I felt I could have pulled out forever and never fallen out of her. (Later, Ginger told me it was her favorite sex scene ever.) You could feel the intensity, the concentration of everyone watching us. In casual sex scenes, you can hear the director talking and people murmuring. In this scene, all you heard was the sound of the car's shocks squeaking.

I like Ginger, but I think the industry has made too much of her. Her acting is cute—when she's placed in the proper roles. Unfortunately, she too often appears in parts that are ridiculous for an actress with her limitations. Ginger's so popular because she seems like the innocent girl/nympho next door. A little over five feet tall, she's a little shrimp who used to be scared shitless. Now she has the world by the balls.

When I met Lois Ayres (a.k.a. Sondra Stillman), we were doing *Surrender in Paradise.* We didn't have sex, but watching her shoot a scene where she was washed up on the beach wearing a long, wet purple gown got me very hot. At one time, she had one of the best bodies in the business.

Lois was always very pleasant, but ugh . . . if you did a "69" with her, it was like exploring an unclean birdcage with your tongue. Lois always seemed to be in pain during sex. Lois was so sweet that I didn't want to get angry with her, but I couldn't perform correctly with her.

We had a scene together in the film *Bootsie* (a takeoff on *Tootsie*). Going down on Lois, I had a hard-on. All of a sudden, a lump of curdled cream slipped onto my tongue. I got so upset and sick that I went into the bathroom and washed out my mouth. I couldn't get an erection after that. And the director was angry at *me!*

Finally, word got around that Lois had a very bad problem with female odor and was told to clean up her act—literally. When I worked with Lois a year after that, she was fine.

Lois was always in and out of love. She's a typical girl from Melrose—you know, a punker who dances and parties to all hours. Half of the time she doesn't show up to the sets when she says she will. She's broke, too, like most of us, but she's still staggering along, happy.

Vanessa Del Rio is my ultimate, all-time favorite porno actress. I remember watching her loops on my dad's beat-up projector. When I met her at a party for Veronica Hart, Vanessa came on to me like a hungry puppy looking for food in the morning. After seeing my first couple of movies, she "wanted to meet me." Laughing, I told her, "Talk to my dick. Your name is scarred onto it from the callouses on my hand."

I saw Vanessa every day for about three months. A joyously plump, abundant woman, she was like a float in the Macy's Parade—unreal. She gave the impression that if she weren't held to the ground by twenty guys, she'd float away. She's that extreme. Her softness got to you. Everything about her body worked. Making love to Vanessa was like making love to the sea on a stormy night. On her knees, waves of flesh would roll from her behind to her neck and back. Vanessa was like my Thanksgiving turkey—and Thanksgiving is every day when it comes to Latin women.

Vanessa's apartment was like a sex-tomb. There were giant posters of her all over the place and life-size cutouts in the windows facing out to the street. We never went out to eat, always ordered food in. It gave us more time to fuck the hell out of each other. Vanessa has a clit the size of a Bic Pen cap, and she was the most responsive lover I've ever been with. Just whistle on her clit and she'd come.

After she took a bath, she'd coat herself with baby oil, and the fur from her two cats would stick to her body. We used to make love on a fuzzy blanket and get cat hair all over us. Sometimes I couldn't tell whether I was eating the blanket or Vanessa. Despite our hot sex, both of us were very lonely and were reaching out to each other.

Like a lot of other guys, a good friend of mine dreamed of fucking Vanessa. One day I took him to her apartment and told him, "Don't worry. I'll set it up for you." We hung around, talked, and drank wine. He was ecstatic to meet her. Before I started smooching with Vanessa, I left him in the corner and told him, "Watch me and I'll give you the signal."

I was kissing Vanessa, caressing her, and making her say nasty things. Like a baseball manager signaling for a righthander, I waved my right arm up over my head and motioned for my friend to come join us. He was so horny, he probably would have fucked the cat. I've never seen a guy so turned on. Without so much as a kiss on the ear, he was ready to stick his dick up Vanessa's ass. The three of us fucked like one big machine and kept it going for hours.

I finally was worn out and took a shower. When I came out, I figured my friend should probably go home to his girlfriend, but there he was, at it again. We didn't get back to Brooklyn until three in the morning. Afterward, Vanessa felt very insulted, used. We worked together after that, but she never really forgave me.

These days, Vanessa's taken up body-building and has lost her Rubenesque womanhood. The last time we worked together, we didn't talk about clits, tits, and blow jobs. We discussed stomach muscles, triceps, and pecs. It really got in the way of the sex. It felt like I was making love to a punching bag. Things change. But sometimes not for the better.

Fourteen

Ladies of Lust

A woman I really didn't enjoy working with was Tish Ambrose, although I have to admit that I was intrigued by that big mole on her tit at first. It looked like a bug that never moved, and it even had a tiny hair coming out of it. You expect breasts to be white, milky, and perfect. Hers weren't bad-looking, except for that hairy waterbug. We got along pretty well, despite the fact that she liked to drink. When she sweated in a sex scene, it was 80 proof. You hear about how come stings when you get it in your eyes. Same goes for alcoholic sweat. After awhile, I had a problem getting an erection with her.

Tish, probably in her thirties now, is also an old-timer from New York. A pretty good actress, she reminds me of the early Tracey Adams—maybe not as pretty, but in the old days, the selection of women willing to fuck in front of a camera weren't as pretty a crop as we have today.

RAW TALENT

The first time I heard about Nikki Randall I was in a Mexican restaurant named Anna's, having dinner with Reb. My friend Buck was supposed to meet us. He had just done a photo layout with a hot newcomer and invited her to have dinner with us. In strutted Nikki Randall. She has an Italian-Latin look about her and turned me on so much that my balls got tight and tingly. Even though Nikki was sort of mousy looking—she had small tits—she unleashed a fire in me. This feeling doubled when I watched her on the set the next day. She was like Fay Wray offering herself to King Kong on a silver platter, and loving every minute of it.

I remember watching her do a girl-girl with Erica Boyer. Erica loves women, and I could see her eyeing Nikki all day. Nikki never worked with a woman before and was a little apprehensive. Right now, just thinking about their encounter gave me a hard-on. When the cameras started rolling, Nikki wouldn't open her legs, so Erica pried them apart and stuck her face between them. Nikki tried resisting, but Erica spread her as wide as she could. Grabbing some oil, Erica coated it all over her big tits and rubbed them against Nikki's pussy. Soon Nikki was writhing and screaming. I knew I had my own sex scene in less than forty minutes, but watching them got me so hot, I just couldn't hold back. I jerked off and came all over the place, watching a beautiful little chick getting tit-fucked by a man-eating dyke.

I worked with Nikki about eight times, and each time it was intense. She has one of those dark Italian-type pussies that I love—you know, one that looks like it belongs on a beach in Brooklyn. Making love to her was like fucking a feather. That's how light she felt. I tossed her all over the place, into every position you could possibly imagine.

We were shooting that film in Palmdale, out near the Edwards Air Force Base. It was Christmas time, and I was feeling shitty because I couldn't go home for the holidays. In Thrifty's, I bought a Christmas tree, decorated it, and put garlands all over my hotel room. Then I made a Christmas card for Nikki, writing on the front, "To a Christmas Carol." (Carol is her real first name.) She was delighted.

Nikki used to drive to my house in a little Japanese car that belonged to her boyfriend. We'd have great sex, but it never went any further than that. I had a lot of wishful feelings about her, but I guess we weren't on the same wavelength. Before Lisa, I was always getting involved with women who were *already* involved. Maybe I was like a vacation to them, but they always went home after the holiday was over.

I met Veronica Hart many years ago, in *Angel Buns.* It was only my fourth movie, but Veronica was already considered one of the best actresses in the business. While she wasn't my "dream lover," I found her to be extremely easy to work with. Polite, accomodating, and professional, Veronica's attitude seemed to be, "Let's get the job done . . . and done well."

Most people don't know that Veronica has terrible burns over about 25 per cent of her body. When she was very young, a pot of boiling water splashed all over her arms, legs, and back, and she was left with scars and welts, some of them the size of pencils. I felt very sorry for her, but it was easy to see the beautiful woman underneath. Technically speaking, the make-up people did a good job of covering up the scars, but if you look closely, you will notice that Veronica is rarely fully naked in any movie—or when she is, she is shot from a careful angle, or a piece of lingerie is draped over her arms or legs.

Veronica and I actually became like brother and sister on the set. Whenever my own private hell was becoming unbearable, she would try to comfort me. We wound up doing a number of films for Chuck Vincent. In *Roommates,* I played a young gay actor who eventually falls for his female friend (Veronica). It was a movie with a lot of heart. Today, it's still one of the best sex-films ever made. I was all right in it, a little rusty because I was so inexperienced. I call it my "hot potato/cold potato" performance.

Even though I felt brotherly toward Veronica, she was so accomodating it wasn't difficult for me to make love to her. Veronica could chip away at the gravel—those personal things that were upsetting me—and find my core. Being inside of her was wonderful, because she truly enjoyed sex and she encouraged my sensitivity. She was one woman who never faked it. On the outside, Veronica might look angelic and innocent, but I've seen her get so absorbed in a scene that she pleaded with the guy to come in her mouth or all over her face.

Veronica's stopped doing sex scenes now, but occasionally she has nonexplicit roles in porno movies. So don't be fooled when you see her name in the credits of a new movie! In 1987 I saw her in Las Vegas, at the V.S.D.A. (Video Software Dealers Association) Convention. I was a little shocked at her appearance. She was parading around in a long T-shirt and pantyhose, wearing nothing else underneath. Veronica was trying to sell a non-sex video she'd just made. I guess she's forgotten how well-respected she was—and is. It was disheartening to see her flipping her butt around just to get attention. Sadly, many people at the Convention didn't even remember a legend known as Veronica Hart. Maybe it's because she doesn't look like she used to. You can judge for yourself in the R-rated Chuck Vincent movie *Deranged,* which is probably in the horror section of your video store. She and I made it in 1986. Veronica used to have very nicely-shaped breasts, but these days she's as skinny as a rail—even after having two children. But if you're curious to see one of the best female adult stars of yesteryear, make it a point to watch as many of her earlier movies as you can find.

Joanna Storm always reminded me of a little clown. But the first time we worked together wasn't too funny. We acted together in the film *In Love,* and she had her period. That's the last thing a porno actor wants to hear. Although the woman's flow is usually kept in check by a sponge, the guy knows she's not feeling up to par. Whenever we worked together after that, Joanna was usually feeling drained. Often, she had bad sores around the mouth.

Buck Adams was in love with Joanna and was always buying her flowers. One night, a bunch of us were all holed up at Reb's house, sleeping on the living room floor. I woke up to the sound of moaning. The TV was still on, and I could see Buck getting a blow job from Joanna in the flickering light.

"Come on, guys," I groaned. "Can't you keep it down?"

With that, everyone in the room woke up, but pretended not to. You could feel the wakefulness in the air. I saw Buck indicating that I should join them. By the time I moaned, "I really want to get some sleep," Joanna had me in her mouth. So there I was, getting a blow job while Buck's taking her from behind. Every time he pumped, I went further down her throat. I was getting ready to come. Joanna looked at me as if to say, "Please don't come in my . . ." But it was too late because I was wedged down her throat. Bam! With a sour face, she swallowed it.

When she gets mad, Lisa reminds me of Laurie Smith. I first met Laurie several years ago in New York. I wasn't doing cocaine at the time, so I couldn't understand why she acted the way she did. Laurie was edgy and cranky and had frequent outbursts of anger and resentment. I sometimes felt like punching her, but I still found her attractive. I was trapped by her flagrant sexiness.

Laurie and I did a scene in *Snake Eyes* where I actually come twice in the same minute. (In the business, it's known as a "double pop-shot"—it's *very* rare.) That never happened to me before, or since. We played a husband and wife who were having a big fight at the dinner table. Laurie threw a plate at me. I took a butter knife and started cutting off her clothes with it. Laurie smacked me really hard and started pulling my hair. After I slashed off her clothes, my cock became an extension of that knife. When I came, she was scratching me and swearing at me like a mad harpy.

After we filmed the scene, the director Cecil Howard was so pleased that he insisted I watch the playback. Normally, I couldn't give a shit, but this scene turned me on incredibly. I was so hot, when I was going home on the "D" train, I jerked off between cars as we crossed over the Manhattan Bridge. I finally came somewhere in the East River. It was like being lost in a London fog and feeling a feminine hand slide down my zipper.

Laurie never seemed to feel guilty about being in the business—a total opposite of her good friend Shauna Grant, whom I've already told you about. Laurie would tell Shauna, "What's so bad about it? We're making money." Laurie accepted it. I understand that she now lives in Las Vegas and has put on some weight. Last I saw her was on the PBS special "Death of a Porn Queen." She looked straggly and wore no makeup. Laurie seemed very bitter—so maybe she *has* changed her mind about her former profession.

Nina Hartley is the earth-mother of erotica. Her real first name is Debbie, and she's married to an older guy. More than just a pretty face, Nina's very intelligent. She's a registered nurse and does porno because she and Dave are swingers. She probably figured," What the hell? I might as well make money at it."

Nina went through a period in 1987 where she wasn't being hired much; some producers felt she was "overexposed." That irritiated Nina, to say the least. When things like that happen, a lot of actors go for the coke, but not Nina. She takes care of herself and hopes to form a fan club. The producers don't realize the kind of performer they have in her. Nina's always been the one to take the new girls under her wing and teach them the tricks of the trade (like the importance of using sponges, douching, etc.) She even helped form a West Coast erotic-actress support group, called "The Pink Ladies."

Nina is the glue that keeps a scene together. She would work with a guy who had a hole in his dick—as long as it wasn't from a disease, because she's very health-conscious—and hold it so you couldn't see the hole. She's very understanding, very cooperative. While she's not the kind of woman I'd run home and jerk off to, Nina knows exactly how to present herself and position her body. She can get even the limpest guy through a sex scene with flying colors.

Honey Wilder started in the business as an older woman. My guess is that she was past forty when she finally left. A little chubby and big-breasted, Honey was always worried about her looks. But I'll tell you one thing, she enjoyed everything you did to her. She was totally orgasmic. Why not? At her age, what did she have to lose?

Although you won't see her face in new movies, you can sometimes hear her doing advertisements on many videotapes. How can you tell it's her? Honey has a very distinct voice, which sounds like a horn being blown backwards or like a duck getting fucked through the beak.

I even lived with Honey for a short time. She was hospitable—and lonely, too. I kept telling her that she took porno too seriously, that she worried too much about her age. I hear she's met a good-looking younger guy, and that they're in love. I hope it's true.

I don't care what the publicity people try to tell you: Tasha Voux is *not* the Barbra Streisand of the business. I *can* say she's unattractive, yet I've had some very hot scenes with her in *Snake Eyes II* and *Raw Talent II.*

Tasha's big problem is that she's always worried about how people see her. When we did a movie out in Nyack, New York (it might have been *Sinners*), she drank almost continuously and then wondered why nobody liked her. Laughing, I'd tell her, "Look in the mirror. You'll see." On another set, she never stopped crying, asking the same question. I felt sorry for her. It's too bad she had this attitude, because she could handle a part pretty well. Now I hear she's more involved in behind-the-scenes production work than acting.

You may have noticed that Tasha's very agile. An exotic dancer, she's probably double-jointed. Tasha can do a handstand or a full split during a sex scene. I've always found that the women who are the most willing to give more actually feel inadequate about themselves. One of the reasons I started doing pornography was loneliness. I was looking for love. And here's Tasha feeling a similar need.

Siobhan Hunter looks like Ray Bolger in drag. She's supposedly studying to be a nurse at U.C.L.A., and she's married to an English rocker who also writes music for adult films.

Siobhan's flesh is kind of milky, substanceless. I feel as if I'm fucking a rubber glove. I sometimes have trouble working with her, unless it's a threesome with another girl eating the hell out of her.

Siobhan likes to rattle on about the "aesthetics" of porn films. Give me a break! I tell her, "Look, baby, you're getting come on your face, and you're getting fucked up the ass. *That* makes you a star, not your precious acting." The best time I ever had with Siobhan was when she picked me up for a shoot. It was a long drive to the set, and I was really able to break down the defense mechanisms she so carefully puts up. She's vulnerable—and down deep, she really is a nice person.

The Damiano people introduced me to Sharon Kane. (Gerard Damiano is most famous for directing *The Devil in Miss Jones* and *Deep Throat.*) She reminded me of my friend Kenny's sister Susan. They had the same ethnic look. But underneath it all, Sharon has a great body and she really gets into sex. She's pumped up my reluctant cock many times. After all, it doesn't matter what the lifeguard looks like, as long as he can swim.

Sharon has been in the business so long, she's like a young grandmother. She had a boyfriend named Michael, who died of AIDS. He was in *Firestorm* and *In Love.* I admired Sharon's strength. She was with him tooth and nail until the end. Luckily, she turned out to be "negative" on her AIDS test.

Sharon's very quiet. Many women who started in New York have a cool, diplomatic way about them and always keep their feet on the ground. Sharon Kane, Sharon Mitchell, Veronica Hart, and Kelly Nichols all have a kind of inner strength. They're more *structured* than the girls of California.

Jessica Wylde reminds me of the Mona Lisa—except that Jessica has unbelievably bad vision and has to wear extremely thick-lensed glasses off the set. She looks like a store window with tits! Another thing that used to disconcert me was her Caesarean scar. It wasn't the scar itself, but what it represented: It said *baby.* Why, I always wonder, is a woman with a kid doing pornography? I've refused to have sex with pregnant women on the set, but sometimes I have no choice. One very well-known porno actress whom I've already mentioned was pregnant, and that was very obvious in a scene we did. (She decided to have an abortion soon after.) I will never understand why a woman allows her body to be used for porn when there's another life inside of it.

I've never had sex with Hyapatia Lee, but I did work with her in *Sexy.* I had already met Hyapatia a few years ago in Chicago at the Consumer Electronics Show. She and her husband Bud invited me up to their hotel room. We talked as she sat there crocheting. I knew they were swingers and was getting tense because Bud kept suggesting that I fuck his wife—with him watching. Porno was one thing, but real life was different. Lying on the bed, Bud finally told me very bluntly, "Maybe you'd like to screw my wife, but I normally like to eat the guy's ass out while he fucks her." My sneakers practically tied themselves, and I ran back to my hotel!

About a year and a half later, Hyapatia and I worked together in *Sexy*. She plays a psychiatrist. I walk into her office and tell her my sex problems. To solve them (I guess), I jerk off on her leg. I don't know why she didn't fuck me. It wasn't in the script, which she and Bud wrote. Maybe I had to go through Bud's initiation before they'd let me fuck her on film.

Hyapatia is a very pretty woman, but all of the fuss made over her is the result of good management and hype. Bud put all his energy and time into selling his creation. After some time off to have a baby, Hyapatia's back doing explicit sex, prettier than ever. Very concerned about AIDS, however, she's one of the few actresses who requires written proof of a negative, recent AIDS test. As for Bud, maybe he's a better man than I am. I could never deal with watching my wife enjoy another guy.

I've always loved Seka. A few years ago, someone gave me her phone number. When I called her, she already knew who I was. I made the mistake, though, of calling her "Dottie" (her real name). "My name is *Seka,*" she said coldly. No personal-professional schizophrenia for her!

Soon after that, I happened to be at the video show in Chicago, where she lives. Ron Jeremy and I were at the Collectors Video booth promoting *Surrender in Paradise.* Seka was walking around with Paul Thomas, videotaping a show for cable TV. Seka approached me and said into the microphone, "Here's Jerry Butler. He's my favorite porno star. In fact, I love to fuck him."

With a big grin, I asked, "Are you talking to me? I've never worked with you."

Did Seka get mad! The roots of her hair were burning. She walked away in total disgust. Damned if she didn't come back the next day and try the same thing. "And here's Jerry Butler," she said with the video camera on both of us. "I've worked with him many times, and he's got a big dick."

"I don't have a big dick," I explained. "And I never fucked you. But if you want to put that camera down, I'd be happy to do it right here." Paul Thomas had to get between us and stop Seka from kicking me in the balls.

The next time I saw her, we were guests on a show called "330," hosted by Chuck Henry. Kay Parker was also on the panel. Seka and I had another nasty go-around when she told Chuck how much she enjoyed working in porn; money was no object, she said.

I interrupted, "Oh really? Then why is your fee $15,000 to $30,000 per movie?"

Seka smiled at me, not knowing what to say. Chuck then asked me about the use of drugs in the adult film industry. I admitted that a lot of the actors, actresses, producers, and directors use drugs because they are under a lot of pressure.

Then Seka broke in: "I can't imagine why people need drugs in the business."

"What about 1978?" I asked her. "I heard you were in drug rehabilitation for a whole year."

Boy, did she get angry! I wasn't looking to attack her, but let's not glamorize an unglamorous business. Since Kay Parker is an older woman, the whole coke thing was beyond her, but she did her best to keep Seka and I in line. Chuck was pretty flustered, and Seka continued trying to put perfume on shit.

In the dressing room earlier, Chuck had told me he had never seen a porno movie. But now, here he was pretending to be so damned knowledgeable interviewing three porno actors. I mentioned his inexperience at the end of the show. He admitted in front of everyone that he'd never seen a porno movie. I told him I thought it was about time he did, took off my mike, and walked off the show as the credits were rolling.

All in all, "the Ice Goddess," Seka, still turns me on. Tina Marie, Pia Snow, and Seka are three women I always dreamed of working with but never did. I guess I was on the right carousel but the wrong horse.

I've only been in two films with the great Marilyn Chambers: *Marilyn Chambers' Private Fantasies #5* and *#6*. We played one scene on top of a table, and I had a hell of a time getting an erection. I felt intimidated by one of her companions, who was constantly at her side, acting like a tough-ass and carrying a gun. Somehow, I managed to start screwing her. Then Harry Reems began yelling at the director about his pay. I thought the cops were raiding the set. My dick drooped. Getting hard enough to get back into Marilyn was a chore. But I finally finished and muttered a "Thank God" to myself and a happy "Oooh, that was good" to Marilyn.

You might remember Marilyn as "The Ivory Snow Girl." Years ago she appeared on boxes of Ivory Snow as this model of innocence. When it was discovered that she was doing porno at the same time, there was an uproar. Sometimes it takes a while before "real" people catch on and discover that you're doing porno. Another example is Stacey Donovan, who did a couple of commercials for "Swatch" and was on the cover of *Seventeen* magazine—at the same time she was fucking on camera. Why are people outraged? I'll tell you: They isolate pornography from everyday life. But I'll tell you something else: Porn *is* real life, as real as I am real, and as everyday.

Actresses like Chambers and Donovan get to enjoy the sneakiness, the adventure of not being caught. It's just like going to the candystore as a kid when your mom tells you not to. You whine, you cry, but you wind up doing what you want anyway.

Fifteen

Porn Princesses

John Holmes once claimed that he screwed over 3,000 women. Of course, he finally couldn't tell one pussy from another. I feel more like Casanova (who also wrote his memoirs), who screwed over 170 women in his lifetime and who, like me, enjoyed "knowing" them as human beings, too. So, let me continue to tell you about the ladies I know in this business. But remember, it's only one man's point of view. Bob Rimmer tells me that my reaction to the "old ladies," like Kay Parker and Honey Wilder, will change in time; I'll love them for their sinking titties and their wrinkles. What Bob doesn't know is that my wife has had two children. Lisa doesn't have the classic "perfect" body, but to me it's beautiful and soft, and she wears it well. As they say, "Beauty is in the eye of the beholder." As long as someone is comfortable with his or her own body, so am I.

I always thought of Kay Parker as a plucked and brittle flower. If you blew at the petals, there might be nothing left. Because she was an older woman in porno, I think that she had to justify herself in some way, and she often came off kind of phony.

Kay actually played *my mother* in *Taboo III*, and I was expected to have sex with her! Part of me was able to respect her—she is very generous, articulate and polite—but I suppose I also resented the fact that a woman about my mother's age was doing porno.

Honey Wilder was also in the film. Even then, Honey and Kay were relics of the industry. Both of them were battling for attention, each trying to be the most vibrant. I guess they felt kind of displaced by a younger generation. Maybe that's why Kay was so calm and polite—she was desperately trying to maintain a facade. (After all, how does a porn queen gracefully "retire"?) Whenever people need an excuse, most of us can find the proper cliché to suit ourselves. If a guy has a small penis, he can rely on this one: "It's not the sword, it's the swordsman." If a person's old, there's always this: "You get better with age." We all justify ourselves with clichés that someone else wrote for a greeting card.

I only worked with Kay that one time in *Taboo III*. Despite my misgivings, we had a hot scene. I wound up tossing this replica of my mother all over the bed. It made me feel very strong to push around this cornerstone of the industry. A guy with a penis twice as big as mine couldn't have penetrated her the way I did that night.

From the very start, I felt sexual pressure from Kay. I was sure she wanted to make me a "kept man," that she would happily take me home to live with her in her beach house. I might have contemplated it with a woman outside of porno, but I wasn't going to be bought by some shooting star who was swimming in the same toilet I was.

Things like that happen all the time in this business.

Women fall in love, promise you the world, and then barely remember your name five days later.

Maybe Kay does not deserve those harsh words. It's nothing about her personally, but I get very annoyed by the people in this business who try to come off as intellectual, as Kay does. Sex is not intellectual. In fact, the less intellectual your approach, the better shape you are in. The more you release, the more you gain. Still, everyone in the business has some sort of argument to convince society that they're really decent people.

Chelsea Manchester (a.k.a. Tigr) would come to the set looking like a wreck. I'd say to myself, "What is this sneaker with blonde hair doing here?" But, strangely enough, I found her sexy because she was so *unattractive*. But wearing makeup, Tigr knows she's transformed, and it magnifies her sex scenes. She has a body like a pink Gumby . . . very hard and wiry. Tigr knows just how to touch me. She definitely can twirl my baton. She is a polished performer in bed, but I sensed she felt self-conscious because her breasts were sort of small. That didn't bother me, though. In fact, in my personal experience, a lot of big-breasted women are lazy lovers. They think their big tits are enough. Women like Tigr compensate for their modest endowment by giving more of themselves. In truth, I've found that smaller breasts are ususally more sensitive, and the way they respond to the touch is more arousing than a handful of Jello that just jiggles and shakes.

Colleen Brennan is like an Etch-A-Sketch. When you turn her nipples, lines pop up on her face. She's such a sweetheart in the morning, but she becomes a cranky old lady as the day progresses. But despite her sometimes-bitchiness, and despite the fact that she doesn't turn me on physically, I've had tremendous sex scenes with her. Colleen's a natural redhead with white, milky flesh, but I prefer darker women.

Colleen would become so wild in a sex scene, she needed more than I was capable (or wanted) to give her. I'd have to tell her, "Whoa!" It was like the horse trying to tell the cowboy how far to go. I never reached a bursting erection with her . . . maybe seven-eighths my capacity, and I had to work damn hard to keep it.

As an actress, Colleen's like a relief pitcher in baseball—very capable, very dependable. The only problems I've ever had with her were because she was always jumping into things that didn't involve her. When we were doing *Raw Talent II*, they worked the actors really hard. Colleen didn't suffer too much, because they made sure she had her beauty sleep. Joyce Snyder (the producer) wasn't paying me right: just five hundred dollars a day for a lead role, and she didn't even reimburse me for the karate lessons she asked me to take. I admit, I was giving Joyce a lot of shit, but I was fed up. While I was arguing with her, Colleen butted in. "Jerry, you're such a baby," she said.

I told her, "Real soon, you're going to start complaining, and when you do, I'm going to give you hell."

Not even an hour later, Colleen was crying because she was being treated unfairly, too. But now, it was justified because *she* was the one being put down. That's a major problem with porno people. They don't realize that we're all in the same pot and that sooner or later we're all going to reach the same temperature.

I've told you that Colleen's insatiable, but she's also fussy about camera angles and makeup. As I'm pumping away, she's continuously demanding makeup touch-ups. It ruins the rhythm. To me, things like makeup don't matter. The important thing is how you look *in character. That's* what makes the audience feel. They get lost in the beauty of the moment if there's nothing phony to distract them. In porno, the camera has an axis and covers every part of you. Sometimes I feel like I'm Saturn and the camera is one of the rings. Women like Colleen only worry about the colors, not about the vibrancy inside.

When I first saw Barbara Dare, I thought, "Who does this little twerp think she's kidding?" I guess she was able to kid me, because she has quite a commanding screen presence for such a tiny girl.

Naked, Barbara's body is very sleek, almost like marble. She takes care of herself and works out a few times a week. Barbara's not what you'd call "feminine"—but thanks to peroxide, perms, and fake nails, she looks good on the screen. She really gets into the sex and is very aggressive. She'll pinch and slap my nipples like crazy because she knows how it turns me on. But there's also a sweet, soft side to her. Barbara's always there to help me out when I need her, to listen. When we were filming *10½ Weeks*, both of us were going through rough times in our personal lives, but we used our time together to sedate ourselves and relax. We became very friendly. We never made love off camera, though.

I went to lunch with her recently, and she told me that she couldn't imagine herself getting AIDS. If she did, "I'd die, and so what?" she said. I think she's too grateful to this business, simply because of all of the money she's earned. She probably feels she owes it something. But nobody gives you *anything* for free in porno. Whatever you get, you earn, and you work damn hard for it. Nobody should have to pay for it with her life.

I've always thought that Barbara Dare was the Big Bitch of the industry. She likes to tell people what to do. She likes to appear tough and aggressive, but underneath it all she's just like anyone else—a Volkswagen trying to be a Masurati. You can tint the windows, add mag tires, and a sun roof, but it's still a Volkswagen.

Fucking Bunny Bleu is like fucking Bobo the Clown. (Remember him?) She stares at you in a dizzy way and makes the silliest faces when you're humping her. Every time I'm about to work with her, I get scared shitless and think, "I can't fuck this girl. Just *look* at her." But a sex scene with her is the softest, creamiest feeling, like fucking butter. She's got a little pussy. Her tiny body can't take much so she screams her heart out. And when she screams, it sounds like you're fucking a squirrel. Bunny sucks cock unbelievably (in one movie, she did it while humming "Old MacDonald"), like she *has* to, as though her life depended on it. That makes up for her "Bobo" looks.

Cara Lott everything to the utmost to complete the formation of a sex scene. I don't consider her a very pretty woman, but she carries herself like a slinky snake and looks great on camera. She's like the kid who doesn't want to go to school yet comes home with straight A's.

My first impression of Janette Littledove was that she was trying to be a junior Joan Collins, because she spends all her money on jewelry. Better than blowing it on coke, I guess. Everyone makes a big deal about Janette, and I could never understand why. Maybe it's her tremendous cantaloupe tits. But, melons or not, Janette's very arrogant.

The story is that Janette's from Oklahoma, a bona fide American Indian straight from the reservation. After winning a wet T-shirt contest back home, somebody brought her to California. I admit she's gone through a lot of mismanagement in her career, but Janette hasn't exactly been the most loyal person in the world—as Buck, her exhusband, can tell you.

One time, when she had a fight with Buck, she moved in with me for a while. I wasn't looking to make her; I was just helping her out. Guys kept calling her day and night. She also wasn't the cleanest girl I've ever met. She kept dyeing her hair and never cleaned the gunk out of the bathtub. Half the time, she didn't even wash.

After Jeanette married Buck, she settled down a little bit, even though they lived like gypsies. They often slept in their Corvette when they didn't have a place to stay. She makes a lot of money, but she'll spend five hundred bucks on hair weaves, six hundred on a ring, and leave herself with one dollar for living expenses. It's almost like she has a cocaine problem with jewelry.

As far as sex goes, one-on-one was never too much fun. Janette has no ass, but big boob-job tits. A lot of women are going that route these days. The competition is pretty fierce out there, so they just do whatever is necessary to stay afloat. Women have limited longevity in this business. Men make less money, but we're more fortunate because we have a longer "shelf-life." Guys like John Leslie have been around almost twenty years, and no one tells him to chop off his love handles or get a wig. As for the women, they have to keep building and improving. After all, how long can you work with a World War I prop plane when everyone else has supersonic jets?

The first time I ever saw Traci Lords was in *Penthouse*, and I jerked off to her incessantly. I'd never seen a prettier pin-up, but in real life Traci was another cup of tea. When I actually met her, I wasn't too impressed. Traci was hyped so well because she had the innocent girl-next-door quality that porno companies loved. You know, the girl most likely *not* to do it. Porky and lazy, her balloon tits didn't do much for me. Then she started to make these orgasmic sounds—before I even pulled down my zipper! It was like fucking a voice-over.

Traci was a big star, who often earned $1,200 a day. Working with her, I felt very limited. She's a sexual billboard. Billboards look expensive and expansive. They demonstrate, but they never move or feel. Like Shauna Grant, Traci mastered that clichéd sexy look for the camera. Guys go crazy over Traci because they feel they have to, they're *conditioned* to.

Traci's another porn starlet to hit all the newspapers. You might recall how she nearly blew the porno business out of the water when she admitted that she was fifteen or sixteen when she made most of her films (about seventy of them). She made all of those movies perfectly willingly, using false I.D. Because she was underage, video companies had to pull all of her tapes off the shelves, and they lost millions of dollars. One theory goes this way: Traci wanted all of her old tapes gone so she could start her own video company and have a monopoly on herself. It didn't work out that way. In any case, Traci came out the winner. Even the IRS pardoned her. The cops excused her from all charges because she turned informer. Rumor was that one of TV's biggest producers promised her a lot of money for her life story. Believe it or not, he said he would clean it up so he could show it on regular network TV.

Traci's early films are collectors' items. Even though she recently turned eighteen and has made a new video—*Traci, I Love You*—she has been informally blacklisted here because of how she hurt the industry. But, since everyone in the business is in it for the big bucks, and a new Traci Lords film would be a big seller, I have a feeling she'll eventually be forgiven.

Kimberly Carson and I don't get along. She's since left the business, married actor Dick Howard, and they have a baby. With her, sex on camera was just a job to do. She yelled a lot and expected to be treated like a prima donna, but she smelled like a fishtail. If I had to name five girls I hated to work with, I'd name Kim twice! What's odd is that I've had some great sex scenes with her. I suppose it's because I dislike her so much that it created a kind of intensity: fucking with hate instead of love. Hate's a strong emotion, so it worked. I tried to make use of anything I could to enhance my work.

Kim and I were making a movie when the space shuttle went down. I watched the funeral ceremony on television, deeply touched. I felt it was important to watch it, out of respect for the people who died. Four of us were watching the funeral on television. It soon became five, six, then seven. Kim was sitting off to the side, partying and blabbing away. I watched the Reagans talking to the bereaved families. One woman held a baby in her arms, and Nancy looked at that little child with such sincere pity in her eyes. Feeling the helplessness of that baby and that family, feeling the sadness for the children who had lost their fathers, I started crying. Jets were flying overhead and the band started playing "God Bless America." Five other people in the room were crying with me. Suddenly Kim said, "I can't watch this fucking shit." She blocked the TV screen. Nobody was going to break in on my sorrow. Nobody was going to deny me my tears. Especially Kim Carson. "Change the channel," I yelled, "and I'll kill you."

Looking back, I don't know how in the hell I fucked that woman, except to say that each thrust was a punch—jabbing her, going for the knockout. At least I didn't have to kiss her. (In fact, very few people kiss passionately in porno. Sure, sometimes there's a quick peck to get things started, but that's about it. Kissing is a very private thing. A lot of women work on that principle: "Okay, I'll fuck. I'll suck. I'll get a dick up my ass. But don't expect me to *kiss* the guy!" That, she saves for someone she cares about. Kissing on the mouth, for me, is more personal than sex on film. I never got paid to kiss. I got paid to fuck.)

When you screw for a living, you want, more than anything else, to get your dick hard as a rock, fuck the hell out of some chick, get your money, and go. But sometimes your dick becomes like Congress. Even though the President puts a bill in to become law, Congress still has to vote on it. Sometimes your penis stalls on the bill. I've had problems working with women like Kimberly Carson; but given enough time and footage, I could always get erect. The ego of a male porno actor is a delicate thing. It doesn't want a sex scene to be good because the editor cut and pasted it to look good. He wants a perfect sex scene at that moment. But sometimes it just isn't like that.

Working with Melissa Melendez was like looking at an aquarium with no fish inside. She didn't belong in the business. Her leg muscles were always so tight that you never felt she wanted to be there. I liked Melissa as a person—she had a good sense of humor and was very sweet—but I hated the producers who hired her. What right did they have to hire a girl like this? She always laughed during sex scenes because she was so embarrassed. It made me feel uncomfortable and unclean.

In *Rockey X*, Melissa and I had what was supposed to be a romantic sex scene. It was late when we shot it, and we both wanted to get the job done and go home, so she didn't have enough time to get giggly or embarrassed. The director, Patti Rhodes, rushed us along and we had to snap it up. I got my dick up fast and it was over quickly. If you think it was a very loving sex scene, great. That means we did our job—you were conned.

Working with unwilling women like Melissa, I felt that I was committing suicide emotionally. Some of our sex scenes were truly awful. When I make love, my whole body becomes a penis. I show disrespect to myself when I make love to an uninvolved woman. True, the woman is 100 percent of the selling pitch, but the man does 75 percent of the physical work in a sex scene. Nobody sees the work that goes into a potter's craft, only the end result. I honestly think most guys in the business *don't* look forward to sex scenes. Most of the time, I didn't. It's always a test—and you wonder, "Can I get an erection in front of strangers? *Again?*" You go into it looking to get out as efficiently as you can.

What a task porno actors have! It's enough work doing a good acting job, but now you have to perform sexually on camera. When you're acting in a regular scene, your energy is contained within your clothing. When you take off your clothes, the energy disperses. People might admire a legitimate acting performance, but when they're watching a sex scene, they figure, "I could do that," because sex is something people do every day. They just don't realize the extreme effort and creativity that goes into it, the pressure, the concentration.

Before I started in the business, I never respected porno. I might have respected the arousing part of what it had done for me, how it tickled and stimulated me, but I never respected the *craft* part of it. I never thought there *was* any craft, in terms of acting anyway. You could say that I came into the field as an innovator, one of the first people to combine serious acting with good, hardcore sex. I make the most of what I do while I'm doing it. I'm not Olivier, but I never stop creating.

Sixteen

A Bittersweet Intermission

I'm not feeling very good right now: I just finished talking with my folks. They're angry and hurt that I'm writing this book and don't want me to include anything about the family. I don't want to hurt them, but I also don't want to lie. As soon as I hung up the phone, I ran to my dresser drawer and took out a fresh cassette tape. I ripped it out of the plastic as if I were a cocaine addict unwrapping a rock of pure coke. I needed to talk out my feelings while the wounds were still fresh.

I still have so many unresolved feelings about my father. I love him, and I'm sure he loves me, but he could never give me what he gives everyone else: friendship. Simple, casual friendship. Years ago, I wrote a movie script called "Masquerade." It's about a boy who disfigures his face and comes home being someone else, just so he could be his father's friend.

I'm also fighting the pain of no longer doing porno films. Something inside of me still craves it. Being involved in porno for ten years made me very irresponsible. I was a butterfly going from woman to woman, from movie to movie. Now, all of a sudden, I have to trade in my wings and become a caterpillar. I have to learn to enjoy life on the ground. The pace is much slower, much more confined. It's tough to forget porno. I always tell Lisa, "You can dive into a pool, but you can't dive out." The transition might have been easier if I slowly tapered down, but this cold turkey isn't easy. In my new life with Lisa I've become a very possessive, extremely jealous person.

People ask me what I'm going to do now that I'm finished with porno acting. I don't know. All I have been thinking about is getting this book out, telling the story of my life as truthfully as I can. Lisa wants me to go into legit acting; she thinks I got a lot of talent. But I doubt I would ever be accepted as a legit actor . . . porno kind of follows you around. But even more than that, I don't know if I *want* to try legit acting again. I don't have the enthusiasm for acting anymore. I'm tired. The life I've led has damaged me.

Yesterday, Lisa went on an acting audition for an R-rated movie. Just reading the script over her shoulder, I saw that she'd have to do a rape scene with three guys. The sex would be simulated—Lisa never has and never will do porno—but she'd have to be naked. I went beserk. I hadn't felt that shaken since I was playing hockey. Standing on the ice as the National Anthem played, I used to be so afraid of failing that my knees would shake.

About three weeks ago, I swallowed a dozen Percodan pills. I didn't want to kill myself. I did it because of mental pain, trying to numb myself because I was going through a difficult emotional situation. I'm so possessive. I know I overemphasize the importance of sex. Now, I have to find some other way to rebuild my self-respect, starting with finding another line of work. But until this book is finished, I can't put the soul of "Jerry Butler" to rest.

More than anything, I need to find truth. I don't want to lie anymore. In porno, I was paid to lie. I was paid to paint a pretty picture. I don't want to fight this painful feeling, yet it's destroying me. All of a sudden, I feel dirty. Try telling a guy who's done more than three hundred porno movies that now sex is a wrong way to earn money. To me, making movies could mean affection, creativity, attention. Because I now have Lisa, I no longer need the affection I sought. But what else can I do to make a living? How else can I put food on the table? I'm petrified as I speak these words. It would crush me if Lisa allowed herself to be kissed by another guy, even in a movie role. And here I am, expecting her blessing and permission for me to continue to work in porno. I'm afraid that one day she'll just get tired of my shit and pick up and leave me.

Pornography is a big word. Within that word you have all different variations: heterosexual, homosexual, transexual, animal, child. So, when people say, "Jerry Butler, porno actor," they're putting me into any and every class.

Some people assume that if you do porno, you'll perform *any* sexual acts with *anyone.* That's not true. You already know that I never have and never will do any homosexual acts on tape. I've never been asked to do a "golden showers" scene (urinating on a sex partner). If I had been asked and the woman was willing, though, I probably wouldn't have had a problem with it.

You see, that's the key: "If the woman was willing." I am respectful of another person's space. I'd be uncomfortable forcing someone to do *anything* against her will. I've done softcore S&M Movies, but I never actually hurt anyone. I never made anyone bleed. That's where I draw the line.

I have rarely refused a sexual act if I was able to perform it. The only exception is anal sex. Although I've done it in the past, I stopped because of the outbreak of AIDS. In fact, I tell women on the set to stop doing it. Directors don't like that too much, but they're not risking their lives in front of the camera, are they?

I've worked with some women who I've speculated were underage, but I never knew *for sure,* so this was never a real problem for me. After all, they said they were eighteen and had the drivers licenses to prove it. But after the Traci Lords scandal and her famous fake I.D., who believes that anymore? But again, these women, these girls, even if they *were* underage, were willing. Along with the speculation comes the excitement, the confusion, the questions. But I never let it get in the way of the job. My job was to get my dick up and fuck. And I did it.

What draws me into the trap? I know all the hazards, the insecurities. I don't think the business is going to last. In fact, I *know* it's not going to last. It's going to end with a lot of people I've worked with, a lot of women whom I've made love to, dying. Cynics might argue that I'm not making love, I'm fucking. But, in a sense, I never fucked or made love to *any* girl in the business. I fucked and I made love to what was missing in my life. Every woman was a symbol of my own striving to find the missing link. I made them into whatever I needed them to be.

Before Lisa, I really didn't know what love was. But one thing was certain, whatever love was, I didn't have it. I was falling for women all the time. It wasn't the greatest thing for me emotionally, but it sure as hell benefited my work. Maybe an actor's insecurities allow him to display great sensitivity and emotion.

You might close this book and end up saying, "Jerry Butler

is a weak person. He just couldn't take it." Whatever you decide about me is fine. Porno was my decision. Maybe it was to spite myself. Maybe it was to spite my father. Maybe it was to spite the gay men who tormented me. But porno was on *my* terms.

For a while, I was tearing down the road to hell. I had the looks, a good body, and people who believed in me. The problem was that I didn't believe in myself. I admit, I wasn't living my life sanely. I was driving my car with my foot on the brake. I needed to have a couple of near-fatal crashes to learn how to drive correctly. Now, when I put people I care about into my car, I know they're safe and protected because I'm safe and protected from myself.

In hockey, every time I skated my blades chopped into the ice and shavings flew all over the place. My body actually steamed and my heart would hurt when I came off the ice. In porno, I didn't put that kind of pressure on myself. I rolled, strolled, lazed into it. In magical sex scenes, I felt like a bow on a violin. When I moved, I hit a string and I made a beautiful sound.

No matter how acclaimed my sex scenes are, if I don't get my cock up tomorrow, I'm worthless. This business has no compassion, no sympathy. The producers don't realize how valuable actors and actresses are. They feel we're dispensable. If a legit actress doesn't want to take a role because she doesn't want to show her tits, there are thousands of other women who will. There are a million guys who are better looking than I am and thousands who can replace me.

Porno people don't have company insurance. They don't have pension plans. If I get hurt nobody pays for it—except me. If I die, a director will just call the next guy on the list. Our union is our feelings and our blood. We share the same bodies—and sometimes the same diseases. We're in the same war.

I have won a lot of awards—like *Hustler's* "Best Porno Actor" in 1983 for *In Love,* or in 1985 from the Adult Film Association of America, *Hustler,* and the X-rated Critics Organization for *Snake Eyes,* and in 1986 for Best Actor in *Star Angel* and *Snake Eyes II.* I was also *Adam Film World*'s "Performer of the Year" for a body of work done in 1983. But the first time I won anything, I was petrified. Where could I go from there? I've never felt comfortable imagining myself on top. When you're on top, it's tough to stay there. I know damned well when I'm really feeling good and I have a couple of bucks, I'll just screw up! I can't stop myself. I put myself back in third place because I have more room to fight, to claw, to gain, to achieve, to progress.

Same thing with my private life: When things are going along nicely with Lisa, I often conjure up a slight bit of annoyance for us so we can have fun bickering. From there, we can make up again. It's like a cat toying with a waterbug. The cat has the bug trapped, then lets it go. Then the cat catches it again. That's what I've been doing, playing "Cat and Waterbug" with my life.

A BITTERSWEET INTERMISSION

Sometimes a porno set is like a strange planet. You see guys talking to their dicks, as though they don't belong to them. "Come on, what's wrong with you? You piece of shit!" It can't belong to you because it isn't getting hard when you want it to. You're so mad and embarrassed that you yell, "I don't know this guy down there. I renounce my fucking dick!" But it's a part of your body and you have to understand why it sometimes ignores you.

Pornography is a boarding house for people running away from themselves. Oh, you wear nice clothes, have your picture in glossy magazines, see yourself on video. But porno people are out of step with the rest of the world. We say, "Love me. Well, at least *like* me." Taking our clothes off, we're not only baring our skins, but we're baring our souls and making ourselves more vulnerable. We have to sacrifice our bodies to gain affection. What's so bad about that? Nothing, so far as some people are concerned. But then there are those quiet moments, those dark days, when your career of promiscuous public fucking comes back to haunt you.

I used to have a dynamite body. I don't any more. I'm twenty-nine, and when I look in the mirror I can see larger love-handles and I can see that my muscles aren't as intense as they used to be. But I'm giving all that away to my talent, to my *inner* muscularity.

I used to be like a lot of porno people, taking pride in the surface vision of my body. When I was younger I used to rely on that vision: I was the best-looking kid in school,

RAW TALENT

I had the best body. But these things became my worst enemies. It became *spooky.* It was if I was nothing more than skeleton and flesh. Now I'm more concerned with the heat beating inside.

Seventeen

Teasers . . . and Thomas

Maybe I'm getting a little too serious for my own good. I notice every speck of dust, every sight and sound, and I magnify it. I'll try to lighten up a bit and get back into the swing of talking about the actresses, but I just want you to see all sides of the business clearly and honestly. Sure, there are beautiful women and glamorous sets, but there are just as many cockroaches and unclean costars. There are men with ten-inch penises and women with no last names, but you've got to remember that we have mothers, fathers, spouses, and, sometimes, even children. And consciences.

When I first met Krista Lane, I thought she was the ultimate sexy woman. She enjoyed working with me, and we had a lot of fun together. The only thing I didn't like was the fact that she had a wire running around the inside of her teeth. Her inner braces didn't show to the camera, but every time she'd suck me, she'd cut the hell out of my prick. Despite that, our first sex scene was one of the hottest ever. (You'll probably say, "Butler always says that!" But, if you take notice, a lot of the hotness has to do with working with a woman for the first time.) I swear, my dick wouldn't go down; I even went home with a hard-on. I asked my dick if it was ever going to go down and it just looked at me and smiled.

Krista likes to act nasty and slutty, but I think she has the eyes of a newborn baby. I felt a lot of innocence in her, but she's a total contradiction. For a while, she was having an affair with a congressman from California. He even sent roses to her hotel in San Francisco when she was shooting a porno movie. Krista also has a pilot's license.

Pornographically speaking, Krista's a real professional. She's clean, she comes onto the set on time, and she does her job well. She's a good actress, very capable of handling lines. She's not one to complain, bitch, or shrink away from her work. Personally, I think she prefers women, but she's always wild, no matter who her costar is.

Whenever Krista and I met on the set, there was always a strong magnetism, even if we weren't working together. I'll never forget the time we fucked off-camera. I was hot and she knew it, so Krista just walked into the bathroom and gave me this inviting look. I walked in after her. We didn't say one word to each other. I just picked her up, put her on top of the sink, and spread her legs.

Angel Kelly. Oh, brother! At first, I thought she looked like Sammy Davis, Jr., in drag. She had one of the smelliest pussies I ever put my nose into. Well, maybe not worse than Lois

Ayres's, but close. Then a funny thing happened. When I worked with her during *In and Out of Africa,* Angel was suddenly very clean. Women have a lot of things to learn when they first get into the business, tricks of the trade, so to speak. They're having sex more often than they probably ever did before, and it's not as easy to keep clean. Some directors don't even give you the chance to shower between sex scenes. Maybe it just took some time for her to learn the ropes.

Angel's really responsive and has one of the tightest pussies in the business. She's a light-skinned black lady, so naturally her pussy's very dark. That kind of turned me off at first, but we always got along very well, kidded around, and joked with each other.

At a trade show in Las Vegas, I told Angel that I really liked her. She didn't take me seriously, but I wasn't kidding—she is a very nice, sweet woman. That's where I always find female beauty.

Lisa DeLeeuw is an abundant, extreme personality. Since I'm pretty extreme too, we were always warring. For some reason, I also found her to be sexy. No matter how much of a prima donna she was, no matter how demanding she was, Lisa was transformed from a big, bold, untouchable landmark into a flesh-and-blood woman when my dick was going in and out of her.

In *Raw Talent,* the character she played was a bitch supreme: a porno producer who wrecks my character's career in soaps. Our mutual dislike for each other worked to our advantage. In the story, her character "Carolyn" forced me to fuck her, but Lisa was upset at my uninvolved pumping, my coldness. She even started crying. But Lisa didn't understand that I was fucking her in character.

RAW TALENT

Directors are always laying claim on porno people as though they're a piece of land and want squatter's rights. Joyce Snyder, the director of the *Raw Talent* movies and many others, claims to have "discovered" Cassandra Leigh. Cassandra's a very sweet, quiet Cuban lady, but neither of us really enjoyed sex with each other. Her long, blonde hair is certainly attractive, but I never found anything glamorous about her. At the time I worked with her, she used to peroxide her pussy hairs blonde. I always bothered me when a woman did something unnatural to her pubic hairs, whether it be shaving, dyeing, or trimming. Furthermore, Cassandra also seemed sweaty and nervous. Otherwise, I didn't mind working with her, because she had a pleasant personality and didn't have an overblown image of herself.

In *Raw Talent II*, I worked with Cassandra again. We had a threesome with Greg Derek, a D.P. (In case you don't know, that stands for "double penetration"—one guy in the front and one in the rear.) Greg's dick kept making a left turn and I kept rolling up my window. Maybe he was more interested in me than Cassandra. She seemed involved in the sex, so that made me enjoy it more.

When some women first get into the business, there's a reluctance. They brace themselves and can't be free and open. After a while, Cassandra loosened up so much that I couldn't believe her scene with Buck Adams in the same movie. She really seemed to have a good time, especially when he flipped her upside down so elegantly.

TEASERS . . . AND THOMAS

I met Samantha Fox in Chuck Vincent's office before we began shooting *Roommates*. She was a historic artifact, and I was just starting out. Before I left, she handed me a card that said, "Wowie Zowie!" and her phone number. She was sweet, charming, and had this leopard-kittenness about her. We never seemed to have sex scenes, though. The more I didn't work with her, the more I wanted to. I had a wild, preconceived notion of what she'd be like. She must have been thirty to my nineteen.

Our first sex scene was in *In Love*. I couldn't wait. In rehearsals, we would look at each other and smile because we knew we'd finally be getting each other in bed. Maybe I had fantasized too much about Samantha, because our sex scene was a disappointment. I had a problem getting an erection and she didn't taste as good as I'd expected. Although we didn't have a great scene, I still found her to be sexy.

Samantha and I kept in touch and had lunch a few times in Manhattan. It was tough for me to start up a relationship with her. At that time, I was a Brooklyn boy still living with my folks, making a movie here and there, rocking around with my friends. Samantha was a real Manhattan actress, and I never lived in that circle. I never went to those parties. I had to take the subway to enter that world.

Still, I sensed Samantha's loneliness. Sometimes we would cry to each other and later smile knowingly. I knew she could give me a lot of motherly feelings, support, and comfort. All I could give her was a big, warm blanket of flesh. We never made love off-screen, although we did talk about it. If I called her right now (like I did the last time I was in New York), she'd want to see me, kiss me, and be intimate with me. Even if I told her I was married, she'd find nothing wrong with making love to me. Samantha's the kind of woman who never feels guilty about *anything*. Why should she? Porno becomes your credit card. It extends your license for living. It dissolves the line between the sacredness of sex and disregard for it. Believe me, it's a fine line.

Maybe four months ago, Samantha and I spoke on the phone. She shocked me when she told me that, more than anything else in the world, she wanted to have my child. She wanted a baby and explained that I was her idea of the ultimate beautiful male, so the kid would *have* to be gorgeous. She's one of a handful of women who have told me the same thing—not just casually, or as a novelty, but very seriously.

Talking with Samantha made me remember that I have a son in New York. I almost never see him. I'm not allowed to. Maybe that's why I try not to think about him too much.

His name is Thomas. I met his mother, Lorraine, on the set of *Naked Scents.* She's a makeup artist. I fell head over heels in love with this big, beautiful woman. Lorraine informed me she was a good Christian and that she would never screw anybody but her boyfriend. Well, before the night was over, I was fucking Lorraine in a hot tub. A few hours earlier, she insisted that she could never be with a guy like me. By the time she said, "I really can't . . .," I was already inside her.

The cast and crew were sleeping at a mansion in Connecticut. Lorraine and I stayed up all night, drank, and did some cocaine. We must have nodded off and woke up about five in the morning. I don't know how I managed, but I carried her out to the back of the house, put her on top of the doghouse, and made love to her. She screamed so loud, she woke up everyone in the entire house.

After the shoot was wrapped up, Lorraine went back to Queens and I went back to Brooklyn. We kept in close touch. Then I discovered that Lorraine hadn't been exactly truthful with me. She was living with a guy named John and already had one baby, named Christina, with him. So much for her being virginal. Despite her ties, we started a serious relationship. She was considering moving in with me, but she worried about how irresponsible I was. She couldn't make up her mind whether to live with me or Johnny. First she'd tell me she was going back to him, so I'd try to forget her. Then she'd call me up again a few days later.

Lorraine and I next worked together in *Dick of Death,* which was filmed in Asbury Park, New Jersey. At that point, I was getting tired of her indecision. I guess she was trying to feel me out and wanted me to tell her I loved her. There she was in my hotel room, saying how happy she and Johnny were. I told her I thought that was great and to get the hell out of my room. At first, she wouldn't go, so I pushed her toward the door. She stubbed her toe and started crying. Lorraine wound up spending the night. I swear, that was the night she conceived. I knew in my bones it was happening.

At six the following morning, there was a knock on the door. It was Johnny. He had driven all the way from Manhattan. Johnny was so cool when he asked if Lorraine was with me. They went outside to talk. What a crazy day that turned out to be! We were supposed to finish up the movie, but never did. (If you watch *Dick of Death* and think it has a patched-together, unfinished feel, you're right, because we never actually finished shooting it.) The cops showed up because Sharon Mitchell hadn't paid a hotel bill, they kept me as collateral for five hours while she gathered the money, and Lorraine decided to go home with Johnny. Again.

Lorraine was pregnant, but I didn't know it. A few weeks after the movie, I met her at Rockefeller Center. It was crisp and cold as I pushed her baby Christina in her carriage. The Christmas tree looked pretty above the ice-skating rink. I felt good inside, until Lorraine told me she had decided to stay with Johnny.

Lorraine called me the next day, but I was tired of her playing with me like a yo-yo. I told her, "Lorraine, let's just forget it. I can't go on like this." Then she told me she really loved me and that she thought she was pregnant. Even though she hadn't taken a test, she knew the feeling. When I spoke to her a few days later, she confirmed that she was definitely pregnant and decided to have an abortion. I told her I'd pay for it. I left the decision up to her because it was her body. If she wanted to be with me and have the baby, I would have supported the both of them. But I just couldn't handle Lorraine's head games any longer. In her next phone call, she told me she'd gotten her period. *You* figure it out!

When Lorraine told me she wasn't pregnant and that she decided to stay with Johnny, I went back to California. I was at Reb Sawitz's office in L.A. when an actress told me she'd just returned from a New York shoot and had seen Lorraine, who was seven months pregnant *with my baby.* Immediately I called Lorraine and asked if it were true. She admitted it was. I flew back to New York as soon as I could. When I saw her belly, I knew there was something inside that was mine. I loved my unborn child, even though I didn't love the woman who was carrying it. After I'd traveled across the country, Lorraine decided that she was going to let Johnny believe it was his baby and leave it at that. When my son was born, Lorraine didn't even call me.

A few months later, Lorraine told me she was coming out to California. She told me that Johnny had died of a heart attack. Believe it or not, she was laughing. She even laughed at his funeral, she admitted. Now, *this* frightened me. I'd always known there was something sinister about her. Many born-again Christians don't live their lives the way they preach, and Lorraine was one of them. She claimed to be spiritual, but only to lord her righteousness over people like me. No thanks. P.S.—Surprise!—she never made it out West.

The next time I saw her, Lorraine did her usual 180-degree turn and insisted that Thomas wasn't really mine. Months before, she had asked me about my blood type and all sorts of other things. Everything matched. Now, Lorraine was trying to be devious. Did she just want to hurt me? But Thomas *is* my son. I know it. I didn't see him until he was about a year old. It was just a fleeting glance, because I was afraid of studying his face. I was afraid I'd see myself in him.

When I was back East filming *Raw Talent II,* I went to visit Lorraine. She told me, "Look, I like you, Paul, but I don't love you. And we can't be together." She always smirked when she really meant to frown, but I could see through those big, dark glasses she always wore. I knew she was horny, but she told me she didn't want sex. I was relaxing on her sofa bed and she sat down next to me, caressing my face. When I grabbed Lorraine's hand, she said, "No." But suddenly, she unzipped me and her mouth was on my cock.

Recently, Lorraine did makeup for *Deranged.* In most of it, I played a zombie and required tons of makeup, so we spent a lot of time together. I told her I wanted to see my son. "Just forget about him," she told me. "He's being well taken care of. He doesn't know you, and he doesn't have to know you. Harvey [her new boyfriend] will be his father."

I know that if I took a plane to New York and knocked on Lorraine's door, I would be in bed with her. For a long, long time, I didn't cry about Thomas. I was able to repress my feelings. But now it really bothers me. *I have a kid running around in this fucking world, a child I don't even see.* And more than anything, I want a child. Lisa and I have been trying, but it has just not been working. I make love, and what comes out of my penis is the solution that also brings the life of a child—to be given my name, to live under my roof, to be united with his mother and his father at all times.

So, my son's name is Thomas. I don't even know his last name. I don't even know what he looks like. It's not so much that I'd *like* to be his father. I *have* to be. I didn't realize this until Lisa drew it out of me one night. She knew I had been hiding and denying my pain for a long time. I pushed it deep down inside because I knew I couldn't be a father to Thomas. Lorraine wouldn't let me. Lisa told me I knew I had a child and that he'd try to find me one day. I couldn't stop crying.

Eighteen

Sex Kittens

When you write *your* autobiography, you'll be bewildered by how much you instinctively want to *avoid.* I've been trying to avoid talking about Rachel Ashley, but Lisa insists I tell the story from beginning to end. I've been down thinking about my son, so this is probably as good a time as any.

It seems I met everyone who's everyone while making *Nice Girls Do.* What an impressive aura Rachel had! She's about 5'10" and busty, with shapely gymnast's thighs. Her strength and grace reminded me of a thoroughbred walking around the corral before a big race.

When we were filming *She's So Fine* in the Hamptons, Rachel and I did something pretty wild with a shoe-shine machine contraption. You put your shoes between these padded wheels and it would shine them up. It didn't take much coaxing for Rachel to squat over this rotating, pillowy thing. She pressed against it, still wearing her panties. When she came, she soaked the thing. I felt sorry for the next guy who wanted a shoeshine!

It wasn't until we made *In Love* in New York that we really hit it off. We had an interesting scene. Rachel made love with her boyfriend as I sat in a chair and watched. All the time he was pounding her, she kept staring at me and licking her lips. We finally did have a sex scene later, but I don't think it was used in the film's final cut. Rachel told me it was one of the first times she climaxed on camera.

That night, Rachel came home with me and met my parents. She stayed at the apartment for two days. We even talked about the possibility of getting married. When we flew back to California, Rachel paid my way. We spent a lot of time together on the West Coast, and I discovered that Rachel was a real party girl and would screw anything in her path that excited her. She didn't understand my kind of morality, my "human policy" of getting to know lovers as people, too. I like a woman who stays close to her guy and isn't promiscuous. I guess I could say that Rachel was just another beautiful woman who passed through my life. I tried to make her more than what she was, to suit *my* own needs for love.

I think Rachel did love me in her own way. I mean, she bought me clothes and jewelry. But being with her was like going to the movies for two hours. You're entertained and captured by the pretty images on the screen. But when it's over, you have to put down the popcorn and get on with your own life. Our "movie" only had a two week run, and then it was over.

Rachel and I have worked together in twelve or thirteen movies, but we only had about nine sex scenes. She was one woman with big, slopppy tits who *wasn't* a lazy lay. It was always a pleasure to fuck her. Maybe it was the angle of her pussy, but it was always especially nice. Remembering Rachel is like hearing a song on the radio that reminds you of sad times. To me, she represented hope and wishfulness, a symbol of what makes people go on with their lives and keep searching.

I suspect Rhonda Jo Petty has had a boob job (to make them *smaller*), but I think she is one of the most gorgeous and sexy women in the world. Her body is smooth. Beautiful feet, and a beautiful pussy.

Rhonda was a Mormon who was excommunicated from the church when it found out she was doing pornos. Just now, Lisa asked me, "How can you be a Mormon and a porno actress at the same time?" Well, it's the fight within yourself that drives you, that makes you go to any lengths to obtain some kind of social acceptance.

Rhonda and I hit it off very well and were kind of in love. But again, it wasn't *real* love. After all, I never spent more than fifteen minutes with her off the set. Maybe what I was trying to see was how close I could come to love. Did you ever stretch your arm as high as you could when you were a kid? It didn't really tell you how tall you were, but you imagined that you were larger than life. Well, that's what I tried to do with many of the women I worked with. I wanted to be in love and constantly tried to get as close as I could. Close, but no cigar.

I called Rhonda up about two years ago. At the time she was living in Agora, California—trying to recover from the wild life. I tried to help her get work, but I couldn't reach her after that. I haven't heard from Rhonda since.

Ona Zee is one of my favorite newer people in the business. Although she claims thirty, I'll bet she's about thirty-six. Either way, she's considered "old" for the business. She's only been doing adult films for a year or so. Even though Ona's a capable actress and a pretty woman, she still does D.P., she ass-fucks, she swallows come, and she works with transsexuals—all the things a homely bimbo has to do. Why? Ona treats herself as though she's not attractive. People take advantage of her because she takes advantage of herself.

I have yet to see a woman as beautiful as Ona have no concern about what she does sexually. A lot of big-name women tell the director, "No come swallowing! No anal! No interracial stuff! No D.P.!"—and they make *more* money. Amber Lynn is one of those women. But Ona's way ahead of Amber because she's pretty and can act, too! She's a little too old to play somebody's girlfriend, but she's perfect for the unhappy-wife roles.

In *No One To Love,* Ona came about five times with me in our first scene. She has a shaved pussy, which doesn't turn me on in porns. When I make love to Lisa, her pubes become a bunch of arms and legs stimulating me. I like to push away the hair and find the buried treasure. When Ona's pussy is shaved, her mound appears big and pudgy. Her vagina looks like a mouth smirking, and it makes me feel small. Without pubic hair, you see every crevice and crack. You can almost see lips and cheeks and eyebrows. With Ona's beautiful black hair, you'd expect to find a great, full bush down below. It's very disappointing to discover she's got a bald crotch. Even though she keeps it shaved smooth, there's always one annoying little nub that'll drive me crazy. It's like getting a great blow job and then all of a sudden feeling a tooth sink in.

I was attracted to Ona the first time I saw her. She has this anorexic Annette Funicello look. When she took her clothes off, I saw stretch marks and other imperfections. (I think she's had a child.) It didn't coincide with the tiny-waisted woman whose breasts and ass were bursting through her clothes.

Ona has so much passion, desire, and hunger. Sometimes,

I got the feeling that she wanted to swallow me up. She reached, gripped, and clawed me, and she kept saying, "You're so beautiful. You're so good." In *No One To Love,* we had an incredibly hot sex scene. It was from the heart.

I think it's great that Ona can give away so much of herself. She's one of the rare women who does. Of course, the business didn't appreciate her fervor and grossly underpaid her when she started. She made only $450 a day! Less than a guy! Top women generally get five hundred to a thousand dollars. I don't think she had the heart to ask for more. Maybe she didn't think she deserved it.

Ona will learn. Right now, she's too eager to become a star in a galaxy that's full of clouds.

In *No One To Love* Ona and I had a threesome with Shanna McCullough. Like Siobhan Hunter, Shanna's too white and snowy for my taste. In fact, Shanna's so fair, when she takes off her panties there are lines and irritation marks on her body. That's how sensitive her skin is. A body like that doesn't turn me on, and neither do red-haired pussies. Some guys go crazy because Shanna's a natural redhead, but I say, "Give me a black crayon. Hurry!" When Shanna's pussy gets wet, it looks like a handlebar mustache.

She was always very gentle, though—the girl next door who's so nice, naive, and gullible, that you feel you can do anything you want to her. The attraction I have for Shanna has to do with her sweetness as a person. She's so sensitive that if you pound her too hard she hurts. She's always kind of creamy when I pull out, like Ivory Liquid. But Shanna receives very well and she's also a screamer. A 5.2 on the Richter scale.

Shanna lives up in San Francisco and doesn't come down to L.A. to work very often. Because she keeps pretty much to herself, she reminds me of a female Mike Horner (a.k.a. Don Hart). What's interesting is that she and Mike have had some very wild sex scenes together. It's sort of like Amber Lynn and myself. We represent L.A., and they symbolize San Francisco. Mike always picks Shanna up and they come to the set together. It's the affiliation, the closensss that makes for a good sex scene. That's what it's all about, or should be, not the positions.

If people look uncomfortable in a sex scene, it's probably because they're following a director's guidelines and not doing it the way they want it. I'd rather see a guy fuck a girl in one position and both of them have ultimate, maximum pleasure than to see them moving around like jumping jacks. I don't like certain positions, and I've told directors that they're not going to get a good performacne if they move me around like a chess piece. But they usually don't understand.

Mai Lin might be someone's Oriental fantasy, but she's not mine. Her pubic hair is so long and stringy that she reminds me of a guy who can't grow a full beard so he tries a Fu Manchu instead. I feel as if I'm eating a paintbrush.

Mai Lin and I worked together in *Sexual Odyssey* in Malibu. The next time we hitched up was in San Francisco. Mai came up to me and said, "You know, Jerry Butler, you gave me the clap."

"I never had the clap," I told her.

It seems Mai came down with it after the Malibu shoot, but I wasn't the one who gave it to her. I was insulted. If I had it, I would have been honest. Gonorrhea isn't something you should hide when sex is your business. I heard that Mai's stopped doing porno because of AIDS.

Recently, I went out for a quick beer with a friend in

L.A. He took me to a place where a woman he knew was an exotic dancer. I found out that Mai Lin was also appearing there, and I thought I'd stop to say "Hello." There she was, dancing in a booth, not even the main act on a stage. It was sad. She was so happy to see me, especially after being stuck in a glass booth with guys jerking off to her. Finally, Mai saw me as a human being—because she wasn't being treated like one.

Sheena Horne is a valley girl from Chinatown: part Oriental, part Californian—and don't ask me which part goes to which! I've had some pretty good sex with her, because she allows herself *to feel.* But out of bed, Sheena's not too bright. In ways, she almost reminds me of Shauna Grant, but Sheena's a little more outgoing.

I wasn't feeling too good about the business (or myself) when we did *Hot Gun* (a take off on *Top Gun*) up north. The circumstances reminded me of Ginger Lynn and the Porsche in *Beverly Hils Cox.* In fact, it was Paul Vatelli's last film before he died of AIDS, and he directed both films. I was down to the wire again, undecided about quitting. Vatelli was saying cold things like, "Okay, you're going to get your dick up now." I was also having trouble with a video technician named Ilo because I used to go out with his girl. In the front seat of that convertible with Sheena, I forgot all of these problems. Maybe it was the car.

I fell in lust with Shannon on the set of *Momma's Boy.* She was a gorgeous woman who looked like Angie Dickenson, only prettier. People started to laugh because I was making a play for her. I asked what was so funny, and they said, "You'll find out." And I did.

Shannon used to be a guy.

I don't know the details, and I don't want to! It's a $10,000 operation. When I found out Shannon had been a guy, I felt a little distaste. I still felt attracted to her, though. She's a beautiful person, inside and out, but when you really studied her body, you could see the mannishness in the way she carried herself.

In another movie, we did an orgy scene where Shannon was only supposed to give me head. I was so turned on that I had an overwhelming desire to fuck her. I wanted to put it in, but she wouldn't let me. Because Shannon was not originally a woman, her "vagina" doesn't get wet. She needs some kind of lubricant. I grabbed a slap of Abolene, which always reminds me of Turtle Wax. I felt as if I was simonizing my dick! Once inside Shannon, I was having ups and downs with my erection because I couldn't forget that she'd once been a man. I finally came, but I knew I was making love to something that wasn't the genuine article.

I always thought Kristara Barrington looked like a Siamese cat. In a magazine interview Kristara once said, "I don't like Jerry Butler because he makes me laugh too much, and I don't think it looks professional on screen." There she was, condemning a part of me that she really enjoyed. The next time we worked together, Kristara said, "I'm so happy to see you. It's so dull around here." When I asked her why she didn't tell the interviewer how she really felt about me, she didn't know what to say.

Kristara always uses a strawberry-scented, won-ton-looking suppository spermicide. It even has a dragon on the box. I felt as if I were sticking my dick into something that was loaded with MSG! Eventually, the suppository would melt like a pat of butter and numb me.

Kristara's pretty good when it comes to sex, but her huge aureolas reminded me of TV knobs. If you look closely enough, you'll notice that one says VHF and the other says UHF.

If you made love to Candie Evens doggie-style, she would sound like a whimpering puppy. I hear she's now working as a supermarket clerk, but when she was in pornos, she was the sweetest, most trusting little creature. You could tell her you had AIDS, but if you promised you wouldn't come on her, she'd smile and say, "Okay." She had the cutest pussy. I was always amazed at how much I *should* have been aroused by her—but wasn't. Candie is so sweet, you often wondered what the hell she was doing in the business. But when you saw her get totally consumed in a sex scene, it kind of answered your question.

Nineteen

More Kiss and Tell

When you hear the name Jeanna Fine, you might expect something out-of-the-ordinary, something, you know, *fine.* It bothers me when a porno actress chooses a name that describes something she *wishes* she were. Jeanna started out with an unflattering, punky look. She has a very nice face, but tree-trunk legs. You can tell it bothers her. That's why she wears mini-dresses. It's like walking into the lion's cage just to prove how courageous you are.

Jeanna had a bisexual boyfriend named Tony. She used to bring the porn actress Keisha home and the two of them would fuck him. Then, when she was making a film with Keisha, almost everyone on the set caught the clap. I was shocked to hear Jeanna blame it on *me.*

After that, I understood that Jeanna left Tony and linked up with the head of Catalina Video, a guy named Norman. Catalina Video produces a lot of gay films and were the first to introduce completely bisexual films, ones where the guys fuck each other and the women, too. Jeanna made quite a few movies like this, so it bugs me that she's also doing straight porn. In a business that's in a high-risk AIDS category for starters, working with women like Jeanna makes it even riskier.

Recently, guys like Jeff Stryker, who was the king of male homosexual movies, have started making heterosexual porn. Stryker has tried to fend off criticism by claiming he was only the fucker, not the fuckee, in gay anal sex. Somehow, though, I'm not too reassured.

I would rather fuck Margaret Hamilton, dressed up as the Wicked Witch of the West, than to have to fuck Chelsea Blake again. She always came onto the set with this pardon-me-but-I'm-ugly attitude. Poor thing, she really had a terrible body. During one particular sex scene, I noticed the crew snickering. She had a floppy stomach and tits, a Caesarean scar, and stretch marks. That's not for porno. I've had maybe three sex scenes with her, and they weren't easy. When I work with unattractive women, I often feel as though I'm being used. When they scream, "More! More! More" I whisper, "Be lucky! Be lucky! Be lucky!" But deep down I feel sorry for them.

Patti Petite's got to be one of the homeliest girls in the business. She's not a bad actress, but she never stops yacking. Sometimes I feel like putting her to sleep with a right hook. The only time I could have a decent scene with her was before nine in the morning—before she was really wiped out. Working with someone like that is when you really earn your money.

Stacey Donovan gave me the impression she'd be more at home climbing trees than doing porno. She seemed like a grown-up tomboy. Everything was fine between us until we started screwing. Besides being unenthusiastic, she was very rough and unfeminine.

The only reason our foursome worked in *Dial-A-Dick* was that I was so hot for Krista Lane. When I switched back to Stacey, I still had some steam left from fucking Krista. I'd pull out of Donovan and go back into Lane for some more fuel.

Toward the end of her career, Stacey appeared on a major network, attacking the industry. If she has any hopes of getting back into it, she can probably forget them.

Sahara *was* as dry as the desert. I was really attracted to her when we met in *Strange Bedfellows;* she had this clean Diahann Carroll look about her. I planned to fuck the hell out of her. She was always displaying an unnecessary amount of stand-offishness, but when I put my dick into her, her ego collapsed and she became helpless.

Strange Bedfellows gave me a chance to play a challenging character. I was handed the script about five minutes before we started shooting. "Genius" was a nerdy scientist. At first, I didn't know how to play him and started to get panicky, looking in the mirror, playing with my hair. Then, suddenly, I had a zany feeling about what Genius should look like. I had the makeup girl tease my hair. Then I put on a pair of glasses and wore a crooked bow tie. I really enjoyed Jerry Lewis when he appeared as *The Nutty Professor,* and as Genius I mimicked the way he talked. Suddenly, everything fell into place.

Sahara was very abusive toward me in our scene, but it was all right because it meshed with the character she played. Genius was a sponge with intelligence. You could say anything you wanted to Genius, and he wouldn't mind. He lacked attention and affection, so even sarcastic remarks were taken as compliments by him. Every time he was insulted, it made him feel uwanted. I really identified with him.

Doing a sex scene with Mindy Rae is like making love to Mulhollen Drive. She used to be very plump, but now she's skinny as a rail. Her sister, Athena Star, is also in the business. They had a porno mommy who pushed both of their careers. The often told story is that on an "audition," Athena wasn't sucking off some sleazy producer the right way, so mom took over and showed her how.

As a porno actor, you accept the job and the hazardous risks. When I came onto the set and discovered I had to fuck Mindy, I'd groan, "Oh shit, not her." It was like a guy who drives a well-tuned cab, but once in a while has to bum around in a wreck.

I recently did a layout with Mindy after she lost a lot of weight. She was looking much better, and I was getting hot. I really wanted to fuck her, but she politely refused. She's married now and doesn't do hardcore. But I remember a time when you could drive an elephant into her and she would have said, "Thanks."

Tarantula, I mean, Tantala. Fucking her was like fucking Magilla Gorilla in drag. Her pussy reminded me of the Lincoln Tunnel with padding. John Johnson used to joke that her pussy was alive and even had its own heart beat. Professionally, Tantala—or "Mistress Tantala," as she's sometimes called—is an S & M mistress. When she played my mother in *Momma's Boy,* we had an "incestuous" sex scene. Although she's not appealing, when I stuck my dick into a woman who is known as a dominator, I felt powerful and in command. In real life, Tantala's sweet and polite. After all, she doesn't get onto the bus, put a dollar in the slot, and start whipping the bus driver.

Desiree Lane was so cute, I wish I could have put her into my back pocket. Desiree finally got out of the business because her boyfriend objected. He wanted her to be a born-again Christian, so he and his family drilled it into her that porno was evil. Now she's totally "reformed" and preaches against the likes of me.

Helga put so much perfume on her body and pussy that I felt as if I were eating all the Chanel numbers from one to a hundred. She looks like Zsa Zsa Gabor with over-stuffed tits. Looking at her, you'd think she'd fuck anything, but she's very cautious and concerned about "safe sex." In fact, on the set of *Wild Nurses In Lust,* one of the male leads had a blister on his penis and she wouldn't screw him.

I found Helga to be sexy in her own way. Remember the lady who only had raisins for the Halloween trick-or-treat? Sometimes I still open my bag for other people, no matter what they put inside. Once you're inside Helga, she's great, very professional and technical. She even jerks you off in a businesslike manner. Helga's an older woman, but she's a real *woman.* There are a lot of girls in this business, but very few women.

Alicia Monet's voice has a raspy quality that reminds me of Ann-Margret's. The first time I worked with her was in 1987, in *Romeo & Juliet,* and she was just starting out. Her husband is almost twenty years older than she is, and his "job" is to manage her money and work her to death. While she's getting fucked and screaming all over the place, he's balancing her checkbook. He seems to be weighing the moans and groans, trying to figure out how much of it's real and how much isn't.

They tell me their goal is to get $200,000 in the bank and quit the porn business. They boast about how they don't do drugs, yet their noses are always running. One of the first times I saw Alicia work, she had to take on three or four guys. She wanted so much to please the director, but she humped and bumped so hard that she hurt her uterus. She overextends herself, maybe just to prove that she can do it. She's still pretty green and is often self-conscious during her sex scenes.

In the 1970s, porn starlets were more natural looking, like the Venus de Milo with arms. In 1987, Alicia was being groomed to become a top porno star. I heard she's going to get a boob job soon. Imagine that, only twenty-two and she is already going to have her tits lifted. The women in this business will do whatever it takes to enhance the assets they have, to improve the product. Boob jobs are unbelievably common. When I'm doing a sex scene, I hardly notice if they feel different or not. In what I call the "business scene" with someone I don't feel particualrly attracted to, I usually don't get too involved. I concern myself with the money area, which is her vagina.

It's a big world out there, and guys have different sexual tastes. The producers and directors make the decisions, and all of the women are tremendously competitive. A woman can walk onto a set and see what she needs more of or has too much of. It's like going to the men's room. While you're peeing, you look at everyone else's dick but your own. When a producer gets a girl under contract, that's it, you've sold yourself to the meat market. The directors and producers will change your hairstyle, your hair color, and the way you dress. Some women seem to enjoy it, because they get a lot of attention. Overnight, they're "movie stars."

Other times, becoming a leading lady is a lot more complicated. I hear that one particularly beautiful woman is going to get a lip job. They're going to take a piece of her ass and put it on the fleshy part of her lips. And this actress has already had a ridiculous boob job. It's disgusting what they put women through, and it's only the beginning for Alicia.

I really believe Alicia Monet will be a big star someday. You might wonder what it takes to be a big star in porno. Usually, it's nothing more than pushing yourself to the limit. Alicia's vagina needs 10WD motor oil to keep it in working order. I'm damned if I could watch my wife fucking and groaning while I sat on the sidelines and counted the money she was earning.

I've done tons of cocaine watching videos of Tina Marie. To me, she's the ultimate porno queen sensation. We've never had a sex scene, but both of us were in *Bad Girls III*. I never got so horny in all my life watching her play with her pussy in the restaurant scene. Even stronger than my dream of fucking Tina Marie is my desire to see her in lesbian scenes. The other day, I saw her on the cover of an all-girl video called *Paper Dolls* and I got an immediate erection.

Back then, Tina Marie was seeing a guy who had formed Video-X-Pix. They've been in the business for years and were formerly Quality-X Video. In the past few years, they've gone back to making "cheapies." Tina called me one day and said she wanted to use me in a film. I asked her if I could do a scene with her, but she said that would be impossible; her boyfriend only allows her to do a little girl-girl. (A lot of guys like that. Maybe they don't feel threatened by a person who doesn't have a penis.) I wanted her to at least be on the set when I did my scene, and she said she'd see what she could do. Later, Video-X-Pix dropped me from the cast because Tina's boyfriend had been listening to our conversation on another line and got angry. There's always *Paper Dolls!*

Getting onto an airplane to do *Broadway Fanny Rose,* I noticed a pretty woman with her baby. When I landed in San Francisco and got to the set, I was surprised to see her there. She turned out to be Lorrie Lovett. Lorrie brings a nanny everywhere she goes so the nanny can watch her kid during Lorrie's sex scenes. Lorrie was still nursing. I was very turned on by that thought and was ready for a good scene, but it didn't turn out that way. Lorrie showed up a little woozy and started yanking on my chest hairs. I yelled, "Oh, great! I know we're going to have a fantastic scene," and shoved my fist right through the prop wall.

Tracey Adams has a really beautiful, classy womanliness. Without her makeup though, she looks like Miss Liberty on the old dimes. Bold and stand-offish, Tracey sometimes seemed to be a mountain. You're in awe of the strength, beauty, and power it possesses. Then you realize that a mountain doesn't move and it doesn't have feelings. Tracey's pretty reserved, and yet she sways and moves you from the inside. I consider Tracey a good actress. The more we worked together, the more feelings we gained for each other.

Because Tracey used to drive a limousine, she got to meet a lot of Hollywood stars. Tracey claims she went out with Warren Beatty. She said that when he saw one of my pornos, he thought I was one of the best actors he'd ever seen.

Tracey *acts* like she's involved in the sex. She'll lie on her back, open her legs, moan, and pant like crazy. But as soon as the camera stops rolling, it's "Makeup! Where's the coffee? Can I have some ice for my pores? My face is opening up." She's a real businesswoman. If you ask her to do anal, she'll say no. Until you pull out your wallet, that is. Then it's, "Should I use the Fleet enema now?" Tracey's one of the most professional women in the busines and treats pornography like a career. In fact, I think she's my favorite female in the business. Whenever I've needed help, Tracey's always been there. She always went out of her way to understand me. I don't know if we could ever be together long-term, though. If I could sew up Tracey's vagina and seal up my pee-hole, I'd be with her forever. Sex is what would ruin our relationship.

Kari Fox had a boyfriend in the business named Troy Tanier. Troy was very insecure about what she did for a living. We had a threesome together in *Rated Sex,* and he allowed her to blow me. In between giving me head and camera roll out,

Troy kept asking her, "Honey, you love me, don't you? You need me, don't you?" Then the cameras would roll. She'd be sucking me and he'd be doing her from behind.

It's interesting that Troy had the hots for Lisa on the set of *Traci's Big Trick,* where we met. At the time, Troy was studying to be a chiropractor and I jealously watched him working on her back. Troy was falling for Lisa, but Lisa was falling for me.

Sexual dominoes.

Solomon Siederman

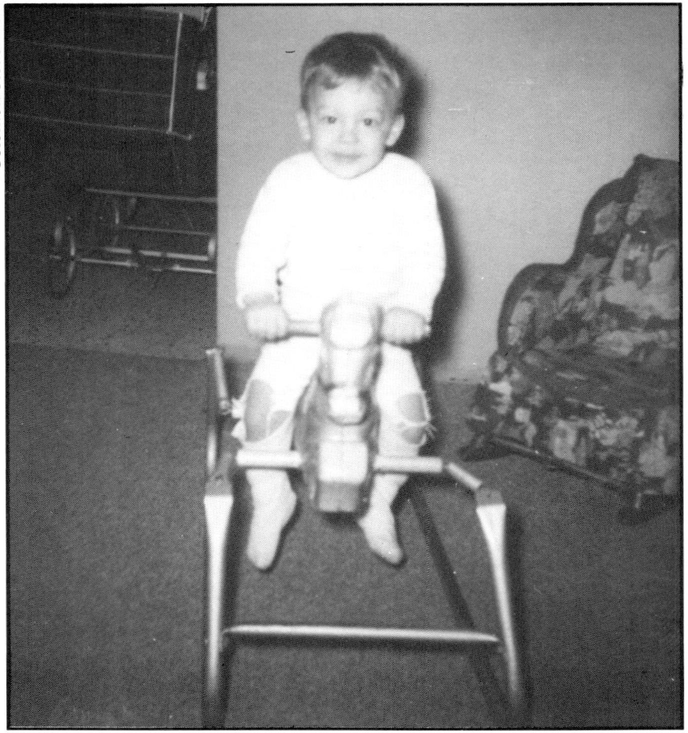

Solomon Siederman

At home with my beloved rocking horse; and with my Mom at age nine

Solomon Siederman

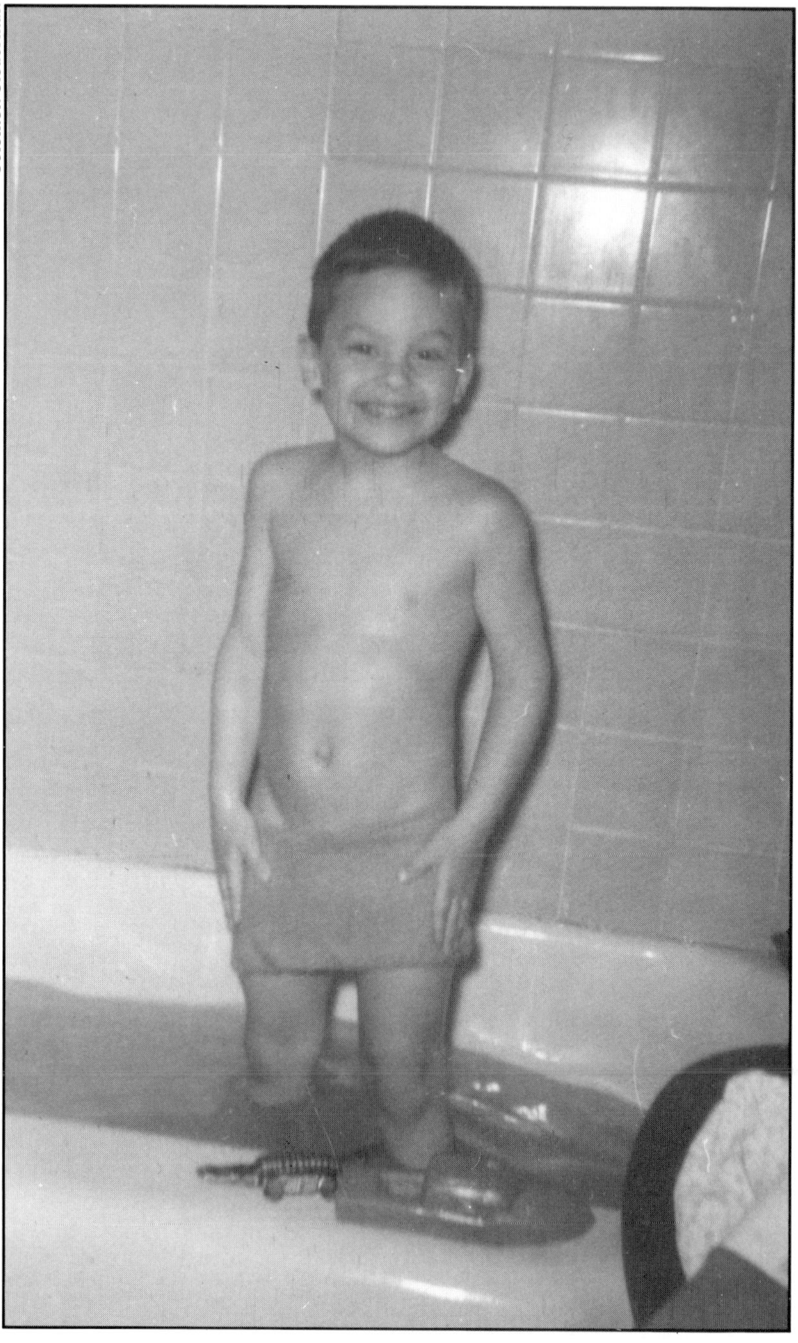

My first "still shoot" . . . the last one I did for free

Platinum Pictures, Inc.

I can go toe-to-toe with any tough guy on the street, but I'm still a child

VCA Pictures

Writer/producer Joyce Snyder and me on the set of *Raw Talent III*, based on my up-and-down life

Reb Sawitz

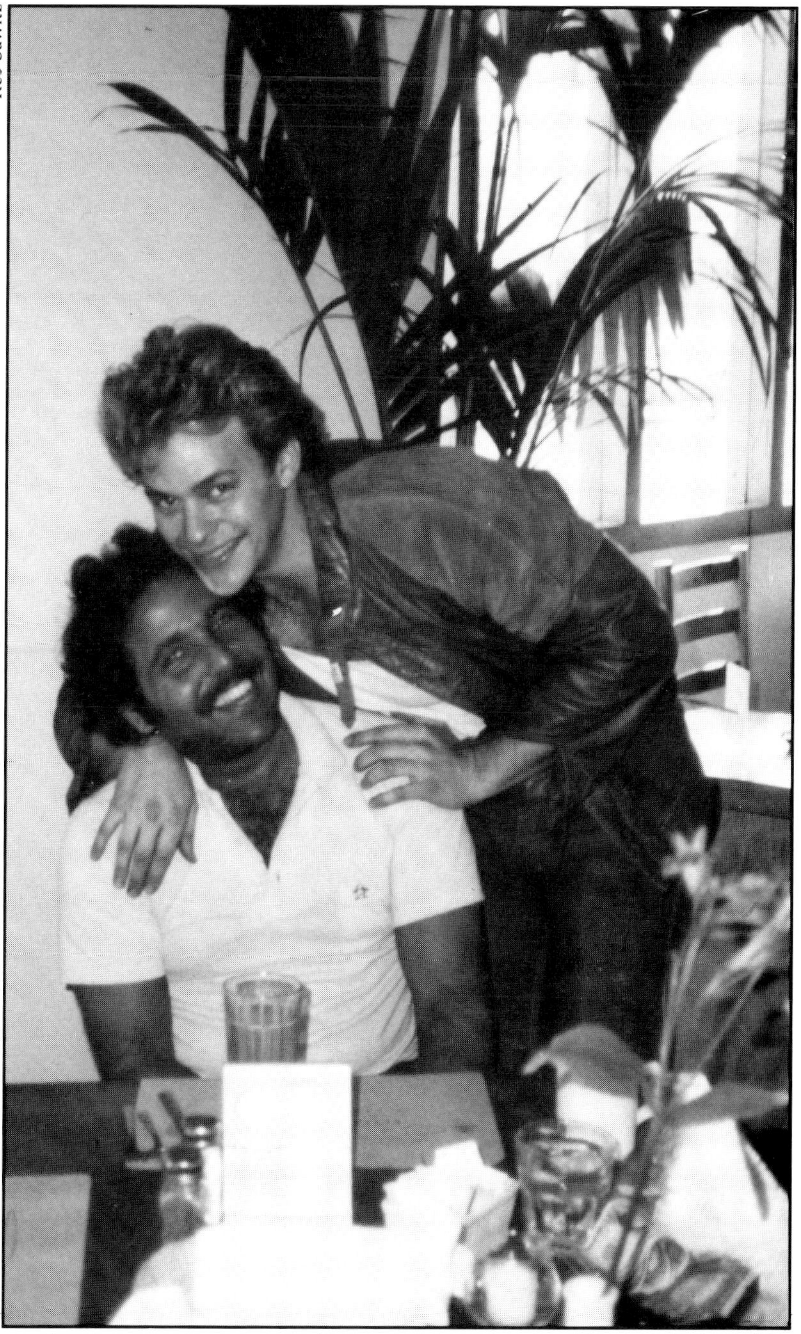

With Ron Jeremy at Stanley's restaurant: Ron has unbelievable muscle control

VCA Pictures

In a scene from *Raw Talent II,* I face off with pal Buck Adams

Femme Productions

On the set of *Femme,* whispering words of praise to costar Rhonda Jo Petty

Peter Martin

Me and Lisa, who says it doesn't matter what anybody thinks of us

Twenty
Shooting Stars

Being a porno actor isn't a dream job. No one knows the pressure of getting an erection in front of a roomful of people, of having sex with a woman you don't even like, or of being told to switch positions in midstream: "Move your right arm, move your right leg, stick your tongue out further!" I'm not saying that women have it easy, but they can pretty much fake it. One can't fake erections or ejaculation, though. Male porno actors are like artists working in the same medium. We're like survivors of the same war. There's a certain camraderie we share that you won't find in any other profession. But there's also a sense of rivalry. We're vying for the same roles. No matter how different we are, most producers and directors see us as almost interchangable. After all, you're only as good as your last sex scene.

Jamie Gillis is a sweetheart. Out of all the guys in the business, I have the softest, gentlest feelings about him. He's one of the most fascinating people I've ever met. I could sleep with that man, cuddle up to him, and not feel there's anything wrong with it. I'm not talking about sex. I'm talking about heartfelt affection. While we were making *Deranged,* Jamie and I took some time off just to be together, to have lunch, to talk, to be human beings. I feel like he's my brother.

Jamie's been in the business practically from the beginning. My guess is twenty years or more. People say stupid things about Jamie. But Jamie is not as crazy as he might appear to be on film. And what's crazy anyway? No, Jamie isn't crazy, just misunderstood. People expect the worst from him and are surprised to discover he's not the monster they imagined. Sure, sometimes he seems like a sleazy guy, but what the hell is porno all about?

I find him sexually interesting because he's so damn sure of himself. When I first met Jamie, he liked to drive down to Hollywood High and check out the young girls. Here he was working with beautiful women his own age and younger, and getting all the sex he wanted. Yet I understood where he was coming from when I found myself doing the same thing at places like McDonald's. It wasn't that I was interested in young girls sexually. I just liked looking at them because they're lovely, budding works of art. I haven't forgotten what I was like at that age and how innocent I was.

Jamie and I must have done twenty-five movies together. He's a very good actor, but I don't relate to the Jamie from films. Our relationship goes much deeper than that. We impress each other and I let myself accept him for what he is.

I first met John Leslie when we made *The Four-X Feeling* in New York. Joey Silvera—my *Raw Talent* costar—was the link between us. About five years ago, Joey told me that John considered imself to be the best actor in the business. I thought I was, so I knew there'd be an undercurrent of rivalry on the set.

John and I were polite to each other. We covered all the macho topics, like baseball and hockey. John likes fine wines, art, and golf. I wondered whether he might have consciously acquired those things to give himself some class and contradict the image people have about porno actors. Maybe he acquired these interests deliberately. I wanted to get beyond the hype and discover the real man underneath. When John and I got into this manly conversation, it was almost like a contest.

In *The Four-X Feeling,* John and I basically played ourselves. He's visiting me from out of town, and, as two porno actors, we decide to make big bucks and direct our own movie. My character's supposed to be in control of the situation, but I was a little nervous working with him. After all, John's been in the business about fifteen years. When I opened the door to let him into my apartment in that first scene, I didn't like the feeling inside of me. I had to get rid of it somehow. Suddenly, I screamed out, "Fuck! Cocksucker! Bullshit!" To this day, no one knew why I burst out like that, but I was trying to dispel the jitters. Being nervous didn't work for me, or for the scene. After that, I was all right.

John and I became pretty good friends. He accepts the fact that I'm wacky. It's something even "King Salami" can't argue with. Lisa always asks me what planet I came from.

If you watch *The Four-X Feeling,* you can see the sense of competition in the opening scene. We improvised all of the dialogue. I was going a mile a minute and John was his usual laid-back self. Throughout the movie, I was off the wall and kept making all sorts of wild comments, like comparing a big, black dildo to a bowling trophy. John was my straight man, and you could see the intimidation on his face. At one point, he gave up and stopped trying to match me because he couldn't keep up with my fast repartée. Very few people can—not even Ron Jeremy, who's very quick and funny. It's almost like I handcuff them and throw away the key. It's my way of being playful. I don't mean to insult people, but sometimes it happens. My tongue is trigger-happy.

I like John Leslie and enjoy working with him because our exchange of dialogue becomes a ping-pong match. He'll smack the ball back and forth and keep it in play. John's one complaint about me was that I "use up other people's energy." I don't want to get too pugnacious toward a backbone of the industry like John, but he tempts me. Although I'm middle-aged in the business, because I've been doing porno for so long, I'm still young in life. John's elderly in the business and middle-aged in years. There are only about eight of us "old-timers" who are considered good actors: John, Harry Reems, Eric Edwards, Joey Silvera, Jamie Gillis, Paul Thomas, Ron Jeremy, and myself. We're sex relics. Because of his world-famous schlong, John Holmes was more of a curiosity than an actor.

Joey Silvera is very serious when he works with John, but together, Joey and I are notorious for being very naughty on sets. Why do we terrorize people? Because it's a lot more fun than just working with some dull woman who sucks you off half-heartedly or with some director who makes you work tedious, long hours. We make our own reality and our own fun.

John can't get that loose with me. He treats me very much like Harry Reems does. They both try to find their own level of seniority, but I don't let them get away with it. Although I wasn't even thirty when we worked together, I was almost their peer in the business. I've made more films than most veteran actors in legit film (except maybe for John Carradine). I know porno is not the exact same medium, but it counts for something. It's matter. It takes up space. It's film footage.

As an erotic performer in his forties, John is concerned

about conserving his energy. He's getting uptight about his hair loss and his thickening middle. You can see time creeping up on him from movie to movie. Whenever I find some animal hair on a set, I pick it up and say in a loud voice, "Gee, it looks like John Leslie has been doing a sex scene." Once I gave him a black yarmulke to cover his bald spot, but he didn't appreciate it too much. His bald spot is his sensitive spot. John also insists on having the first sex scene of the day and won't work more than eight hours.

John Leslie can say anything he wants about me, because I know what he feels deep down. I bring a lot of playfulness out of him. I encourage people to let loose within themselves, to make jokes about themselves.

The only thing I don't like about John is that he'll never totally relax or ease up. He's got a "Hollywood star" complex. To me, he seems like expensive china that gets washed carefully and handled even more carefully. I'm more like a plastic plate. Sure, I get banged around, but I get used and enjoyed more often than the classy stuff. People feel more at home with me. For every bad thing John Leslie could say about me, he has three times as many nice things to say, except he keeps the good comments inside. A lot of people are like that. But it's those unspoken feelings that give me something to work with.

Buck Adams was the most peculiar-looking person I've ever seen. With his jutting jaw, his oddly shaped face, and his tight thoroughbred body, I didn't know where he was coming from. Yet his manner reminded me of a little kid who comes to the schoolyard and hopes he'll be chosen to play basketball with the big guys. Buck and I became good friends on the set of *Momma's Boy*. He had a lot of rowdiness in him, and

I liked that. We have similar qualities, except I don't have an Adam's apple the size of St. Louis.

Together, we have a lot of power. I have the craziness, the zaniness, the bulk, while Buck exudes a quiet, solid, Charles Bronson-like quality. We lived together for a few months in a one-bedroom apartment and switched off on who slept in the bed and who slept on the couch.

We both had our share of problems. We'd make the rent and pay the bills, but we spent every other cent to party. Buck's sister Amber Lynn used to hang out with us. Being high, I was fascinated by the fact that Amber looks just like Buck in drag, and vice versa. And like Clark Kent and Superman, you never see them in the same room together.

Both Amber and Buck were adopted by step-parents. Their biologial mother died of cancer. They led a pretty shabby life in Orange County, California. Redneck, poor white trash, they grew up stealing and driving fast cars. (He claims he was an amateur boxer and knocked out Thomas Hearns in a bout in Texas.) So this tough Brooklyn boy really clicked with Buck. We create a certain chemistry on film; but lately, directors won't hire us on the same shoot together because we create such havoc.

Buck is a follower. Whatever I did, he did and sometimes even took it a step further. I'm very pragmatic about my obscenities and my practical jokes, but he's impulsive. If I'd pee in the corner of a hotel room, he'd take it too far and pee off the balcony and get us thrown out.

Buck always bragged about the number of sex scenes he could do in a day. In the beginning, it was five or six. Now people expect that of him all the time. Recently, Buck's been having problems with his sex scenes. (I even stood in for him and did a come shot for him once.) With his wife Janette, he can still always perform. Before you find someone special, your penis acts like a thermometer. It reacts to any piece of climate. Once you fall in love and settle down, porno becomes more difficult. The guilt settles in. The enthusiasm is out. Now Buck can rarely knock out two scenes in a day, which is fine, but people have come to expect more from him. I always told him not to boast, not to throw in extra sex scenes for free, but he didn't listen. He was looking for that extra acceptance. In porno, it's always better to leave people hungering for more.

I'll talk about Paul Thomas as an actor first. Although he might sometimes overact, PT (as he's usually called—his real name has the same initials as his porno name) is one of the most polished and professional actors in the adult film business. He must have been doing it almost twenty years before his new wife made him quit. In my opinion, his best work was in *Space Virgins.* Paul, Herschel Savage, and I played three hillbilly brothers. We were fucking our sister (Kimberly Carson, without the black wig for once) when three space virgins visited our farm.

These days, PT's directing adult movies, and I sometimes feel he's forgotten where he came from: He used to be an *actor,* in the same sense as we were, quibbling with some director over day rates. Now he's on the other side of the fence. He probably gets around $15,000 to make a movie, and whatever he doesn't spend, he pockets. I understand that, but it doesn't give him the right to underpay the talent, especially someone who knows what an injustice it is.

Sometimes I've helped him direct by suggesting camera angles and setting up shots, and he's really grateful about that. Even though we've never had a big fight, I've had a lot of disagreements with PT. I dislike how he tightens up and becomes too demanding on the set. All he ends up doing is constricting the people around him. The business part of him has become tough and arrogant. To find the sweetness in him, watch the films, but stay away from his sets.

Every time Harry Reems tries to pull his "seniority" bullshit on me, I put him in his place. Basically he's a nice guy, but he's also arrogant. Maybe it's because he's been in classics like *Deep Throat* and *The Devil in Miss Jones.* Harry's a well-known name, and I don't think "Jerry Butler" will ever be a "name" like that. But I'm not a guy on a podium like Harry is.

I met Harry at a screening of *In Love.* He was impressed with my work and I must admit I was touched, because this praise was coming from one of the relics in the business. Once I worked with him, though, I realized that he was just like any other jerk. He drank on the set and went on partying binges. I tried to find the niceness in him. It's tough for him to give in, but he finally does. Too often, Harry's like an old lady who keeps hitting you with her pocketbook when you're trying to help her across the street.

Ever see a sloppy Jewish kid who acts like an Italian? That's Herschel Savage. He always wanted to be Italian, but he had no choice other than to defend the Jewish faith. Herschel and I are both from Brooklyn, and his cousin Willie lives in the building next door to my parents. Herschel and I both drove cabs for P.D.Q. Car Service, but we never met until porno.

His real name is Harvey. A big, husky guy, I find his body unattractive and can't bear to watch him in a sex scene. But as a person, I do like him, even though he's always on the defensive. Defensive people are always on guard with me, as if they're trying to prepare themselves for something nasty that might come out of my mouth. You have to peel Herschel's red skin back to get to the juicy apple underneath. But if you leave a peeled apple out in the air, it turns brown.

Tom Byron is the Scott Hamilton of porn. You know, the ice skater. Tom's pretty skinny. The industry's joke goes, "What do you get when you put an earring on a stick?" The answer: "Tom Byron." But he has a huge prick, and I envy him for that.

Tom and I have had some good times, but since he was from Jim South's agency and I was from Reb's, there was always a silent feud underneath the surface. He's always trying to pick up on new women in the business. The only problem is that he doesn't hold onto them too long. He's not as cool as he tries to be.

There are so many bad things I could say about Ron Jeremy, but I could never dislike him a full 100 percent. You just can't hate the guy. There's some weird thing about him that makes you forgive him. Alone together, we've had wild and funny times. He changes totally, however, the second another person walks in the room.

I met Ron about ten years ago, when I was a pup in the business. I was always amazed at what he could do sexually. Ron has a ten-inch dick and unbelievable muscle control. He can make his dick jump, bounce, or wiggle like a snake. He can get his dick hard for *any* kind of pussy, and it stays up until he comes, whereas I have to keep shoveling in the coal. But if I had to rely on a face like that . . . forget it!

As you've probably noticed, porno lets me run wild, but

I only reach that point when the cameras are rolling. When the camera's off, some of the craziness stops. But even off the set, Ron uses his porno position as a credit card. He's very pressuring and persuasive with women. I really feel lousy about being in the business when I seem him hound women to the point of making them cry. Someone once told me she'd never been to a party with Ron where he hasn't lured at least one woman off to the bathroom.

Ron just doesn't know when to stop. Doing *Pink Lagoon,* he was with his girlfriend Tanya Lawson, but he started bothering Lisa Marie, who was John Johnson's girlfriend. It got so bad they had to fire Ron from the shoot. And I've been in hotels where women just want to talk to Ron about the business, nothing more than that. Before you know it, though, they're in his hotel room and he's locking the door. Because Ron has a big dick, he identifies himself mostly through his sexuality and isn't happy until his pants come down.

Still, Ron's a bright person as far as managing his money is concerned. He's been in the business well over ten years and he's made a lot of it. I only wish I had managed mine half as well. But then again, I'm pretty lucky because despite all the stupid things I've done and the mistakes I've made, they've led me to find and marry the woman I love. On the other hand, look where Ron is today. He has no one special in his life, as far as I know.

Here's a typical Ron Jeremy story. I was on Ventura Boulevard at a restaurant named Stanley's (a big hot spot in L. A.). The hostess—Barbara—was beautiful. I couldn't believe she was coming onto me—she was wearing a wedding ring. "Have you fucked her yet?" Ron asked.

"Look," I told him, "I may fuck on-screen. We may fuck in the same sex scene, but my private life is none of your business."

I told Ron I really liked Barbara. He shrugged, put his hands up, and said, "I'm not looking to do anything. I just thought she might want to go to the Comedy Store." That's his ploy. He thinks he'll be respected more because he knows people like Sam Kennison, Robin Williams, and Whoopie Goldberg. Ron feels that because they're his friends, it makes *him* more likeable. But I always thought it was okay to be with Ron no matter who he knows or doesn't know. He's too insecure to realize that.

In any case, I went to Barbara's house that night, after I found out she wore the wedding ring just for effect; she wasn't really married, but it helped to keep creeps away. I couldn't believe this gorgeous creature was going to give herself to me! While we were making love, the phone rang. I knew it was Ron! I fucking knew it! And when Barbara said she didn't want to go to the Comedy Store, I was absolutely sure it was him. Ron was shocked when I grabbed the phone, blasted him, and then hung up.

Despite all of this, I feel sorry for Ron. He has a lot to learn about himself and women. He's afraid to be married. If he stuck with one woman, it would shut down all the mechanisms he needs to convince himself he's a man.

Buck Adams and I were working on a film up in San Francisco that Ron was directing. We were the usual practical jokers, and Ron was trying to be serious about directing. He was standing at the foot of a hill, and Buck and I were at the top. There's Ron with his shirt off, his belly hanging over his shorts. He's trying to act like a pro, calling meetings with the crew. Watching him from the top of the hill, I was bored shitless. I turned to Buck and told him, "It's play time." I started jerking off. Still holding my cock, I ran all the way down the hill and shot a load all over Ron's leg. There he was, trying to gain respect from the crew. Buck was laughing so hard he practically rolled down the hill. Everyone cracked up. I said to Ron, "Why don't you stop this 'meetings' shit and shoot the fucking film." Because Ron couldn't take control of the shoot, we all took control.

Another time, we were shooting a movie in one of those canyon towns outside of L.A. Ron had just finished a sex scene, and I was up to bat next. Ron had all that time during my sex scene to take his shower, but he was taking his time. I was hot and sticky, so I took off my clothes and started scrubbing next to him in a little two-by-four stall. It didn't seem to bother him. Then I slowly edged behind him and started peeing all over his hairy back. Ron had nowhere to go. All he said was, "Butler, is this really necessary?"

Mike Horner (a.k.a. Don Hart) is like a screen door. It's not very sturdy, it doesn't keep the house warm, but it keeps the bugs out. Like that door, Mike's a very sound, professional actor in this business, but he's not what you'd call a backbone. His acting is a little stagey, and sometimes he appears extreme on film. But if I were shooting a movie, I'd like Mike to be in the cast because he's solid and he's prompt.

Mike's a harmless guy and never says anything bad about anyone. I can see that my craziness sometimes gets in the way of his cool, collected manner. Mike chugs along at 55 m.p.h. and gets to his destination at a leisurely pace. I accelerate until I hit 85, make hairpin turns, and take more chances. Sometimes he seems out of place on the set, almost like a giraffe in an elevator. Mike gives the impression he's a tall, lanky creature who doesn't know what to do with himself.

On March 13, 1988, John C. Holmes died of colon cancer. It was probably AIDS related. He had been in intensive care in a Veteran's Hospital in L. A. for many months.

You already know that the first time I ever saw John was when I worked my Dad's projector. John was kind of my idol. Because of his huge penis, I almost worshiped him, worshiped him devilishy. The pleasure he gave to women was almost painful. Still, it wasn't really John Holmes whom I admired so much as his . . . artillery. I was intrigued.

In *Rockey* X (a takeoff of Stallone's *Rocky* movies), I finally met John in person; he played rival fighter Buck Adams' manager. (I was "Rockey.") I told John how much he had meant to me as a kid, and he got a real kick out of it. I was surprised that John was so down to earth. Sometimes people with reputations like his act like a slab of marble—cold and resistant. I don't mind, because I have my hammer and chisel. I want to find out where the veins and arteries are hiding. So there I am, chip, chip, chip. And they're saying, "No. No. No." I chip away some more, and they're grateful at what I dig out of them. But John Holmes was all right there on the surface.

John also had the "Ron Jeremy Complex," except his dick was even bigger: thirteen or fourteen inches—but when you're that big, what's an inch or two? It becomes a novelty. How good can you feel about having a tremendous cock? In porno, it's the most valuable thing about you, but it doesn't even have a brain. After a while, people don't even look at the person behind it. The real person who suffered was John.

As you know, I never suffered from the "big dick syndrome." People didn't hire me for my dick, because mine's just average. I knew there was a lot more to me than that. John's treasure chest was a bag of money between his legs. Mine is overflowing with emotion. There are gold doubloons and strings of pearls hanging over the sides.

Twenty-One
Studfest

Eric Edwards is another porn landmark. He's the most level-headed guy I've ever met in my life. A few years ago, he married a porno actress named Rene Summers, and now they have a baby, a cute, little thing with a bald head. Eric doesn't like me too much, because he can't put up with me, especially when I'm running in sixth or seventh gear. He operates in automatic and I'm a stick shift. Although Eric's directing more these days, he'll never hire me. If he can avoid Jerry Butler, he will.

Even though he denies it, I can swear I've seen Peter North in gay magazines. (Maybe he's got an excellent impersonator out there.) No matter what he's done in the past, you can't deny the fact that Peter's a consistent sexual performer. His come shots are legendary, both in volume and in distance. As for his acting, it's pretty limited. But on a person-to-person level, I don't mind rooming with Peter on a shoot, because he's a lot of fun.

Randy West is so debonair that, if I were directing, I'd dress him in a cape, spats, and top hat. That's the type of image he projects. When you meet him, you imagine that he has a high set of morals and thinks pretty well of himself, but Randy falls into the same category as all of us. He'll do anything, or almost anything, for the money. Yet I feel the elder wisdom in him, and I respect his dignity.

I've always seen myself as stucco. I chip. I'm flawed. I'm filthy dirty. But Randy always seems to be made of solid polished marble, no matter what the surroundings. We're a good team, though. He's articulate, reserved, and immaculate; I'm a ranting, extroverted mess. He's the wall and I'm the Spaulding basketball bouncing against it.

In all the times we worked together, he usually played my brother or my friend, but we never had any meaty or juicy roles. I always hoped to work together in very emotional scenes with him. With his bold exterior, Randy's like the John Wayne of porn, and I've wanted to see him let go of that helium balloon and be himself.

If I meet Randy fifteen years from now, I'll probably shake his hand. I will hug Joey Silvera. I will hug Billy Dee. I will even hug John Leslie. But for some reason, with Randy it'll only be a warm handshake and a sincere pat on the back.

Bill Margold—a porn veteran and critic whose business card reads something like, "God created man and Bill Margold created himself"—once called me "the new Richard Pacheco." This didn't help my relationship with Richard any when we finally met in California. I knew he was a good actor who had won praise for his role as a retarded guy in *Nothing to Hide.* I also knew that Richard was married to a woman who allowed him to make porno movies.

I remember the sex scene Richard had with Shauna Grant in *Bad Girls III.* It was the last day of the shoot. He thought Shauna was beautiful and kept anticipating the joy of working with her. Richard was so keyed up, it added twenty pounds of extra pressure to his head—and his cock. When the crucial moment arrived, he couldn't even get his dick up! That kind of thing happens all the time, but it really embarrassed Richard. To cover it up, he pretended he injured his knee during the scene.

We had to go back to San Francisco to complete the film. Richard invited me to his house one night. We were drinking wine and he was getting drunk. I was about twenty-two and my body was huge from working out. It was probably the most fit I've ever been. Drinking at his house, Richard was admiring by muscular body. There was nothing homosexual about it. But I sensed he was searching for something negative, some *flaw* in me. I remember him playing with his son, tossing him up in the air. "This is Jerry Butler," Richard told the kid. "He's going to take all your Daddy's work away."

That really crushed me. "Oh, come on, Rich."

"No," he told me, a little drunk. "You're a good actor. You're going to take all my parts away. But that's all right. I had my day."

I felt Richard had really thrown in the towel at that point, and there was no need to. I have always tried to create my own space. I'm a totally different type of actor than Richard. I have a different "look."

It still puzzles me why Richard said that to his son. It probably comes down to the insecurities of people in porno. We're only insecure until the director yells, "Action!" Then we know exactly what to do.

I understand that Richard's considering quitting the business. These days he won't do a sex scene unless it's "safe-sex," with a condom. And those are few and far between.

To me, Robert Bullock is *really* the "new Richard Pacheco." They look alike and both have the same aura of craft and schooling behind them. Robert's also married and his wife also lets him do movies. Like Richard, he often plays nerdy characters. Yet even in their nerdiness, you can still see the royal scepters in their hands.

All in all, Richard Pacheco is a friend of mine. However, he *did* once tell an interviewer once that, even though I'm a good actor, I'm a goof-ball. Then again, that's not *too* far off.

Steve Powers looks like the kind of guy who'd belch when he says, "I love you." I had a preconceived notion that Steve would be very tough and aggressive, and I always felt that kind of behavior was out of place on a porno set. To me, porno is like a flower garden, something soft and gentle. And you shouldn't need boxing gloves in a garden.

When I finally met Steve, he turned out to be a plush pussycat with the stuffing coming out of the back of his neck, as though someone had hugged him and wore him out.

Steve Drake is the Tom Selleck of smut. He's a solid foundation, a skyscraper with a mustache. One film we did together was *Dial-A-Dick.* We played two guys who couldn't score and so set up an escort service for women. In one scene, I got Steve laughing so hard that he couldn't say his lines. (The director even left that in.) Trying to hide it, he buried his head in Krista Lane's shoulder. Again, I tried to bring the aroma out of the artificial flower.

Steve's like the heaviest chess piece on the board. You can play chess just the same with plastic pieces, but Steve's were always metal. It doesn't really matter, though, because king always takes queen.

François Papillon cuts an impressive figure: muscle on top of muscle. A native Frenchman, his acting often seems wooden—he doesn't have great command of the English language.

François is a health nut, and he'll preach against coke and other drugs, yet he takes steroids to build up his muscles. When people tell you what you should do with your life, it's usually because they're not too happy about their own. It's always the guy who said he gave up coke who has a straw in his back pocket and crystals in his nostrils.

There are a lot of people I'd like to have the chance to direct in movies, people who cover up a lot of their beauty and sincerity. I think I could get them to reveal the real parts of themselves. But I wouldn't even try with someone like François. To me, he's a stud and that's all.

You'd never know it, but Jack Wrangler has an artificial hip. He's one of the few actors who very openly did gay films and then crossed over into straight movies. There's an "elder statesman" feel to Jack, because he's a real gentleman. Jack doesn't do porn anymore and is married to Margaret Whiting, the 1940s pop singer, who's at least twenty years older then him. I don't deny that Jack has talent, but there's not a whole lot of weight to his bag of tricks. He's like Felix the Cat, skinned.

When we made *Jack and Jill 2,* I really saw the great guy underneath. I could tell we both wanted to get to know each other better, but it never happened. Jack's a few years older than me and we didn't have too much in common. A funny thing about porno is that on the set you answer yes to almost every question. You wind up changing that yes to a no when you hear the word "Wrap!" You never keep in touch with anybody, although you make promises. It's so easy to make promises on the set, because you seem to be at the circus. How can you not smile while you're at the circus? It's filled with cotton candy and peanuts. But once the tent goes down, you don't have the reason to keep up that festive front.

Yes, porno really is like carnival time. The actors are the animals. The directors are the ringmasters. The crew members pull all the magic together. But when the circus tent comes down, you can't bring the circus to your house, so you leave it all behind, knowing that soon you'll raise the tent again. It'll always be there.

Blake Palmer's penis looks like Stevie Wonder did the circumcision. Ever take a salami, rip the casing off the top, and see the beef swell up? That's what his dick looks like. He's actually hurt women because they think they're going to have an easy time when that small head slides in so smoothly. Then, wham!

Women have found vowels beyond standard phonetics when Blake enters them.

The big dicks are important in the business, but I judge their owners by how they are on the set. Is it the penis or the person that's more important? You'd be surprised at the answer. I think John Holmes was more popular than he deserved to be—and he'd be the first to admit it. A few people have told me that I have a pretty, nice-looking penis, that it seems friendly. It sounds funny, but I really appreciate that: It shows that the swordsman is using his weapon correctly. I have tried to keep my penis and my acting evenly matched. In great sex scenes, I've felt my penis was huge. During terrible ones, it felt like a thimble. But my penis is always an extension of the way I feel about the woman I'm with.

Blake and I worked together in *Taboo III,* and some people said we looked enough alike to be brothers. I give in and my hands sort of soften when I work with him. I joke around with a lot of people, but I cool it down with Blake because I sense a lot of seriousness and loneliness in him. He's very quiet. Sometimes I worry, wondering whether he's taking all my antics personally.

Buddy Love is like a totem pole that never smiles. It is a great challenge to get him to crack up. Buddy was rooming with me for a while. I suppose we both needed each other's friendship, because we were lonely. When I brought him to my apartment though, it was like bringing in a homeless cat. He just didn't get the message when it was time to go.

Jose Duvall has an Adam's apple bigger than my erection. I've seen that guy get a hard-on faster in his throat than in his dick. In fact, he usually has a problem getting erect. It's rough seeing a man who weighs sixty pounds lose seventy during a sex scene. Jose is also a male exotic dancer and wears a lot of leather. We get along well, and he almost worships me. To me, Jose is an old comic book with a ripped cover. You know what to expect. You know just what's inside, and you call him over when you want to have fun.

Tony Montana is a toilet bowl that will not flush. The man is just plain obnoxious and rude. I don't think he even knows how to be himself. Maybe he's afraid he won't like what he sees. His big claim to fame was that his actress/girlfriend Blondie would fuck only him on camera. After a while, even she dumped him.

At a video convention in Cherry Hill, New Jersey, Tony grabbed Lisa's ass in front of a roomful of people. After she yelled at him, he played coy and said he was only joking. I called Tony after he goosed Lisa and told his message machine, "You'd better apologize. If you don't, I'll know that you really are an asshole. The next time you see me, you're going to have to deal with it." At least Tony returned my call, but he'll always be an uncolored crayon in my book.

Bobby Astyr reminds me of a guy you'd find working in a Brighton Beach deli who makes great corned beef sandwiches and tells jokes while he does it. I found him to be a very natural actor and a comfortable person to watch.

Bobby and Samantha Fox lived together for a long time. They were the Sonny and Cher of porn and often appeared in the same films, happily screwing each other. They don't live together anymore, but they're still good friends. Today, Bobby is pretty much phased out of the business. If you've never seen him in a porno movie, you might want to look for him in the many films he made in the 1970s and early 1980s. He has a real New Yorkerness. I always wished I could have appeared in more films with him because he had a quality that I wanted to work with and react to in a story line. But the industry never cared too much for establishing positive friendships and relationships between guys. The characters were always too busy trying to take women away from each other.

Michael Knight and I were very close at one time. While Buck Adams and I terrorized the West Coast, Michael and I were a team on the East Coast. I could make him laugh as no one else could. We were buddies, and I wish we had more of those "buddy roles."

Mike's girlfriend really fell for me when I met her, though. I remember driving her back to Brooklyn, alone. I took her up to the rooftop of my parents' apartment building. We climbed up the ladder to the chimney and fucked up there. She begged me not to tell anyone and Mike never knew . . . until now. But hell, it was a long time ago. They've since gotten married and are still together. I think they even have a baby.

Mike's acting wasn't too bad. Sometimes he tended to be wooden, but I think he gave a good performance in *In Love* as the guitar-strumming hippie. If you put anybody in the right role, or right position, they'll do a good job. You can't put Reggie Jackson on first base, but he makes a great designated hitter.

R. Bolla reminds me of Bob Newhart. A very good actor, he no longer makes pornos. Older guys in porno are usually cast as dirty old men—and he's way too good to be limited just to that. Bolla really gets into the role and stays within character, even when he's fucking. He's very studied and has appeared in quite a few legitimate productions. In porn, Bolla enjoyed playing straight man to my nuttiness. He always seemed to have a kind of casual and collected attitude—but sometimes they're the people that go home, take twenty Valiums, start screaming and wear ladies' underwear. If you haven't seen any Bolla films, check out *Naked Scents,* in which we appear together.

George Payne was one of those who did gay porn and didn't hide it. George deserves this a place in my book because he introduced me to the joys of jerking off using baby oil. (He's probably swum through gallons of the stuff in his life!) But, baby oil aside, as an actor with a hollow, sinister appearance, George has always done his job well.

Twenty-Two

Love and AIDS

By this time, you're well aware that sex is *the* driving force in my life. I'm just not sure I know how to integrate it with love. I don't think most porno people know what love is, either. I don't think they really love themselves. It's like we put a handle on top of our heads and someone leads us through the scenery that appears to be life. We're nothing more than walking fantasies.

I used to come home after a shoot and desperately try to find my own reality. At my old apartment in L.A., I had all these toys and games, like "Mousetrap," "Monopoly," and "Candyland," as well as little dolls and clowns. I came home to a fictitious world that kept me sane. My toys were remnants of what life used to mean to me. When I went back home, I needed to see these things. They were objects that went back to my roots.

I am a child, an insecure little child. I can go toe-to-toe with any tough guy on the street, but I can also sit in a kid's room and play with Big Bird. I had a great time last night, for example, getting into a cream-of-wheat fight with Lisa's young daughter.

I hope I've made people happy. I like to think I have explored dimensions of pornography in ways nobody had before. I'm not just a guy who fucks a woman. I've been able to find the soul in the characters I played, which is why a lot of producers and directors were afraid to hire me. I wasn't just a penis. I added a creativity, an authenticity that intimidated them. In porno, you just give someone $15,000 and a clipboard, and suddenly they become a director. Fucking on film is a lot more complicated than that.

I've spent years. I've spent my life. I've spent pain. I've dripped blood. I've got the scars to prove it. Did you know that at least half of my lines in porno movies were ad-libbed? Made up by me alone? I would get a script, look at it, then throw it in the garbage. Directors used to get angry with my freewheeling attitude, but when they saw the results on tape, they were overjoyed—not that it mattered, because after all, they got paid whether I gave them a black-and-white or a technicolor performance. They're happy enough when my dick gets hard and I fuck. But now, I've added color. I've added a rainbow to the business, to my characters, to the videos, to the audience's delight. A few directors praised me, but most of them took all the credit for what I've done.

I realize that I couldn't have made it in Hollywood ten years ago, even if someone had believed in me. I didn't have a grip on acting, or more importantly, on life. I had the tools and the toolbox, but I didn't know how to put the tools in the right compartments.

Things changed when I met Lisa. Now I look at sex differently, even though I still occasionally use it to earn our daily bread. I just did a soft-core S & M movie in Palm Springs. Even though there was no screwing, just dry-humping, I hated doing it. But there's still a part of me that can't let go of the business, even though I'm very much in love. Sometimes I feel I'll always be a bathroom in Lisa's mansion. I know she won't accept that analogy, but I have to. A bathroom may not be loaded with antiques and fancy things, but it's a necessity to life. We'll always be like Lady and the Tramp.

In that S & M movie, I was selected to do the hardcore scene. I refused. I thought it would be a contradiction to the kind of life I want to live with Lisa and her daughters. So the director and I compromised: I didn't have actual sex, but I was required to jerk off on a woman's body. I had trouble getting an erection. I was amazed and proud that my body was finally protesting sex with strangers. Loving Lisa and trying to be faithful even made something like this movie difficult to do. It's tough to be close to another woman in a physical sense when you're in love.

Porshe Lynn and I were talking the other day, and I realized that I will have something with her that I will never have with Lisa. As porno performers, we share the same *degradation,* and that is a deep, deep bond. But it's not *love.*

Will I ever be able to put love into the right compartments? Although I always knew I loved Lisa, I was terrified of making a commitment. Then suddenly, at the V.S.D.A. Convention in Las Vegas, I asked her to marry me. We rushed off to a chapel (we even have the Polaroid to prove it). Part of me feels secure, yet another part of me is afraid. For some reason, I still hang on to my little apartment in L.A. It's my emergency escape hatch. Lisa has her children and her grandmother's house filled with memories. She has vestiges of her life before me. I have nothing—except Lisa.

Now I'm starting to find a new direction for my life. For a long time, porno was a second family. I was told where to go and what classes to take. "Oohs"and "aahs" were my report card. My gold star was cold cash. I had no real responsibility. Being a porno star really kept me as a child. I didn't want to grow up. Porno became a hammock that would swing and sway in the breeze. A hammock isn't the greatest thing for your back. It's relaxing, but you can't sleep on it forever.

When a regular guy goes to work, he has to worry about meeting deadlines or getting a seat on the bus. I had to worry about some woman's vaginal odor and not being able to get an erection. Until AIDS, those were my *only* concerns. I never caught anything in this business, not even the clap. I've lied about having it, though. I've told producers I had the clap when I didn't want to work with a particular actress or wasn't feeling up to par. It was the greatest excuse in the world, and I used it about three times. I've even worked with girls who had herpes and never caught it. What was my worry?

I was talking to a cameraman today about why he thought porno actors don't get married, or don't stay married, if they continue in the business. "Our worst enemy is love," he said.

"But it's the reason we get into the business, and it's the reason we don't want to leave." Love—or the *desire* for love—is the unspoken piece of hardware in the machinery that makes the industry tick. We enjoy the attention, the glamour, being a *somebody,* a visual celebrity. The cameraman admitted that even he loses perspective and sometimes considers himself to be the third person in a sex scene. Although I respected where he was coming from, I had to disagree. I don't mind the crew laughing and sharing in the sexuality when I do a scene—but they don't share the same hazards.

All I try to do is add another couple of colors to that great big box of Crayolas. But these days, the business is down to just sixteen tints and shades. And the crayons are broken to stubs. The paper is peeling off. This business has lost *more* than its color. It's dying. I'm amazed when I see the new, beautiful women flocking in every day. Because they're willing to fuck on film, they're also willing to risk their lives.

Every time I talk about AIDS on the set, one or two people try to shut me up. Then I get the attention of everyone else in the room. They become instantly reminded of how serious it is and they want to quit, especially if I bring it up during lunch.

The subject of AIDS came up on the set of *Divorce Court Exposé.* Cyndee Summers became very upset and told me to change the subject—as if not thinking about AIDS were protection in itself. This was about the time my open letter urging the business to wise up about AIDS appeared in *The Hollywood Press.* (Years later, in September of 1988, I read it on "The Morton Downey Jr. Show.") At the time, I was very concerned, because we needed to do something to protect ourselves as porno people. I was tired of being led around by the nose by producers and directors who didn't give a shit. As performers, we had to stick together. We had to form a kind of union of sexual safety. Cyndee didn't see it that way. She started yelling that she didn't want to hear it any more.

"Yell and scream all you want," I told her. "But I'm talking about it because I really care, not because I want to ruin your next sex scene."

The terrible truth is that AIDS is going to hit the business hard. When it does, a wave of actors will quit—and they'll be the lucky ones. Many more will die. The business will go underground and lose its direction. The party will be over. AIDS has already taken more than a few people in the industry. Rumors flood the sets about who has it and who has already died.

AIDS makes us all Roman gladiators. In the arena, someone has to get eaten by the lions. Everyone thinks, "It can't happen to me," and it hasn't to most of us—yet. When I was a kid, I'd run across the highway in between the cars and know I wouldn't get hit. If I tried it today, I'm sure I'd get picked off. As kids, we're fearless. And porno people, as I've said again and again, are like children. It's a different world. A porno actor builds a terrarium within himself and wanders happily through the garden of porn, enjoying all the fragrant flowers. But how big is a terrarium compared to the earth—the *real* terrarium? We're all afraid to leave our little glass boxes and face the world.

I never felt I had to defend my choices in life. The more I was able to expand, the more satisfied I was. I could always crawl back inside to my terrarium after I did a film. But looking through the glass, I know I've learned something. Life is my teacher. The world is my schoolbook. I don't mind being hurt and I've always survived pain.

But AIDS is something no one survives. To fight it, everyone in the industry has to cooperate—the producers, the directors, the video companies. But they don't care, they just don't care. Most of the biggest companies don't require proof of negative AIDS tests for all actors. Why the hell not? That should be a *standard procedure*—no *ands,* no *ifs,* no *buts,* no exceptions. Producers know damn well what a high-risk category porno is. Not only has there been a lot of anal sex, but a lot of people have been shooting drugs and sharing needles, too. It frightens the hell out of me. It's like walking into a shooting gallery wearing a blindfold.

What else should be done? The video companies should pay for the AIDS testing and force the actors to comply. It's for the companies' own good, because pretty soon an actor who gets AIDS will sue them and they could be held liable for all medical expenses. It will hit them where it hurts—in the pocket. Why shouldn't it? They're making the bucks while the fuckers and the fuckees take all the risks.

The producers are going to have to do something about "safe-sex." Personally, I don't like wearing condoms, but it's not a question of "like" any longer. It's a question of *life.* Wearing a condom is like eating spinach. You don't like it when you're a kid, but when you're older you realize that it's necessary.

Amazingly, not many people are leaving the business. I have a feeling that 80 percent of the people in the business would go down to the wire even if they *did* have AIDS. They wouldn't admit that they had it until they couldn't work anymore. It all comes from an insane sense of pride, of not giving into the disease. But that crazy sense of pride can hurt—even kill—other people.

Before AIDS, nothing scared me, except maybe myself. Now I have a lot to fear. Although I took an AIDS test about two years ago and it came out negative, I've made a lot of movies since then. Now I can't help but wonder. All it takes is another test to dismiss the wonder, but I'm afraid of what the answer might be.

Twenty-Three

The Western Front

I know people wonder about the dynamics of how porno movies are actually made. For the the most part, a video-distribution company puts up the initial money. The one who usually handles it is the director. If he's hired to make a video, he might have a shooting budget of $15,000. In the old days, when movies were shot on film, it was much higher, but because of the so-called video revolution, shooting budgets are getting lower and lower these days. I hear they've even made some tapes for as low as $5,000. Of that bulk of money, the scriptwriter usually gets about $250 to $500. Actresses make between $500 to $700 a day, sometimes more, depending on who they are. Actors get about $500 or less. Then there's the crew to pay, which includes people like the cameraman, the sound man, and the makeup girl. Whatever's left is the director's salary. So, the less directors spend, the more they make. Some directors underpay the actors or have very small crews so they make more of a profit. It's not unusual to see the director's wife helping to move furniture to cut corners. That's how bad it gets.

Videos are either shot in studios or in houses rented out for the shoot (sometimes even hotel rooms). If you're really on the ball, you'll notice that the same houses are used over and over. Some directors, like PT, shoot as many as three videos at the same time, making slight changes within the cast. The average shoot lasts two or three days, but the "One-day wonders" of the 1960s and 1970s are becoming more common. It isn't unusual to work eighteen hours straight and then call it a wrap. The quality of porn has therefore gone down drastically.

I had a bad—and typical—experience today at Western Visuals, a video distribution company. I've done a lot of work for those guys. I've made them a lot of money, but today they were making me feel like a pinball. I was getting bounced around. I was hitting metal. It's all right when the metal ball hits the rubber. It may get worn and streaked, but it doesn't get nicked or scratched. But today I was nicked and I was scratched.

Jerry Tannenbaum is the head of Western Visuals. He directs under the name Jerome Tanner, and he has a partner named Elliot. They owed me a small amount of money for a still shoot, and I went down to pick it up. In porno, getting to see the big guy is like getting an audience with *The Wizard of Oz.* To reach the damn Wizard you have to survive all these crazy obstacles, survive all these unnecessary shenanigans—risking your life, sanity, and welfare along the way. But when you get to the big man, he's even smaller than you are.

The second-in-command at Western, Elliot, doesn't like me. The first thing he said when he saw me was, "Hey, Butler,

I hear you tell people that I don't like you. That's not true. I like you." I had no business with Elliot. I was on my way to see Tanner. "Let's see how much you really like me, because you guys owe me a couple of bucks," I told him.

Right away, he lashed back: "What about your plane fare to Chicago?"

A few weeks back, they had put me on a Super-Saver flight to Chicago while Lisa was there on business. They didn't tell me it was only for a two-day stay, and I was out there four days. The return ticket was no longer valid. Stranded, I called Elliot from Chicago, and he told me it wasn't his problem. Now he wanted to know why I thought he didn't like me.

Here's a guy flying in my face, annoying me like a mosquito. I have a lot of resentment for people like Elliot, who make piles of money on porno actors but refuse to treat them with respect. Elliot made it very clear that he was "doing me a favor." I saw it differently. "Standing here talking to you right now, Elliot, I could be infected with AIDS. I've done good work for your company. You have your Mercedes and your house, but only because some guy is willing to stick his prick into some woman's pussy. Everywhere I go, people know what I've done, and I accept it. I accept the consequences. I'm not some chick who testified against you in court."

Western Visuals was having a lot of problems with a court case because Jerome Tanner was busted about three years ago. He's been going through a lot of hell. There's another case against him in which he's accused of hiring a minor. When the cops called and asked for information about Tanner, I refused to testify. Now Elliot didn't even appreciate my loyalty, so I took my grief out on him.

After I was browbeaten at Western Visuals, I picked up Lisa from work. I was looking for her to make up to me what those people took away, wanting her to take care of me. Sometimes I stick my nose in too deep and come home muddy. Then I expect Lisa to clean me off and make everything all right again. Sometimes I don't realize that she's got dirt on her own face and has to tend to herself. Why do I always expect someone else to fix things up for me? I don't have all the answers. Maybe I ask too many questions.

Driving home afterwards, I explained the whole story to Lisa. Reliving it, I felt the hurt and the anger boil to the surface again. Earlier that day, I had the entire building at a standstill because of the viciousness I displayed. I was a ferocious animal, two notches away from being an out-of-control monster. I was getting nowhere with Elliot, so I called Jerry Tanner on the phone and reminded him that he owed me some money. He told me his accountant wasn't in town. "Can't you give it to me in cash?" I asked. He told me he was on his way down to the office.

So I waited, talking to the receptionist. And I waited. It's important to people like Jerry T. to keep someone waiting. Practically everyone in the office was floating around, but there was still no sign of Jerry T. First, they'd tell me he was in a meeting. Then they said he wasn't in yet. Finally, I spoke to his girl-Friday—not a pretty sight, but when you discover she's in charge of casting, she immediately becomes more attractive. I put a smile on my face and gave her a hug, but she coolly turned her back on me.

To give you an idea of what an idiot this woman is, I'll digress a bit. On a Jerry T. shoot in Mill Valley (right outside of San Francisco), I was approached by two cops asking all sorts of questions. Immediately after, I told Lori about it because I trusted her and also because she was the Production Manager. Instead of doing something about it, she just sighed, "I don't want to hear about it. Jerry T. is already up on charges. He doesn't need this crap."

When I told her she didn't know the time of day, she ordered, "Keep your mouth shut or I'll send you home."

The makeup man heard us. He was nervous, too, because he noticed the police hanging around in the local restaurant.

When you see a lot of cops near a porno shoot, you automatically get paranoid. Paranoia's what saves your life sometimes.

Sure enough, the shoot was busted. The police didn't book us, but they scared the shit out of us. We packed up our stuff in a hurry and drove to "The Sound Stage" in San Francisco. A helicopter hovered above us on the highway as two cops escorted us. Lori still acted as though there was nothing wrong. "You dumb ass," I told her, "We're being followed."

"No, we're not," she said.

When we arrived at the Sound Stage, the police ambushed us as soon as we stepped out of the car. Jerry T. came up to me with the saddest expression on his face. He looked as forlorn as a St. Bernard on three legs. "Jerry, you knew about this," he whined, "Why didn't you tell me?"

I started to cry and yell at the same time. "Because of that fat pig of yours," I told him, motioning to Girl Friday. "I put my trust in her because you put your trust in her. Your whole shoot was destroyed because of this idiot."

And there she is, still working for Western Visuals, turning her back on me. "What's your business here?" she asked me, very coldly.

"Look," I said, "It's none of your business. The last time you involved yourself, you screwed everything up."

She insisted I tell her why I was there. I explained that Jerry T. still owed me money for a still shoot I did.

"He told me he wasn't going to pay you," she said.

"I just spoke to him on the phone and he told me he was." I could see she was annoyed that I'd gone over her head.

Elliot appeared on the scene again, muttering about how I didn't like him. There was a touch of sincerity in his voice, though, so I appealed to his compassion, this time with a joke. "I'd like you more if you'd give me what you owed me."

With a sly smile, Elliot said, "Yeah, but what about the flight to Chicago? You owe us eighty-one bucks."

I was fuming. "If I were one of your female stars, you

wouldn't make such a fuss. Of course, I'd probably have to suck you off. And what's eighty-one bucks to you? This is a multimillion dollar operation. The fucking pants you're wearing cost more than the damn plane ticket. What about all the things I've done for you?"

"Look at the favors we've done for you," Elliot yelled back.

I was getting angrier by the minute. "Favors?" I screamed. "You did me a *favor* by hiring me? I could be dying of AIDS right now. What are you guys doing about protection against AIDS?"

I'd taken a lot of shit from Elliot over the years, but I wasn't going to swallow his garbage any longer. I could see that Elliot was scared. Another guy in the office stepped in and tried to calm me down. "Don't worry about the plane ticket," Mark said. "I'll take care of it."

"I don't want your money," I told him. "I just want your respect."

I didn't feel great about disrupting the whole office and shaking poor Elliot up. But after all these years, I owe it to myself to stand up for my own rights. If Jerry T. had taken me aside and discussed it with me like a man, there would have been no problem.

"I'm very disappointed in you," he told me when he showed up later.

He was disappointed in me! Here's a guy who thought nothing of hiring young girls, treating his actors like animals, and shooting unprotected anal sex.

I'll never forget something that happened during the filming of *Nymphette.* Ron Jeremy was screwing Careena Collins in the butt and really rammed it in deep. Careena's a delicately built lady, and I saw the pain wither her face. Careena collapsed and doubled over. Instead of bringing her to a hospital immediately, Jerry T. just said, "She's all right. Just give her an aspirin." Maybe Careena had her period, but I could swear she was bleeding anally. Before she had time to get angry, they made her feel like a heroine wounded in battle. Jerry not only convinced her to finish the scene, but he made Careena go directly into another scene with myself and another woman after that one was done. I was expected to make love to a woman who was in a great deal of pain. I tried my best to be gentle with her, but it didn't compensate for what had just happened with Ron. And Jerry T. was disappointed in me!

Twenty-Four

Burning Questions

No matter where I go, people recognize me. Before they even say anything, I can always tell by the looks on their faces. First, there's an embarrassed smirk. Then I imagine the following crazy conversation zooming through their heads: "It's him . . . that porno guy! I forget his name . . . I'm not going to look . . . but I just did . . . I swear, I won't look again . . . I just saw him in a video last night . . . Shit, I looked again!"

I create a vicarious thrill in other people's lives. If they're not too shy, what usually follows is a mouthful of questions. They want to know all about the adult film business—how, where, and why. Especially *why*.

I think the business is going through a dieting process, actually a serious anorexic phase. It doesn't know exactly where it wants to go, yet everyone still wants to make money. Shot-on-video productions changed the time frame of the shoots because videotape doesn't have to be sent to a lab to be developed. It's instantaneous. Indeed, video made me a more popular actor. I worked more often, but it didn't make me as much money as in the old days.

The companies can't afford to make big movies anymore. Shot-on-video productions made it possible for smaller companies, like Video-X-Pix, to materialize and shoot $15,000 movies. They drop their selling prices per tape and offer their products to consumers at a much cheaper price. A few years ago, X-rated tapes were selling for $38 to $47 each. Now it seems that the video stores would rather buy something for $20 or $25, no matter what the quality. These cheapies often turn out to be something shot in two days or less, and they're usually lousy. But the sex is still there, and that's the only thing that matters to some renters. People like Ron Jeremy (who's also directing these days) forget quality and just give you wall-bangers. Some people feel cheated by the quickies, but I guess they're in the minority, because the rest of the audience just wants hot sex, and that's what they'll get. Most cheapies are nothing more than loops with sound: no plot, no characters, no drama, just bare bodies squishing together.

With so many videos being shot, a lot of cases are pending in court charging video companies with something called "pandering." What exactly is pandering? It's a paradox. The law states that it's illegal to make any hardcore movie that shows penetration. It's the same when a woman dances onstage. She can even take off her bottoms (if it's permitted in the particular state, and state laws vary), but if she inserts anything into any orifice, she's committing a crime. According to new city laws in Los Angeles (which change almost every day), you can't make a porno movie, because porno's the same as prostitution—you're paying people to perform sex. The pandering charge was originally created to arrest hookers, not people who made erotic films. However, if you're caught with the tape (evidence) on the set (more evidence), and the law knows money exchanged hands, they insist it's the same thing as prostitution.

Making these films is illegal, but *selling* them isn't. The right to sell and view them is protected by the First Amendment. The problem is that no one, not even the Supreme Court, has been able to define what's "obscene" as far as film-making is concened. So selling and viewing become matters of personal choice. If you asked me what I was getting paid for, I'd tell you I was getting paid for sex. Believe me, if I showed up for a shoot and told the director I wasn't going to fuck, I'd get replaced!

Another reason the business isn't ready to go back to five-day shoots is because the actors and creators have become so damned lazy. We've quickly been conditioned to knock out a movie in a day or two. The stamina isn't there anymore. I've done films recently where I've struggled to work three days in a row. Years back, I could do seven days straight and still go home at night and jerk off.

As I said, I can't explain why beautiful women are still flocking into the business, even more so than in the old days. I think we're in a desperate time of life. It's unbelievable what these beautiful mannequins will do of their own free will, especially in this age of AIDS. I remember reading somewhere about two young women who had watched "Death of a Porn Queen" on television. Instead of being turned off by the industry, they went to a casting office, mentioning that the documentary was their inspiration! I admit that making pornos is a quick way to gain notoriety, but they don't see all the consequences. They just see the prettiness and the money.

Lots of money.

I was on a set recently with some newcomers, who were telling me how much money they had in the bank. Alicia Monet was one of them. Her husband acts as her agent and he brags that they've saved $36,000. At one time, I had money in the bank, too; but one day you reach a gap, trying to justify what you've done. You try to fill that gap with whatever you can: cocaine, alcohol and other drugs. When you hit some turbulence, you'd be surprised at how fast you crash down and how soon the cash is gone.

People wonder how watching porno movies affects marriages. If couples watch them for the same reasons—to get aroused—then I think it's fine. But often the man gets more turned on by the woman in the film than by his wife, who understandably gets jealous. Before you know it, they're fighting. If Lisa watches a porno movie alone, I wonder whether she masturbated, and I immediately get jealous at the thought. If we watch one together, I get aroused watching her reaction. The first thing I want to know is what the hell's going on in her mind and body. I try to measure and mathematically weigh out something that should be natural, and soon I'm missing the point of the whole thing. People shouldn't worry about what arouses their partner. They're with you by choice and you're the one who's going to give them the pleasure, no matter how the arousal started.

People might think it feels odd to do a threesome with a woman and another guy. Take the girl out of the scene and naturally the two guys become self-conscious. Keep the girl in and everything you do is okay—because you're aiming at the same target. It's like playing darts. Once in a while, your dart misses the board. Once in a while, you get hit with another man's come. I'd always get so involved in what I was doing that I didn't have enough time to worry about things like flying come.

I wasn't nervous the first time I did a threesome. It added more to the excitement. To me, porno has always been a fantasy anyway—it was happening, but it wasn't true.

I'm always bothered when I don't have control in a sex scene. Add another guy and your control goes out the window, especially if the other guy has trouble getting it up or if there's double penetration. In D. P. scenes, I usually opted to be the ass guy. I liked it that way. That was the dirtiest part of the job, the most crucial, strenuous part. Entering a part of a woman's body that isn't commonly used excites me. In a D. P., the pussy guy usually has to lie on his back. And you know that's not my favorite position—especially if you don't have a bone-hard erection.

Being in the rear, I also had the best vantage point. I became a spectator along with the home audience. If you knew the other guy well, it could be a lot of fun, like riding a human roller coaster. If not, however, it could be a disaster.

Most people in the world consider anal sex to be sodomy, the ultimate no-no. But the things your mother told you not to do were the first things you tried when she wasn't looking. It makes you feel bigger than the world. Most women have never been doubly penetrated, but by watching it on film, they can fantasize about it and compensate. Video anal sex is the safest sex in the world for the audience. But as an actor, I refused to do it toward the end of my career because of AIDS.

In *Raw Talent II*, Greg Derek couldn't even get his dick hard enough to get into Cassandra Leigh's pussy. I'm in her butt, fucking away, and suddenly I pull out a tremendous lump of clay. If a woman agrees to do anal (which pays more), she should know enough to give herself an enema or go to the bathroom before the scene. It's an unspoken law in porno, just like having the courtesy to wash her pussy before a regular sex scene. I know it's a lot easier to clean a dick than to reach all of those crevices a pussy has, but it's common porn etiquette that can't be ignored.

I remember Taija Rae's first anal scene on camera. It was a special occasion, like graduating to a higher level. What more can you do after you've been fucked in the pussy and eaten? Anal sex becomes the challenge. After a while, I'm sure a woman starts to feel that her vagina's like a bank and craves other ways to draw out the cash.

Taija was really excited, but she didn't know what to do. Like a lot of other girls, she thought she just had to stick her behind in the air and you're in. Billy Dee was on his back and she sat on him. I crouched behind them. When I finally squeezed the head of my cock into Taija's ass, she was uncomfortably tight. I said, "Taija, it's just like a tunnel that's caved in. Sweetie, you've got to relax."

So she relaxed her cheeks—the cheeks on her face! Every part of Taija's body was as hard as a rock because she was terrified. Then she squealed, and I wasn't even an eighth of an inch inside. "It's bleeding," she said. She couldn't even see it, but she started wiping herself and whimpering. This is on tape and in front of the crew.

The crew suddenly became the Dallas Cowboy Cheerleaders: "Taija, go! Yeah, Taija! Relax! Open your hole!" It didn't do much good, though, because she was still tense. Then I saw a tiny speck of blood and insisted we stop the scene.

A lot of actresses are really hot in regular sex, but when it comes to anal, they're babies. However, there *are* a few professionals who know how to take it in the behind and love it. Women like Brittany Stryker, Penny Morgan (a.k.a. Rachel Ryan), and Sheri St. Claire are almost as good, or better, at anal than regular sex. The rectal tissue stays firm, and behinds don't get wet like pussies do, so it stays tight to the tip. When you pull out your penis, it's so hot that you can start a fire.

In *Despicable Dames* I had a threesome of sorts with Siobhan Hunter and a transsexual (sometimes known as a "trisexual"—a man with a partial sex change—because, although he has breasts, for some reason he still hangs on to his penis). The he/she couldn't get an erection (from the sex-change hormones?), so the make-up man devised a fake dick that fit over the real one. They painted it with flesh-colored makeup and even put artificial hair on it. There was a piece of tubing going under his/her legs and he'd squeeze it, pump it up, to get it hard. Although I was attracted to this he/she, who had the face of a pretty Spanish woman and nice round little tits, when the director asked if I'd let the he/she suck my dick, I refused. But I did let the he/she touch my nipples. I may act like a homosexual for a role, but I've never done any homosexual act on camera. I've been accused of it many times. As I've said before, if a guy can show me concrete evidence, there's $1,000 in it for him—plus a blow job from me!

A lot of people wonder why women in porno rarely finish off the guy in a come shot; nine times out of ten he jerks himself off. Porno acting is still "acting." The emotions aren't real, although you try to make them appear real. You try to carry it to any level to make it seem real. In contrast, sex is real. When you try to mix acting, which isn't real, and sex, which is, there's a gap. As soon as the man comes, you'd be surprised at the silent click that happens in the minds of many actresses. They think their work is over as soon as the actor climaxes.

People lose their composure in moments of orgasm. They must be the most free moments we have in life. You have no control. You're totally paralyzed in your uninhibitedness, in your defenselessness. The natural thing for the man to do is grab for control, to grab his cock. It's like a pilot coming down in a crashing plane. He grabs the controls to try to correct the malfunction. When I come making love to Lisa, I'm much more quiet. On film, I go crazy, and there's a typical face I always make. You have to be more audible for the camera. You have to raise the temperature to enhance the product.

I remember doing *The Debutante,* with Ali Moore in Palmdale. When the cameras weren't rolling, she wouldn't let me touch her. That caused a problem because my dick had to stay up. Let's face it, when you shut the heat off under the kettle, the water stops boiling. I didn't care whether Ali liked me or not. That wasn't the point. She agreed to do a porno movie and was making $1,000 a day to my $400. Keeping my dick hard was *her* job as well as mine. But a lot of actresses don't share that attitude. Once the guy comes, it's as good as yelling, "Cut!" No woman, unless she really enjoys the man, or if she's new in the business, thinks she has to or wants to do more. When a guy comes on them, the expression on their faces sometimes reminds me of a soldier bracing himself for a barrage of bullets. That's why the guys often give them the "I'm coming!" alert, to give the woman ample time to get the hell out of there.

In *Pink Lagoon* I had a scene with five women (Lois Ayres,

Raven, Ginger Lynn, and two others). A lot of guys might think I was lucky, but I remember feeling outnumbered when I walked onto the set. I was confused: There wasn't enough of me to go around! There was a lot of pressure being the only one with the cock, the focal point of the scene—so I was going up and down, getting hard and soft. I could only concentrate on two women at once, at the very most. Finally, I just took care of myself. With five women hovering over me, I wound up jerking myself off. That's where the editor becomes important. He has to make that come shot look like *something.*

If I was having trouble with a "one-man orgy," I'd focus on two girls playing with each other. I'd use anything to enhance myself. Many times, if I was humping a girl (I wouldn't even tell *her* this), I would straddle her leg and have the back of her heel stimulate my asshole. I used everything I could to heighten my arousal. I created my own sexual wonderland.

My guess is that at least 70 percent of the people in this business have herpes. Women can easily disguise it if the breakout occurs inside, but it's amazing what men will do to try and cover it up. On a set a few days ago, I ran into a particular actor who's also done gay films. I won't mention his name, but he was acting odd, and I sensed he was going to do something. In the past, I'd done still work with him and another girl and noticed blisters on his penis. They're not easy to see on tape, but if you look closely, you'll be able to pick them out. (After reading this book, you may never want to look closely again!)

This guy suddenly went into the bathroom and yelled out, "Oh, shit! I got my dick caught in my zipper!" Yeah, right! He'd pulled that one before. I bet the makeup man that when this guy did his sex scene, you'd see blisters on his prick. And not from getting it stuck in his zipper—from herpes. If people are going to fuck with herpes sores, then what's going to stop them when they have AIDS?

I've worked in the business so long that I've seen just about every type of physique, smelled just about every kind of body smell. I've seen chubby, nipped-and-tucked, and perfect midriffs. Because of that, women outside of the industry often look to me as some great judge of beauty. Sometimes they flirt, but other times it's very innocent. The other day, I was at the Foursome Diner talking about the business with a bunch of waitresses. One of them was in awe of "Jerry Butler" and asked me, "How's my body?" Then she lifted her skirt and showed me her pink panties!

In porno you don't really have to be good-looking. You certainly don't have to be a great actor or actress. You just have to be there. If a performer is *really* feeling what's happening, that's all a viewer should ask for.

Some reviewers make a mistake. *Penthouse* praised my performance in a particular film, but commented on how out-of-shape my body was. My weight fluctuates, but that's not too relevant to what I'm trying to do in front of the camera. You might see me in one video looking trim and tight. In the next one, I might have put on five or six pounds. The world scrutinizes me under a magnifying glass. It concentrates on one flaw and misses out on what's really important.

You can't always help things like dirty feet or dirty socks, because sometimes the sets aren't too clean. In scenes where I've left my sneakers and socks on, it was because I was concerned about the smell. But I think grayish sweat socks add to the authenticity—it reflects the unavoidable dirtiness of life.

I'm still annoyed by the fancy lingerie and garter belts you always see in porno movies. They're porn clichés—very few women wear them in everyday life. For once I'd like to see some chick slide out of her control-top panty hose. Now *that* would turn me on, because that's *reality*.

In the early days of porn, there were "fluffers" on the set, women who got the guys hard for their scene. Today a director may ask an actress to help an actor get an erection if he's having trouble, but there are no professional fluffers anymore. If a guy can't get it up, the director cools the set down for a few minutes. That means they'll turn the lights down, give you a break, and ask if you'd like some orange juice.

But most directors make you feel terrible. Just because your dick is down, you've let *them* down. They don't actually tell you that you're holding up production, but they make you feel it. The girl you're supposed to fuck looks pretty sheepish and wonders if it has something to do with her. If you've worked with her before, she'll usually understand. I tell you, a guy who is pretty boisterous suddenly becomes very shy when his penis won't cooperate! He'll look around the set to see who's within ear shot and then whisper to the girl, "Stick your finger way up my ass" or "Play with my nipples."

Some of the wildest-looking, hottest encounters are the most difficult and exhausting. If you look at my scene with Krista Lane in *The Boss*, you might think it was a lot of fun. In reality, I couldn't get it up. Luckily, Krista helped me out by playing with my nipples and using some baby oil. When you really have to work for a sex scene, it often ends up flowing more smoothly on your television screen than it did under the lights.

Porno watchers often ask whether they use things like whipped egg whites to fake come in movies. Usually not in videos, but sometimes in still shoots or photo layouts. There, you're only simulating sex, so there's no real come shot. The most popular substitute for the real thing is Tame Creme Rinse.

In *Delicious,* they attached me to a "come machine." In gore movies, it usually shoots out blood and guts, but in porno it sprays out a mixture of half-and-half and gelatin. I held a tube next to my penis. I had to be careful not to hold it against my balls, because it shoots out at such a great velocity (sometimes 20 m.p.h.) that you could easily injure your balls. There's a similar scene in *Jack & Jill 2,* but in both of those instances the buckets of come were part of the story line.

A lot of people compare horror movies and porno movies. Some people say they'd rather have their kids watch two people making love than seeing somebody getting blown away in a cop movie. In an R-rated film you can see a woman's breast get mutilated, but you can't see a penis giving a woman pleasure. I won't make that porno/horror comparison. First of all, in horror movies the actions aren't real. But in porno you're watching the real thing. A penis really goes into a woman; a fake knife doesn't. Which is more offensive? That's a matter of personal choice. The law says you can see either one at the age of eighteen, so the argument's moot anyway.

I've often wondered how I'd feel if, someday in the future, I had a teenage son or daughter watching my movies. That would be a delicate situation! I think it would force me to be very honest with them about myself. I wouldn't tell young people to get involved in porno, but I would tell them the truth. It's like the Army. They show you beautiful posters of guys sailing off into the sunset with beautiful women waiting for them at home. They show you macho TV commercials. But they don't show you mangled bodies and helmets pierced by bullets. They don't show you the heads rolling.

That's what I'd tell young people about porno: how you can die . . . or commit suicide . . . or become a drug addict . . . or how you can become even more lonely and insecure than you already are.

They might look at me and say that I came out all right, that I'm happy with Lisa and her kids. That's true, but it will never wash away the damage I've done to myself. I carry those scars around on the inside. I still do cocaine; and when I do, I jeopardize my health, look like hell, and feel like shit. I know I've done too much coke. I've done it for the same reason a lot of porno people do it: to get outside of myself. We coke up and we feel like we're not the people who have done what we've done on camera. We try to understand why the hell we're doing it, why *us.*

When I do coke by myself, I do it to have personal fantasies. I have given so many of my fantasies to the industry that I need to keep something for myself. Sometimes I grab a *Cosmopolitan* magazine and cut the heads off the pictures of some women and put them on other bodies, and I jack off to that. It is brief relief, though, and expensive.

Before Lisa, before love, I did cocaine more often. I had to find other things to sexually arouse me, because I'd done it all. I'd been with three women, five women, two guys and a woman. I'd done everything in every combination except cause physical harm to someone, or be with another man. Now I have a beautiful wife whom anyone would want to be with, but I still have to battle my insecurities. At one time, everybody wanted to be Elvis, yet Elvis didn't even want to be himself. Nobody's ever satisfied.

With Lisa wearing no perfume, just the lovely smell of her clean flesh, we have ultimate sex. During those times, Lisa can be my sweet, little girl. But sometimes something called reality sneaks in and ruins it, and despite our beautiful sexual and emotional relationship, I sneak out, get a little coke, go into the garage, snort, wear Lisa's panties, and jerk off.

I can't imagine what all of this is like for Lisa. I've told her that if I were her, I never would have married me. I know I'm no prize. I have to understand that Lisa loves all of me, even the sidewalk part, the dirty part. What she fell in love with goes beyond any suit and tie.

Still, it's been tough for Lisa knowing what I've done. I realize that she's changed her life to be with me. Sometimes it tortures me to realize that Lisa gave up security for a man who's fucked to earn his keep. Now I'm struggling to pay the rent without using my dick. During arguments, she never stops pointing out how difficult it is for her. Lisa's been an actress since she was four years old and has rubbed elbows with big Hollywood people (sorry, she won't let me mention names, but one guy she dated is now a star of "L.A. Law"). Now she's with me.

We've had our rough times and we've had our beautiful times. Hell is hot, red, and aggressive. Heaven is cool and pillowy and light blue. There is no in-between for us. It's either one or the other. I'll put it this way: I've never thought heaven and hell could be so close to each other.

Twenty-Five

Another Direction

The people behind the scenes in porno are a mixed bag. The receptionist at the front desk in a video company usually has no idea what she's doing there. She's like the sweet old lady who's selling gum in the front of the candy store while a bookie in the back room is taking numbers. Besides people like that, you'll find a lot of unprofessional inexperienced producers, directors, and screenwriters who have never written a screenplay. They think because it's pornography they can be nasty or sloppy. In contrast, the crew—the camera and lighting people, for example—are all pros. They have to be. They have to know how to work a camera or how to light a scene. Most of them do legit work, use fake names in porno, get paid cash on the side, and don't tell their unions.

Right now, the names of specific directors might not mean much to you, but it's the director who's responsible for the "feel" of a film or video. For the most part, he or she tells the actors how to move and when to change positions. As much as the performers or the story itself, a director can make or break a movie. Most of the best directors are known for their own personal styles and unique trademarks: Henri Pachard's bathroom sex scenes, Anthony Spinelli's realistic characters.

A good director is someone who leaves his actor alone and lets him develop his character, emotionally and sexually. The director should stay neutral, offering guidance only when it's needed. The director shouldn't have to feed his ego on the set. His turn for that will come later, when his picture gets good reviews. The actor's turn comes when the camera is rolling. Too many directors try to show off and tell you how to do your job. Some are even jealous of their actors. Here are a few I love . . and a few I don't.

Driving home from Palm Springs a few days ago, Lisa mentined Anthony Spinelli. Of course, that's not his real name. In real life he's a nice Jewish man named Sam, and his brother is a popular comic actor who has been in films like *The Ritz.* For those of you who don't know him, Sam is sure he's the best adult film director around.

I've worked for Sam many times, and it's like working for a big teddy bear who proceeds to lock you in a room. You can have a lot of fun with the stuffed animals, but if you don't have the freedom to get out of the room when you need to, you start going crazy. When Sam tells you that you're working for a day, you're working for twenty-four hours, baby! Although he does look for quality actors, I don't think he tries hard enough to make the sex hot. He emphasizes acting and forgets that he's making a fuck-film.

If you don't do something exactly the way he wants, Sam won't yell at you. He'll fire you! On one occasion I called him a day later than I should have. I didn't think there was a rush, because the movie was supposed to start shooting two weeks from that day. When I did call, Sam told me, "Sorry, Jerry. You didn't call me, so I hired someone else." On the set, he'd let me fool around and act crazy, but then suddenly he'd blow his top. It was tough to know just what would set him off.

I respect Sam's intentions, but I don't believe he's the best director in adult films. I'm not really sure who the best is. My first impulse is to say Cecil Howard, but I may be biased in Cecil's favor because I won two "Best Actor" awards working in his films. J. D. (John Derick) is *one* of the best. He did *Bootsie.* His personal ego doesn't get involved in the work. Any time a director injects his personal ego to give himself a booster shot at the expense of others, I automatically become resentful. He doesn't have to prove anything, because he already has a chair with his name on it. His job is to sit in it and let things flow.

Sure, I like acting, but I don't like working twenty hours, sleeping four, and then having to work six more hours the next day. That's what a typical Anthony Spinelli shoot is like. Still, some of my best acting jobs were done on schedules like that. It reminds me of when you have a tremendous fight with your lover. Right after you reconcile, you make incredible love. But look at the circumstances you have to endure Sometimes it's not necessary or even worth it.

Back to quiet, sheepish, and paranoid Sam. He never tells you where he's shooting, just gives you a plane ticket and has his son pick you up at the airport. I guess you *have* to be paranoid in this business. But still, he puts a lot of pride in his work. He tries to use his actors for all they're worth, often expecting two sex scenes in a day. Believe me, if you have to work nineteen or twenty hours straight, it's not easy to perform sexually.

Sam's been in the business well over ten years, and he finally sought me out about four years ago. Many directors would come to Reb Sawitz's office, sit in the back of the room, and watch you audition. That's what Sam finally did, and he was very impressed with my work. The most generous of all directors, he was always willing to give me whatever money I wanted. Sam would give me advances of a few hundred dollars before I even shot a movie.

Sam recently tempted me with an offer to make a porno movie for $1,000 a day. "Anything you want, Jerry," he told me. I would have done it only if I could have gotten away with simulated sex. But hell, X-rated films don't pay you for make-believe. How can I do a movie knowing my wife would leave me if I did? I didn't accept the offer.

At this point, I'm really troubled by my porno past. For so many years, it didn't matter. Now if I do another sex film, I'll feel like a criminal. If I make a movie, I lose Lisa. If Lisa and I don't make it, I'll probably put a gun to my head and blow my fucking brains out while watching one of my videos.

Lisa just had a fit. She didn't want me to say what I just said on tape, but I'm not going to censor my emotions from you either. We're in an amusement park, running from ride to ride. There are big dips and hills. Sometimes we're so scared and dizzy that we don't think we're going to survive. But, so far we have. And tomorrow, who knows?

I just got off the phone with Ron Sullivan (a director who uses the name "Henri Pachard"), and he's going to lend me some money. Last week I had $1,000 in my pocket. Now I'm down to pocket change and there's hardly any gas in the car. With that call to Ron, I picked up some behind-the-scenes production work for next week. Although I'm very grateful to Ron for what he did, I'm just starting to feel that the industry *owes* me something for the past work I've done. When you see a video labeled "produced and directed by Henri Pachard," you see the actors he's chosen to represent himself on film or video. I've given him a good product, and I've put money in *his* pockets.

Ron's a big man in a big business, but he's small in the eyes of the respectable film business. Porno's a limited world, getting more limited all the time. By coming to the aid of a porno person, Ron's just preserving himself. He needs me because of who I am and what I've done, whether or not I do another movie for him. Sometimes he's gotten sick and tired of my crap on the set and shouted, "Damn it, Jerry!" (He captured that aspect of our relationship brilliantly in *Moonlusting.*) But despite the garbage I give him, Ron knows where my heart is.

Last night I watched *Peeping Tom.* I made that movie during a period of great rhythm in my life, when I was going to San Francisco about once a week to make movies—even though I didn't feel very sunny about the business. *Peeping Tom* was directed by "Robert McCallum." I usually don't get along with him, but that film was an exception. We respected each other's talent. Our first movie together was *Beverly Hills Exposed.* Another notable flick was *10½ Weeks.*

Robert is a very attractive, sweet man with a shark-eyed face. One of my favorite directors, his shoots are free and unrestricted. He's like a rancher: He doesn't mind the stallions running around within the corral, because he knows the gates are locked.

During sex scenes, Robert leaves his actors alone and does his own job: directing and camerawork. His camera always sought out the core of the scene and stayed with it, while most other directors are too mechanical, making you change positions every five minutes.

Robert's doing legit movies now. Lisa even worked with him on a video for cable TV and found him to be nice, pleasant, and respecting of her talent. In fact, she had no idea he had ever done adult-film work; Robert was that professional.

Guys like Robert live in fear that the world will find out what he's doing. In fact, I promised him I wouldn't reveal his real name, and I always keep my word. Well, at least I try.

F. J. Lincoln is an odd-looking guy. He has shoulder-length whitish-gray hair and a beard. The first time I met Freddy, I was grossed out: He looked like a snake with hair! So immediately I distrusted him. But boy, was I wrong! Freddy had looked so closely at my work, it seemed as though he really knew me. But by seeing films he's directed, I didn't know anything about him. That's a major difference between actors and directors.

Freddy really has a sincere respect for his actors. Sometimes he may seem as if he's being overly sensitive, but it really reflects the style and effort he puts into being a director. At one time, Freddy was married to the former porn actress Tiffany Clark. Now, he lives out in L. A. with Patti Rhodes, who's also a director.

With his rugged, raspy voice, Freddy sounds like a gangster, but he's really a sweetheart. In all the films I've done for him, he never argued with anything I did. The only thing he ever demanded was that I behave on the set when the producers—the money people—were there. I could understand that, so I complied.

Freddy's also doing legit movies now. I don't know how good they are, but I do know that Freddy knows how to shoot and edit films. When you work with him, you may work over twelve hours, but he knows just what he wants, so you're not sitting around wasting time. Freddy has great intuition about how much energy to put into his prductions. His budgets are minimal. Lunch comes in from the deli and everything's down to the last penny.

But don't think Freddy's meek or conservative—he's a pretty daring guy. He's shot movies with the cops almost outside the door. He's actually very cocky when he shoots. Like a snowball rolling down a mountain, he picks up speed and gets bigger on the set. It makes you feel he's with you all the way, that he's not going to abandon you, no matter what. Freddy gives you the impression that if the cops ever did raid the set, he'd say, "Handcuff me first."

Damon Christian (a.k.a. Richard Aldrich) used to have his own company, called Gold Medallion, until he merged it with Fred Hirsch of AVC. Richard reminds me of a pudgy David Letterman, not only in appearance but because he has a square, firm style. He was always the "money man" on a set, so no one ever dared argue with him!

When we were doing *Debbie Duz Dishes,* I roomed with him in San Francisco. I flew in from L.A., but Richard drove up in his big Bronco pick-up truck. I could see he was apprehensive about sharing a room with a crazy porno actor, but after a while, he relaxed and we had a good time.

On the set, Richard kept telling me how I saved that movie. He couldn't believe the extra quality I added. He was really enthusiastic. "You bailed us out," he told me. "Your character is the highlight of the movie." Before he hired me, Richard obviously didn't know much about me, but he was really pleased when I created the character of Kirby, a zany salesman who sold the Wonder Vac, a machine with twenty-seven different sexual attachments, plus his own. The character was so popular, I played Kirby again in the sequel. But when *Debbie Duz Dishes III* was made, Joey Silvera took over the role. Why? There's a little story behind it.

Richard's producer, Jim Malibu, had originally asked me to do Part III of *Debbie.* But Jim and I were having problems because of something that happened during the shooting of another film. The entire cast had stayed at the Bayside Motel in Brisbane. At the time, I knew one of my costars, whom I will call Keri, was doing lots of cocaine, but I stayed in my own room, minding my own business . . . until Keri called me on the phone to offer me a half gram of coke, which of course I accepted. Back in my room, I was all set to watch Delta Burke on an HBO series. There I was, jerking my dick off to Delta and doing the coke. I was trying to keep it under control, because I knew I had several scenes to do the next day. The phone rang again. This time, it was the hotel clerk. Did I know Keri? When I admitted I did, he told me to get to her room in a hurry because she'd just tried to hang herself.

Half dressed, I ran to Keri's room. There she was with a lampshade cord around her neck. She had written her name all over the door. The cocaine had made her totally paranoid. She imagined that some guy had come in and tried to kill her. I didn't know what to do. Cocaine was scattered all over the place and I knew the police would be there soon, so I tried to clean up the drug residue as best I could. When they came, the cops didn't seem to notice anything out of the ordinary. I explained that Keri was going through an emotionally tough time and that's why she was a little depressed. Somehow I convinced them I'd be responsible for Keri and take her back to my room to keep an eye on her.

First, I called Jim Malibu and told him that we had trouble at the hotel. He insisted I go back to my room and forget about her. When I told him cops were all over the place, he said he didn't give a shit. I knew Keri was capable of destroying his whole production, but Jim didn't seem to realize it. Besides, I couldn't ignore another human being in trouble. Jim was angry with me: "Jerry, I'm giving you an order right now. Stay in your room and forget about her."

"Fuck you," I yelled and hung up on him.

Back in my room, I kept snorting coke. Keri was really getting spaced out and refused to sit down and relax. Finally, she went to bed, leaving three grams of cocaine in her purse. I wound up doing it all. By morning, I was miserably fucked up, too.

At least Keri was finished with her work and was going home to L.A. I still had a full day to go. When Jim's production assistant left with Keri for the airport, I noticed an unmarked cop car right outside. I didn't know what the hell to do. Twenty minutes later, there was a knock on my door. It was one of the detectives. He claimed he was looking for Keri, but I told him she'd already gone. Next, he asked me what I was doing in San Francisco. I said I was visiting friends. After he left, I knew I was in trouble, so I called a cab to bring me into the city. That unmarked car was now following *me.* So instead of going to the set, I went to an old girlfriend's house. With my heart palpitating, I told the cab driver to let me off at the building's side entrance.

Luckily, my friend was home. I had her call Jim and explain what had happened. If I went to the set, the cops would have followed me and busted everyone. I didn't want Jim to blame my not showing upon the coke, so I didn't talk to him until later, when my high wore off. Jim Malibu was so angry that he fired me. Many times, I've tried to explain what happened, but Jim didn't seem to care. He agreed to pay me for the day and a half of work I'd done, but that was all. Even though I saved his ass, Jim still saw me as the bad guy. Still does.

That's the reason Richard Aldrich didn't use me for *Debbie Duz Dishes III.* It's no skin off of my butt. I'm no angel, but I'm tired of being blamed for things that aren't my fault.

I mentioned earlier that Paul Vatelli died of AIDS. At first, people in the industry were trying to cover it up, saying Paul had been in Vietnam and was a victim of Agent Orange. Then Caballero announced he died of pneumonia. Some people try to blame Paul's death on the fact he was free-basing, but the truth is he fucked a lot of women in the business. That's like playing "Wheel of Fortune" with "bankruptcy" in half the notches. The big shots in the industry go out of the way to make themselves smell rosy. After all, it's not good publicity if one of their top directors dies of AIDS.

Adventureland Studios in New York was—and still is—the East Coast's main porno studio. Even the cops know it, sometimes coming by to watch us work. That's fine with me, but it pisses me off when they expect to get blown by the actresses to keep their mouths shut.

I met Gerard Damiano at Adventureland. He's a very solid guy, the Leonardo da Vinci of porn. Almost everyone knows him for directing both *Deep Throat* and *The Devil in Miss Jones.* In 1983, I did a nonsexual role in his *Night Hunger.*

The worst thing that happened to Gerry was video. Shooting on video is a lot like using a Polaroid camera—any idiot can do it. A 35mm film feature takes great care and skill, both of which are missing in today's product. Because of video, shooting budgets fell and it wasn't profitable for directors to put the same time and effort into their work. Damiano still shoots an occasional adult video, but they don't have the class of his earlier films. Things change.

ANOTHER DIRECTION

I still can't get over how attractive I looked dressed as a woman in that last scene of *Mad About You.* I wore high-heels during my entire sex scene with Porsche Lynn. As a transvestite, I try to seduce Billy Dee in another scene. Billy was so bewildered that he forgot his lines. He looked like he was afraid I was going to kiss him on the lips.

Ned Morehead directed that video, and I always enjoyed working for him. For some reason, he reminds me of the Hindenberg. Maybe it's because his hair shoots out like a zeppelin. Ned is an easygoing director who appreciates his actors as people. He keeps his mouth shut until he sees that something's not clicking. Then he steps in.

After every shoot Ned would tell me, "Jerry, this is my last movie. I can't take it anymore. I'm going to quit the business and go legit." If there's one director who wondered why in the hell I ever got into the business, it's Ned. And I wondered the same thing about him. Like almost all of us, Ned's a victim of circumstance. He finally took up porno because he couldn't get started in legitimate filmmaking. Broke, with no clear direction, he had little choice.

In the last scene of *Mad About You,* all Ned told me to do was look into the camera and blow a kiss at the viewer. Dressed in full drag, I felt the character was so outrageous that he/she should do more. The camera pulled in for an extreme close-up. I squirted a hypodermic needle into the air, laughed like a maniac, then put on a serious face and blew a kiss. I wanted to show the crazed yet *respectable* power the character now possessed as the Head Nurse in an asylum for the sexually insane.

Working for a woman director is like working in a sexual threesome. As a man, you might find it's intimidating, but after a while you get used to taking your clothes off in front of a lady director. You no longer see the difference between men and women or notice who's wearing clothes and who isn't. When a person stays dressed, you can't really see what their body is like. They can create all sorts of illusions, so the bullshit really flows. But millions of people have seen me fuck. They know how big my dick is, how I kiss, how I eat pussy, and how big my love handles are. When you're stripped naked, there's nothing left to hide. It's the same thing working with a woman director. I just see them as people. They just see me as "Jerry Butler."

To put it very politely, Roberta Findlay's homely as hell. Everyone has a lot of fun doing her movies, but they take advantage of her good nature. The crew tapes signs onto her back that say things like, "Suck me, I'm lonely," or "Eat me . . . if you dare." She just laughs and gets on with the show.

Shauna Grant and I did *Glitter* for Roberta in 1983 and were cast as the shy young lovers. In 1985, she wanted to use me in a movie called *Shauna, Every Man's Fantasy,* which was a documentary-type movie supposedly about the suicide of Shauna Grant. I was very against doing the film, because I felt they were using a dead woman to make money, not to tell what a porno star's life is really like. I lost a lot of respect for Roberta when she did that Shauna film—especially because it had such a sick, sleazy feeling.

But I guess Roberta's had a tough life herself. You may remember hearing about a helicopter accident on top of the Pan Am Building about ten years ago. The helicopter's rotary blade flew off and decapitated a man. That man was Roberta's husband. She's still waiting for the lawsuit to be settled.

Candida Royalle was an actress when we did *Delicious* together. Then, we were just a lion and lioness in the same arena. But when she's directing, it's a whole different story. She hasn't acted in sex roles for at least eight years and formed her own video company called "Femme." I did a scene with Rhonda Jo Petty in their first video, which is also called *Femme.*

Candida's husband Per Sjostedt is her partner and cameraman. Their couple-oriented videos don't show a lot of graphic lovemaking. They're probably a good introduction for the female viewer who has never seen an erotic film, because they present the sex very delicately.

Candida means well, but I think she's taking an abstract route to clean up things she might personally feel dirty about. Movies were raunchier in the days she was acting in them! When you've been splashed with come on film, then how sophisticated can you really be? Maybe she got sick and tired of that, so now is trying to redeem the industry. I understand the approach, but I don't think romantic sex will sell. Like it or not, most men enjoy seeing raunchy, animalistic sex. A lot of women are probably the same way, even if they are afraid to admit it.

Women are so determined not to be seen as sex objects today that it sometimes gets in the way of their sexual response. Passion should not be too deliberate or thoughtful. They divide their identities in two. I'm still amazed at how ladylike Lisa acts, for example, when she's not in bed with me. You'd never believe the things she says and does when the door's closed.

Candida is the *only* director in the entire industry to exclusively use "safe-sex" techniques. If the couples aren't lovers in real life, they use condoms. Since she doesn't have too many genital close-ups, you usually can't tell. She concentrates mostly on the faces and the emotions. I don't know, I still think that both men and women want to see hot, aggressive, loving sex. At this moment, Cathy Tavel and Lisa are yelling their disagreement at me. They insist that romance turns them on more than close-up fucking. "Anticipation is a greater turn-on," they're saying. I guess women *do* feel differently. Well, for those who do, there's Candida Royalle. She's sterling silver in a world made of tin.

Kirdy Stevens works with his wife, Helene Terrie, who writes scripts for his movies. They live next door to Michael Jackson. During the filming of *Taboo III,* I stayed with them for a few weeks. I never saw Michael, but I did meet his sister La Toya and his mom. I see Kirdy and Helene once in a while. They're very family-oriented and have a beautiful home and three kids. The *Taboo* series made them a mint, so now they have the luxury of hiring other people to shoot their movies for them. I guess they don't want to take the chance of getting busted themselves.

John Bowen is the classic example of a director who makes pornos for his *own* jollies. This guy sometimes even works his way into the sex scenes! I remember an incident when Alicia Monet flew in directly from Europe to L. A. for a shoot. She was so exhausted that she almost fell asleep during her masturbation scene. Sleaze that he is, Bowen had his wife, Misty Regan (who has made a few pornos), lend her hands to Alicia's "masturbation" scene. Then *he* joined them! Amazingly, he got away with it by only showing Alicia's body and not her conked-out face. Isn't that weird? I guess he didn't want to waste the tape.

ANOTHER DIRECTION

I never made a movie for Hal Freeman, of Hollywood Video. Years back, Hal wanted to see me, so I drove to his office in the Valley with Amber Lynn, Buck Adams, and Jessica Wylde. When we walked in for our appointment, Hal's daughter, Sherry, and his wife, Cynthia, looked at us as if we were animals under exhibition. Then they took turns grilling us about our appointment with Hal. Here we were in a business where we fucked our asses off so that people like them could make a lot of money, yet they had no regard for us as people. They were giggling as they whispered things about us to each other.

I'd had enough. "What the fuck is so funny?" They stopped laughing. "If you don't get off your ass and tell Hal I'm out here, I'll go berserk. And you won't like what you see."

Hal called me inside immediately. He seemed pretty friendly, so I told him about the snotnosed cunts he employed in his front office. Even when he told me they were his wife and daughter, I didn't apologize for what I called them. "Hal, I can't say I'm sorry," I told him. "They treated us like animals."

Instead, he apologized to me. But in the next breath he asked if I'd do an anal scene for $350, which is far below the standard. (Because it's considered a "specialty," anal sex usually pays much more.) I agreed to do it. But on the day of the shoot, I never showed up. It was my way of getting revenge.

We're all kids in the business. We all wear these imaginary baseball caps. But when a director takes off his cap, puts on a big chest protector, and tries to decide what's a strike and what's a ball and who to throw out of the game, I lose my patience. If I get a chance, I'm going to swing my bat at him and knock his head into the stands.

Twenty-Six
Mammary Lane

Now that you know all the industry slang, the low-down on some of the best-known actresses, actors, and directors, and the mechanics of a sex scene, my recollections on specific films will make more sense to you. I've done so many films, my memories are sometimes hard to organize, though I can recall specific pieces of dialogue for a lot of films. It all depends on what was happening during that part of my life, I guess.

Winding down toward the end of my story, Lisa and I flew to New York to consult with Cathy Tavel and Bob Rimmer. Cathy's husband Al, a professional musician, was enthusiastic about the book and told me how much he enjoyed my movies. When people compliment me, I feel a little a awkward and uncomfortable. If I brag about my accomplishments, that's one thing, but when someone compliments me, I feel a touch embarrassed. I told Al I appreciated what he said and I hoped that even in my vulgarity I've contributed something to humanity! I even hope that some people think, "This business can't be so dirty if a clean-cut, talented guy like Jerry is involved." If everyone in the business dared to be as open and honest, the industry would be different. I think it would throw a new light on pornography. True, some actors have added black to a world that's capable of an unlimited amount of creativity. I like to think that I've found the rainbow, even in a dark sky.

This trip East gave me a chance to watch many of the movies I've made in the past ten years. You'd be shocked to know how few I'd seen before working on this book. I was surprised to see how poorly some had been slapped together and, in contrast, how professional others looked. For what it's worth, put on your bedroom slippers for a trip down my memory lane.

Seeing it complete for the first time, I thought Henri Pachard's *She's So Fine* was one of my best films. It has a strong sense of what movies used to be—before video came along. Although most of the film was set in two houses, there were a few outdoor scenes. I always like the use of "exteriors" in porno. They're a breath of fresh air in an industry that's locked underground. Still, sometimes you can sense the tension: The cast is all worried they're going to get caught fucking in the woods! In this film, there was no outdoor sex, but the people walked easily back and forth from house to house in a suburban setting, just like real neighbors would.

To shoot *She's So Fine,* we all bussed up to the Hamptons and stayed in a big mansion, which was owned by a Madame. It felt like going away to summer camp. The cast got to know each other *very* well. In most shoots, people come in and out and go home to their regular lives at the end of the day. In this one, everyone partied together and drank after each day's work.

You get five points if you guessed that the Madame had a crush on me and I wound up sleeping with her. A small woman and not too attractive, what made me fall for her was the *power* she possessed. She even offered me a job as her "main stud," for $2,000 a week. All I had to do was make love to her—and deal a little cocaine on the side. I couldn't see it as a long-term relationship, because she was unclean personally and sexually. One night, I went upstairs to bullshit with the crew, who slept in the attic. They were curious about how this powerful mystery woman was in bed. "Guys, it's not so great," I told them. "She's really a pig. When I was screwing her, and pulled my dick out, a fly landed on it and dropped dead."

All of a sudden, the door popped open. The Madame had followed me upstairs! "I heard what you said about me. How dare you!" she screamed. At first, she was so insulted that she tried to throw me out of the house, but she finally took me back down to her bedroom.

As usual, I created some excitement on the set. Out of sheer boredom I put a big, stuffed German Shepherd toy into the freezer. The next morning, the cook let out a bloodcurdling scream when she opened the freezer door. That brightened up an otherwise slow day.

The movie was filmed during a time when I had no one special in my life. It was a project, an important piece of work that kept my body and mind occupied. Whenever there are people, emotions, and time invested into something, it means a lot to me. My part wasn't that big, but it had substance. The story line concerned all the crazy guests (invited and uninvited) at a wedding that never happened. Critic Jim Holliday called it "Wedding for Godot." Every role contributed to make it a wonderful ensemble effort.

Ron Sullivan/Henri Pachard wants to use me for the sequel, which they're shooting in a few days. I don't think time will permit me to work in it, even though Lisa gave me her approval. She thought it would be all right if I did simulated sex with Sharon Kane. Since Sharon and I worked together so much in the past, it would be like visiting with an old friend. I was hoping Ron could hold up the shoot until after I get back from my visit to Brooklyn, but I don't think he will. Although I don't want to, I'll probably end up standing Ron up. I know he'll be angry, but this book is the most important project in my life right now. I'm going to miss reprising my character, though.

In *She's So Fine,* I played a conservative, vulnerable character—Roger, a checker-shirted middle-class guy from Detroit. Roger's very excited about his hobby: taking videos of everyone against their will.

I had three sex scenes in the original. The first was with Sharon Kane. Whenever I arrived on a set and knew I'd have to work with her, I wasn't thrilled. But once they applied her makeup and I saw her slinky, receptive body, she became much more attractive. Sharon really feels the sex and gives great head besides. Just like a palm tree in the wind, she never snaps, just swings and sways with the breeze.

Sharon Mitchell was also in *She's So Fine.* This was the one where she was made up like a punk rocker. That added to her freakiness. My character was supposed to be mesmerized by this dominant, abusive woman—and I know I was personally.

She's So Fine was a five-day shoot. That's what porno used to be about, actually *going* somewhere and shooting in different locations. You felt you were really creating something. Today, you arrive in the morning, finish by nightfall and have $600 in your pocket. In the early days, you came home with a $3,000 check and had time to air out a little bit, sit down and think about what you'd accomplished. You bang out a one-day movie in San Francisco and are flying back to L.A. after dark. Before I quit, I was banging them out so quickly that my dick hardly had a chance to dry off between videos.

Late After Dark was filmed during a more difficult period of my life. Stuart Canterbury was the director, and boy was I leery the first time I met him. First, he's a white South African, and I felt a sneaky sort of conspiracy in his attitude. On top of that, he's very prejudiced and walks around with a big chip on his shoulder.

There was a D.P. with Shone Taylor and Brittany Stryker in that flick. I don't do too many of them. It's a little awkward because you get so close to the other guy. Shone's a good friend and I like him. He has a funny-looking dick; I always tell him to get a hard-on because I can't stand looking at his dog prick. In that scene, I could see why I was so happy that I came first. When I came, it dripped down Brittany's ass and unintentionally showered Shone's balls. After he came, he shot up and hit the Goodyear blimp. For once, I was the blaster and not the blastee.

Watching one scene in that film bothered me, and it wasn't even a sex scene. It was the part where I was walking aimlessly through a playground. In the background, you could see a couple of kids innocently playing in a sandbox. I remember feeling that they didn't belong in a park that was being used for a porno exterior. Feeling pretty shitty, I walked up to them, but they ignored me. It worked well for the isolation and desolation my character was supposed to be feeling. In another way, I guess I *wanted* those kids there because I felt they had something I was grasping for, something I'd lost to porno.

The night before we filmed that scene, I did large amounts of cocaine, trying to numb my sadness. Until the early afternoon, I was fighting that woozie feeling you get when you come down from blow. I knew we'd have an exterior day (all outdoor shots, with no sex scenes or dialogue), so doing coke the night before probably wouldn't hurt my performance. When Tracey Adams looked into my eyes, however, she was very worried, so she spent time with me and helped bring me back up again, giving me love, understanding, and concern. I think you could feel that intensity just by looking at the scenes of us walking in the park and wandering through San Francisco. We were two pigeons—just hanging out, traveling around, bumping along.

That day, Stuart told me he was very attracted to Tracey. I knew she was pretty open and friendly, so I suggested he approach her. If she's doing porno and has sex with any guy you put in front of her, she might go for this rich, balding South African, right? But our enlightened director was shocked at the thought. "Me?" he said, "Not me. I don't want fucking AIDS." Here he was talking to a guy who should have more to fear than he did. It bothered me to realize that the Captain would probably take a helicopter to escape his sinking ship. I swore never to work for him again, though I finally did when I needed money badly enough. Eventually Stu apologized for his ugly statement, saying he was only kidding. It didn't matter. I knew he didn't respect his actors.

We shot a couple of movies at the same times as *Late After Dark.* That's a pretty common economical porno practice. Both were shot at "The Sound Stage" in San Francisco, where approximately 70 percent of the Northern California shoots are done. *Sex Life of a Nerd* (a.k.a. *Lucky In Love)* had an almost identical cast. In *Sex life* I had a bathroom sex scene with Melanie Scott, who was half-drunk and sucked my penis like it was a corkscrew. I had a rough time getting it up. Stuart was glaring angrily at me—as though I had personally insulted him by not getting a hard-on! Of course, he didn't stop to think that maybe my problem stemmed from having seven sex scenes in three days.

Watching some of these movies, I've been very disappointed with the background music they throw in. It's often so bad that it becomes annoying. Directors go out of their way to get good come shots and hot sex scenes, so why not back them up with decent music?

The cast and crew credits also bother me. Why the hell do people use names like "Sandy Beach?" I can understand not using your real name, but I don't think you should ridicule the industry with stupid names. It insults the intelligence of the audience. *We* stereotype this business, not the public. As long as you show women taking off a nurse's uniform to reveal a black garterbelt underneath, you're not authentic.

Naked Scents was produced by a woman named Chris Toomey, and it was shot in Connecticut. I already told you about how I met Lorraine, the mother of my child, on that set. Another outstanding memory is the terrible fight Richard Bolla had with the cameraman Larry Revene during Richard's foursome with three other girls. There's Larry shooting close-ups of Richard's face, and in between they're having a fistfight!

I played a tennis pro/stud employed on a rich estate. In one scene I had sex three separate times—with Tish Ambrose, Taija Rae, and Sharon Kane. The director had them lined up outside the door and sent them in one by one. The way you see it in the movie is the way we actually shot it. They didn't even let me shower between women. I literally fucked them one after the other. I hadn't had a sex scene in three days and they gave me three in forty minutes the last day. I only came twice. (I never finished off with Taija.) Doing that scene made me feel awful, as though I were taking advantage of my costars. I was the director's human cat-house. Afterwards, all three women told me they felt used, too.

An hour after that last scene, the mini-bus was set to go back to Manhattan. The van was packed with equipment, and the director told me I had to take the train home. Naturally, equipment is more important than a person. It costs more to replace than I did. I made a big deal and told them I wouldn't sign a release form giving my consent to use me in the movie. Despite that blow up, I still wound up taking the train. They didn't even pay for the ticket.

Years later, watching the videotape, I was amused by my performance, especially the part where my character is drunk after a wild bachelor party. I hobble around near the swimming pool. Although it wasn't in the script, I thought it would be appropriate to take a bad step and fall into the water. At the expense of my favorite jacket, I got soaking wet in 25 degree weather. Everyone was laughing hysterically, and the director loved it. That made it worth it.

Jack & Jill 2 was another movie I did for the famous, ever-ready Chuck Vincent. It was a three- or four-day shoot and was a typical Chuck Vincent movie. That means there was a lot of dilly-daddling and fussing with costumes. With the exception of *Roommates* and *In Love*, Chuck's movies have a cartoonish, merry-go-round feeling. They don't dig deep. He wipes the window nicely, but he never gets inside the house. Chuck's too good for porn—he's stylish, and he tries to make his stories gripping—but his R-rated Hollywood releases have something missing.

Even though it was made in 1984, yesterday was the first time I watched *Jack & Jill 2.* Yet even without seeing it, I knew it was going to be a film I'd like. When you work for Chuck, it's on a professional level . . . in a very unprofessional industry. An interesting aside is that Samantha Fox and I never had sex in the film, although we had two "sex scenes." She'd quit the business, and she would no longer do hardcore penetration. On the other hand, she had no objections to me eating her pussy. So, I never actually entered her, just rubbed against her pussy—you can't even tell by the way it was shot—and then jerked off on her belly.

There was an odd scene in *Jack & Jill 2* where I'm having sex with another woman while a drunken, hallucinating Samantha watches. She imagines a mouth being imbedded in the woman's pussy hairs. They shot it by using a mannequin and putting another girl's mouth in the false pussy hole, sucking me. It was kind of freaky, but when I do things like that in movies, I can let the oddity of it arouse me.

My sex scenes in *Jack & Jill 2* were odd, but not really hot. I've mentioned earlier that Chuck is gay. There's nothing wrong with that, but how can a guy who's a softball expert coach a hardball team? There are similarities, but it isn't the same game. Sometimes Chuck seems very sheepish about heterosexual sex. He does care about the look and the presentation of his works, and he always dressed me very nicely, but he seemed a little confused about how to dress women. In *Jack & Jill 2,* for example, the women wore picture hats and frilly dresses—pretty, but not . . . *tasty.*

All in all, I was the plug in the bathtub in *Jack & Jill 2*: I held in the water and kept the toy boats afloat.

Jack Hammer was shot in Oakland by Vinnie Rossi for Zane Brothers. Vinnie is the king of the fifteen-to-eighteen hour shoots. A tall Italian guy, I always made fun of him because he's shaped like the Liberty Bell.

In at least three-quarters of the movies I've done, the script is given to me on the set. *Jack Hammer* was no exception. I knew I was playing a bizarre character, a transvestite named Peter Pussy (a contradiction in itself) who owns an adult bookstore. I always wanted to play a role made up as half-man/half-woman and thought this would be the perfect opportunity. Vinnie gave me permission to do whatever I wanted, so I had the make-up girl do one-half of my face as a woman and the other half as a man. Since we were only working with one camera, I had to be sure to reveal only half of my face at a time as I talked. To my knowledge, something like that's never been done before. It was a great challenge. I did it in one take.

Jack Hammer itself didn't get too much attention, but my performance was singled out. I was nominated for "Best Supporting Actor" award from the XRCO—the X-Rated Critics Organization—but I didn't win.

Because I've been watching so many of my movies, it was starting to get pretty monotonous—and depressing, especially when you can see four more pounds of meat growing around your waist over the years. I was actually getting a little bored watching myself screw. Suddenly, though, I was turned on by a scene I did with Nina Hartley in *Passion Chain*. At one point, you just *knew* she climaxed. I watched my face when I was eating her pussy and remembered I really enjoyed it. Nina was so relaxed and encouraging—a refreshing change. A lot of women harden themselves to such a degree that their clits become knuckles.

This might surprise you: I usually don't like going down on a girl on camera. After a while, a porno actor just sees it as something that has to be done to finish the scene. You become a human stop-watch—four minutes of pussy-eating and five minutes of pumping. Very rarely do you see a guy going from fucking to pussy-eating. You also never see a guy coming and then making the woman come by eating her. Porno has such a stagnant sex system that it often gets monotonous. A guy pulls down his pants . . . a woman sucks him off . . . he eats her . . . he fucks her . . . he comes on her ass/belly/face. "That's a wrap."

The real difference is that real sex boils down to the most purified form of love. When you take a pot of water and boil it, the vapors that rise are the most pure, clean parts. Lisa and I have vaporized sex. It's amazing how minimal sex on film is compared to what I share with my wife. Without doing drugs, Lisa becomes my big package of cocaine.

In fact, I filmed *Passion Chain* just after I met Lisa. We met in L.A. on December 5th and I flew back to New York to shoot *Passion Chain* on the 10th. Coincidentally, Lisa had to go to New York on business. Needless to say, I was thrilled.

But I wasn't thrilled being on the set. Damien Cashmere, the other male lead, wasn't much of an actor. He had trouble learning his lines, his performance bounced all over the place, and he screamed and yelled like a spoiled kid. Besides that, it was cold in New York and I had to travel on the subway. L.A. has a totally different atmosphere. You're picked up and driven to sets. It's the difference between being dry-cleaned and being hung on a clothesline. Compared to the West Coast's, New York's facilities are stifling. There's a dungeonlike feel.

It was hard for me to concentrate on this shoot. All I could think about was Lisa. We were supposed to meet after work, but the shoot was running later than I'd expected. Filming in someone's apartment, their kitchen was set up like a laboratory. In one scene, the phone rang unexpectedly. I couldn't let it keep ringing because it would blow the scene. When I answered the phone—it was Lisa.

Twenty-Seven
Love Story

Today, I'm living a very domestic life with Lisa and her two daughters (ages three and thirteen) in California's San Fernando Valley. Here I am, struggling to write a book about the past ten years of my life as a porno stud. I'm talking into a tape recorder about things like come shots, erections, and herpes, while the baby watches *The Wizard of Oz* in the next room. Yes, I know it's a paradox. The little one knows me only as Paul, the man who sings her songs from Abbott and Costello's *Jack and the Beanstalk* and reads her bedtime stories. When I drop her off at nursery school, she doesn't notice the way the other kids' parents stare when they recognize me from porno movies. I know they're silently wondering about the welfare of this child, this child who has no idea who "Jerry Butler" is.

Lisa's older daughter does have some vague idea. One day, when I was making cheese sandwiches for their lunch boxes, she asked me how I could be happy with this kind of life, taking care of them, making lunches. I had to laugh. I didn't know what to answer, but this is the kind of life I always craved.

Yesterday, Lisa asked me whether I liked California. I quickly said yes, but I wondered why she asked. I've always said that people from Brooklyn are the most insecure creatures on earth, even though they appear to be aggressive as hell. On the outside, they seem to be obnoxious survivalist warriors, but on the inside they're kings and queens in a plastic bubble. It's like being in porno. Within a little pond, you're a star, but take that talent and expose it to the world—to Hollywood—and you're nothing but a grain of sand.

Last night, I told Lisa that I was in love with Mary Hart on "Entertainment Tonight." My wife handled it pretty well and then went into the kitchen to finish cooking dinner. At the end of the show, when they cut to Mary Hart, her legs were crossed, her dress was way up on her thighs, and she was wearing dark stockings. I fell in love with her fucking legs! I couldn't help but pull my dick out and start playing with myself. Then I stopped because I realized that Lisa's kids might come into the room and dinner was almost ready. I went into the dining room and told Lisa that I was a piece of shit, but she didn't know why I'd said it.

I'm a slave to sex. In one way it creates an amazing spectrum of color, but the fire that starts in that brilliance can unexpectedly flare up and hurt people. I was feeling unsure of myself, so I wrote a letter to Lisa—because I've been so rough on her lately. I'll read it to you:

> My dearest Lisa,
>
> There I go again, stomping on the prettiest flower in the garden. I love you. I need you. Life would be minimal without you, is extravagant with you. I always have, will and must fight for the respect that this greedy, insensitive world takes away. I am

a bold, defiant swordsman who raises his sword in victory, but cries even when pain is inflicted beneficially.

I don't always like what I do, but I always stand behind it. I go beyond seven layers of skin. It's only when I stop to catch my breath that I realize something isn't right.

Today, Lisa and I went to the supermarket. Believe it or not, that's one of my favorite things to do. I don't go there to shop, like normal people do. Maybe the managers and checkers always look at me so strangely because I'm there almost as much as they are—two times a day at the very least, but sometimes it's more like six. I eat so many grapes in the fruit department that they should weigh me on the way out and charge me for the difference. I enjoy taking Lisa's little daughter in the cart, running down the aisle with her and then sliding to stop. Sometimes I take cans and chuck them into different aisles. Lisa says I'm not like a kid, more like a juvenile delinquent. I actually egged some poor guy in the dairy department. I took a Kareem Abdul-Jabbar hook shot and hit him on the shoulder. Blame it on the full moon!

At the supermarket the whole world is at your fingertips—food, cleanliness, warmth. You need money to buy those pleasures, but they're all there. Rich or poor, everyone goes to the supermarket. It's a microcosm of society, of the universe. Well, maybe not, but I still want to go back tonight. I'll find a reason to go . . . a quart of milk, a six-pack of Coke Classic. That's right, I'm a crazy, nutty, moron, dope, idiot, jerk. I'm out of control. I'm a nice guy.

You decide.

A few days ago, Lisa and I took some photographs together. During the photo session, I told Lisa to take off her blouse, but she wouldn't. I was so happy she said that, because I was just testing her. I didn't want the photographer to see her breasts. I'm very jealous and possessive. I wouldn't want anyone to touch my wife, yet it would turn me on if somebody did. Even though I've taken off my clothes and fucked in front of ten or more people, because Lisa was my wife, my privacy, I was feeling a little uncomfortable as the photographer (who was her long-time friend) was touching her and positioning her.

After what I've done for the past ten years, how could I be anything but insecure about Lisa's love? I'm so afraid she'll just pick up and leave one day and take up with another man who's a lot less complicated, a lot more under control, than I am.

Only now do I know the importance of privacy and secrecy, of being alone and making love with my wife behind a closed door in a darkened room. But Lisa is also an actress. There's always the possiblity she'll take a role that will require her to be fondled, kissed, touched. In many ways, that intimacy is just as hardcore as some of the things I've done. I've never been jealous before because I've never been so deeply in love before.

How did this love start? When? Where? It seems as though there's always been a Lisa. But there *was* a "before." Before was an unchanging cycle of cranking out movies and doing cocaine. One day a guy named John Keeler called. At first I thought he was a cop. "I only worked with you one time," he said, claiming to be a sound man. John explained that he wanted to use me for a film called *Traci's Big Trick.* It turned out that he was telling the truth.

At the time, Lisa was working for *High Times* with a lady

named Honey Weber. Since Lisa's own mom had died when she was pretty young, Honey was like a second mother to her. Lisa had been helping John with the script for *Traci's Big Trick* and now they were casting it. John couldn't get the actor he'd originally wanted for a particular role and asked Lisa what she thought about using me. Although Lisa had only seen me in *Late After Dark,* she told him it was a great idea.

The shoot was set to begin the next day, but luckily I was free. The location was a beautiful home in Topanga Canyon, the same place used in *Strange Bedfellows,* so I knew how to get there. When I arrived, I met the cast and crew. All of a sudden, I turned and saw the back of a woman. Rear view, she was sensational! Before I actually saw her face, I felt a tremendously strong vibration from her. I could feel her aura before I saw her. At first, I wondered—hoped—she might be a new girl in the business, but she wasn't. The woman turned out to be Lisa.

As an unofficial production assistant, one of Lisa's jobs was to see that things ran smoothly. She was talking to Allison, the woman who had written the script. They were having problems with Jacqueline Lorians, who was also appearing in the film. When I finally saw Lisa's face, my first thought was, "What's a *Vogue* magazine model doing on a porno set?" I trembled. I've met a lot of beautiful women, but I was totally enamored by Lisa.

We exchanged a few words. Lisa stressed the fact that she *wasn't* a porno actress. She was only there with the production. Furthermore, she was a S.A.G. member and proceeded to rattle off all the movies and TV work she'd done. This was her first time on a porno set. I was a little upset, not at her, but because she felt she had to prove herself. Lisa didn't have to hold a resume in front of her face to prove to me that she was a lady.

The fact that I wouldn't be working with her didn't discourage me. I knew that even if I never made love to her, even if I never saw her again, I was glad just to know such a beautiful person. Allison later told us she'd never forget the looks on both of our faces when we first saw each other. She claimed that Lisa looked as if she were walking two feet above the ground.

Just to get close to her, I pretended I needed Lisa's help learning my lines. When we went over the script, I could see she was shaken—and that amused me. After all, we had just met and were reciting pornographic lines to each other. I felt as though we were doing a cerebral sex scene. I ravaged Lisa with a porno script. Little did she know that I was spiritually and emotionally surrounding her with my desire to fill my emptiness and loneliness with love.

There was no need for Lisa to come back the next day. The only reason she did was because I was there. I had no sex scenes that first day, but on the second day of the shoot, I had to work with Jacqueline. During the scene, Lisa was sitting on the side, holding a script. She had kicked off her shoes and I could see her beautiful polished red toenails through her dark stockings. Lisa didn't know it then, but she was "fluffing" me without even touching me.

The early part of my sex scene with Jacqueline didn't go smoothly because I was uptight knowing that Lisa was in the room. How could I be a sexual animal when the woman I really wanted was watching me? But I had a job and I had to do it well. My emotions were magnified because of Lisa. As I made love to Jacqueline, I kept glancing over at Lisa. She was trying to look very cool about it, but I knew she was aroused. I couldn't wait to come so I could be with Lisa, just to talk to her again.

After I showered, Lisa was still there. I sat on a floor mat beside her. Props were set up for a pretty Oriental scene. I was wearing a red satin robe and had doused myself with Lagerfeld cologne. For the rest of her life, when Lisa smells Lagerfeld, she says it will remind her of me. I handed Lisa a love letter. I'm sure she still has it tucked away somewhere.

As we walked to the door to drive to the next location, I spun Lisa around and kissed her. Lisa was still married at the time, but very unhappily. Her husband had moved out two or three times. The only reason they hadn't divorced was because of their baby and because their financial situation was so bad. Lisa knew her marriage was over, but she still wasn't prepared for what she found in me.

The first afternoon we moved to the new Malibu location, the attraction between us was so intense that everyone on the set felt what was going on. Our energy overshadowed the entire shoot. I had a sex scene with Melissa Melendez and Jacqueline, but Lisa couldn't bear to watch it. She went down into the living room. A few minutes later, Allison came down to her and asked if there was any baby oil.

"Jerry is having a tough time," Allison told her. "He's in love. He does not want to be fucking those girls."

Instead of going straight home that night, we met at a place called Twain's on Ventura Boulevard. It turned out that Lisa and I lived only a few minutes away from each other. It was amazing that we hadn't met before. We both went to Stanley's and all the same restaurants. Early morning at Twain's, we ordered breakfast, but neither of us could eat.

The next day (the last day of the shoot), our emotions remained intense. Finally, I told Lisa I thought we should cool it, because even though we'd just met, I felt that the relationship was more than we could handle. But I couldn't keep to my word. I followed her onto the balcony and told her, "If I die right now, my life will be complete because of meeting you." But I had to see her away from a porno set.

The following day, Lisa came to my apartment. When she walked in, I could see she was shocked when she saw all of my toys and stuffed animals. I guess she didn't expect to find a little boy's room. We went out to dinner, talked, and kissed. Lisa was going to New York on business in a few days. I turned down work in California and took the role in *Passion Chain* only because I knew I could see her in New York.

After the shoot, Lisa and I met and I gave her the little love braclet I had bought. We agreed to spend the night at her girlfriend Erin's place. Not for sex, but just to hold each other. We had a vast need to communicate and really know each other's feelings. Sex wasn't important, but we just wanted to spend some quiet time together. Lisa was staying with friends in the Village, and she couldn't bring me there. At the last minute, we couldn't stay at Erin's either. We had no choice but to go to a sleazy hotel called the Iroquois. Walking down the street, Lisa told me she loved me—but I couldn't accept it . . . I wanted to be the one to tell her first.

At the Iroquois, we made love. Awkwardly, tenderly, as if it were the first time for both of us. In a sense, it was.

Twenty-Eight

Raw Talent Retrospective

You might consider why I decided to call this book *Raw Talent.* There are many reasons, but one of the strongest is that *Raw Talent* is the name of a movie that is closest to my heart. In many ways, it's the story of my life. The character Eddie Czeropski is me. He has a violent temper. He wants to be a legitimate actor. He is harassed by gay men. He stumbles into porno almost by mistake and finds himself trapped. His life isn't turning out the way he had planned. And Eddie is desperately searching for love.

Raw Talent was conceived when Joyce Snyder treated me to Chinese food and explained that she wanted to write a movie about me. I told her all about my days of doing legit theater in the Village and doing porno at the same time. She found it fascinating. Joyce patterned the *Raw Talent* script after my life. Ironically—or fittingly—she underpaid me to play the part.

A few days before we were ready to start shooting, Joyce

had me come up to her apartment to rehearse. The Rangers were playing the Montreal Canadiens for the Stanley Cup, but I still went to Joyce's to run lines. I rushed there . . . and waited. My costar, Lisa DeLeeuw, was busy with her wardrobe. Sitting there waiting for her to finish, I was pretty aggravated that I was missing the Rangers game. Instead, I was watching a fat redhead squeeze in and out of clothes. There was nothing else to do, so I wandered into Joyce's bedroom and started flipping TV channels. I settled back to watch the greatest wrestling match ever—Sergeant Slaughter against the Iron Sheik. With his metal-toed boots, the Sheik was kicking the shit out of the Sergeant. All of a sudden, the Sergeant got up, took off one of the Sheik's boots, and started cracking him over the head. Then Joyce called, "Jerry, we're ready for you."

"Fuck you," I yelled. "I waited here four hours, and I want to watch the Sheik get his ass kicked."

I was so riled up and now they wanted me to rehearse with a pudgy redhead. Lisa started to complain. I told her if she didn't shut up, I'd give her a body slam. Two seconds later, I heard, "Okay, let's take a ten-minute break."

Sergeant Slaughter plastered the Iron Sheik. I saluted him one more time and said, "Excuse me, but I've got to go shoot a porno movie."

The script far surpassed anything I had ever done before. I knew the significance of what it represented both to me personally and to the adult-film industry. Usually when I took a part, I proclaimed it and made it mine. *Raw Talent* proclaimed me the minute I held the script in my hands.

Driving into Manhattan, I saw a beautiful hooker on 43rd Street and 8th Avenue. I didn't even know who she was, but

I was smitten. At rehearsal I asked Joyce if she'd do something special for me. "I'll do anything you want," she said. I told her I wanted that hooker.

The day before the shoot, Joyce and I drove up and down 8th Avenue in my white Beetle, looking for the hooker, but she was nowhere in sight. Suddenly, I spotted her getting into a cab. Joyce jumped out of the Volkswagen, ran up to the cab, and slid into the back seat with her. A second later, Joyce leapt out, climbed back into the Beetle with me, and told me to get going, *fast!* I noticed a police car, but still swung the car onto 9th Avenue at top speed. Sirens were blasting all around us. Five cop cars surrounded us and screeched to a halt. The cab followed us, too. It turned out that the cab driver was an undercover cop and Joyce had innocently walked into a trap set up to nab the hooker's pimp.

Whatever a porno movie producer looks like, Joyce definitely didn't fit the description. With her polite manner and her cute Southern accent, she looked more like the kind of a lady you'd see on a veranda sipping a mint julep. When Joyce had stepped into the cab, she told the girl, "Excuse me, but my friend is terribly in love with you." Still, to the cops, Joyce appeared to be soliciting, which she was. What complicated things even further was the fact that my car was filled with all sorts of things for the shoot, scripts and all. If the police discovered *any* of it, we'd be in big trouble. But Joyce had balls. Without batting an eye, she told the cops that she was a photographer and was shooting layouts for a men's magazine. I backed up the story.

"I saw this beautiful woman and wanted to do a layout with her," I told him. We were almost safe, but I had to carry it a step further. I couldn't help adding, "And one more thing, I want her to have my baby."

Instead of taking us in, the cops believed our crazy story and burst out laughing at my remark. We could have been nailed, but they let us go.

The next morning, without the hooker, we started the *Raw Talent* shoot. The opening scene is perhaps the most remarkable opening in the history of porno. It starts with an extreme close-up of my face. I'm crying hysterically. The blank cosmos seems to be my only audience. I appear on the verge of total despair. The camera then pulls back to reveal I'm auditioning for an acting role. Since nobody is paying any attention to me, I pull out my dick and start jerking off. When a woman (Joyce, in a bit part) finally realizes what I'm doing, two guys throw me off the stage and out into a pile of garbage on the street. That starts Eddie's odyssey.

You might wonder what prompted me to cry like that in the first scene. I started thinking about my mom, and I really broke down. With that extreme, jarring close-up, you don't know what's going on at first—and then you meet Eddie. Like me, he means to do well, but he always fucks up. Like me, the casting directors don't give two shits about what Eddie's putting his heart into. To get back at them, Eddie plays with himself and tries to prove the point through a very vulgar act. I've done things like that many times, as you are well aware, now that you know me.

Eddie is searching. He searches throughout the entire movie for something to believe in. Because he's an actor, he can only hope someone else will believe in him. But other people always make the final decisions. He has no power, no control. But Eddie's determination carries through the entire movie. He never stops thinking he's going to make it. He tries to smile through the rain, tries to peek over the clouds and find the sunshine. In real life, I was trying to do the same thing.

The plot and characters of *Raw Talent* mirrored my own life. In *Raw Talent* my best friend is played by Joey Silvera. He tries to help me, comfort me, console me. In real life, my best friend was Vinnie. He tried to help me, console me, and comfort me. In the movie, Joey told me to get involved in porno because it was a good way of making money. Vinnie always told me the same thing.

It was so important to me that this movie be done right. I couldn't imagine *anyone* else as Eddie. The movie ended as I ended: stuck doing porno. Carolyn King (Lisa DeLeeuw) always reminds Eddie that since he's done porno, he'll never be able to do anything legit. Eddie has to kiss her ass, and he finally lashes out and attacks her in an uncommonly vicious scene. That part didn't happen in real life, though. In real life, I was Carolyn, too. *I* put those limitations on myself. *I* was the one who told myself I couldn't do anything else because I'd done porno.

On the last day of the shoot, the crew was setting up a scene in a restaurant. I was feeling forlorn—something I cared about would soon be coming to an end. Wearing Eddie's Army jacket, I was sitting on the steps outside, drinking a cup of coffee. It was a Friday afternoon and the 9 to 5 people were going home. Two well-dressed couples were talking excitedly about their plans for the coming weekend. They stopped and stared at me for a moment, sure I was a bum or some lost soul. All of a sudden, the truck pulled up with the movie equipment.

Guys were jumping off the truck, taking out these big floodlights. Larry Revene, the director, talked to me about a scene with a camera slung over his shoulder. In a matter of a second, those four people changed their attitudes about me, because now I appeared to be someone important. After Larry went inside, one guy came up to me and asked if I were an actor. Loud and clear, I told him, "What difference does it make? Two seconds ago, you looked at me as if I were some kind of animal. As soon as you see a camera, suddenly I'm someone important." They just scadaddled away to their weekend in the suburbs. I felt great, because it was something Eddie would have done. I sauntered inside, ready for my last scene. I had to fuck a turkey carcass.

The movie done, I felt relieved, but I also felt despair. There's an absence, an emptiness when something important finishes. There's *panic:* What are you going to do next? Kind of like the panic of finishing this book.

But this book will never be over. I don't want to walk out of Cathy Tavel's place and think that's it. Every time I leave, it's a new beginning. When something you put your heart into ends, you have a fearful responsibility for your life again. You look forward to that next job, the next time the phone rings.

Well, the phone did ring, many times, after *Raw Talent.* I just finished watching *Raw Talent II.* It's probably the last movie I did that I really felt good about. It picked up where the first one left off. Eddie finds love, but he doesn't know what to do with it.

I feel dirty right now. Dirty compared to a woman who has watched what I've done. Dirty compared to a woman who has two children. I thought I could do porno forever, but then I met Lisa.

This damn book is the only thing that's keeping me afloat right now. I never thought writing it was going to be easy, but it's a lot more painful than I had ever imagined. My parents probably won't understand that I still love them despite everything I've said. I'm afraid they'll disown me. I'm afraid Lisa will leave me. And then what will I have?

After the videotape ran out, I realized that this book is a continuation of that film. It shows what happens before and after, the things they don't show in the movie. *Raw Talent* showed my enthusiasm. *Raw Talent II* showed my reality. And a few days ago, Joyce Snyder offered me the option of making *Raw Talent III*.

Making *Raw Talent III* might mean my losing Lisa. I'm very reluctant to talk about Joyce's offer with Lisa because I know she'd be really upset, insulted. Recently, we've been arguing a lot about my wanting to do more porno movies. It's difficult for me to sever myself from what I've done for the past ten years.

But, like I said before, I'm *married* now. I finally sold the little apartment I had in Los Angeles, the one filled with toys and other childish things. When my head's on straight, I know that I want to be living right here with Lisa and her kids. But there's also a frightened part of me, because something's just not right between Lisa and me—something I just can't talk about.

Watching *Raw Talent II*, I can't help but recall certain things. I never realized how much I miss Buck Adams. I miss laughing and joking around on sets. I miss creating something. Though it was only porno, I really miss acting. I'd like to see what I could do in a legitimate acting career. I know that I'm a good actor. I take chances: I'm serious. And I had the opportunity to prove it in *Raw Talent*.

Lisa watched *Raw Talent 2* with me. She was fine during the first few sex scenes, but when it came to the part where I'm cornered into having sex with a female casting agent, she became upset. It was too close to home, I guess. Here was my character, Eddie, who didn't really want to do fuck-films but was being suffocated by them. Lisa really recognized the Eddie in me. The scene reflected all the emotions I was feeling about the business. It went from A to Z, then back to B. Lisa appreciated my talent as an actor, but accepted the sex only because she had to. At the same time, she thought, "Damn it! He's much too talented to have ever done all of this." But I *did* do it. I'm the man she loves and that's just the way it is. I'm sure Lisa wishes it were different. But if it were different, I'm sure you would not be reading this right now.

A few nights ago, Lisa prepared a quiet candlelit dinner. It was just the two of us and her grandmother. Here's a woman from the old school, who's almost eighty years old. When she looks at me, I think she sees a little bit of what Lisa sees. She's amused by me. I told Lisa's grandmother all about the book. I explained that I knew I was going to alienate a lot of people and offend a lot of friends, but I didn't want to come out looking like an angel. I was also going to offend myself, but for the last time.

It's late at night.

Lisa and the girls are sleeping. Maybe I'll watch *Raw Talent* once more and cry my eyes out. But right now, I'm sitting in the kitchen eating some cookies and wondering whom I should dedicate this book to. Then I realized that I wanted to dedicate it to Lisa. Without her, I never would have lasted.

More than anything else in this world, I want to have a child with Lisa. With her help, I've given birth to this book. Now I want to give Lisa something in return.

An Epilogue

by Lisa Loring Siederman

After reading Paul's often shocking book, Bob Rimmer thought it would be appropriate for me to write this epilogue, to reveal emotions and insights from a woman's point of view. But I am not just any woman. I am Jerry Butler's wife, and I hope I can express the true depth of my feelings for this man.

Jerry came into my life when I was nearing the end of a marriage that had started out with hope and joy, as most marriages do. This was not my first failed marriage, either. I had been married at age fifteen, but that was doomed from the beginning.

At the end of my second marriage, I was close to twenty-nine and I had two children—ages thirteen and three. If I ever married again, I promised myself, it would *not* be for love alone. Still, family and love remained on top of my list of what's essential to life. Then came the experience of meeting, loving, and dealing with a man and a situation I could never have imagined.

As he has written, the magnetism between Paul and me

was incredible when we met. I was intrigued and enchanted by his need to reveal himself, by his search for love—the same kind of love he wanted to give back. It wasn't at all about sex at first—it was about two people with an overwhelming need for each other and for communication and understanding in a world that lacked both. Well, enough said. We found what we were looking for in each other and are still discovering it every day.

In the beginning, there were many times when I said to myself, "Get the hell out!" But then I realized that I was running away from Paul only because I was afraid of what other people would think. My own conscience and my feelings for Paul kept pulling me back to reality. And so did Paul, because he's an extremely powerful individual. His ability and capacity to understand and give was incredible.

Our relationship was battered by many difficulties. Even as our love grew, there was always the question in the back of my mind, "Could we make it? Was it right?" I haven't spoken to my father for almost two years, because when I told him that Paul and I were dating, he insisted I stop seeing him. My dad swore that being associated with Paul would ruin my own acting career. I wonder how he feels now that we're married.

People keep asking me, "What are you doing with him?" How can I explain the richness of love within a man who has had sex on film with scores of women? I have had to fight feelings I had about traditional morality and decency. By those measures, Paul was worthless, perhaps evil. Still, I couldn't deny the good, kind, and generous person Paul was or how his talent always shone above the sleaze. Our love was a double-edged sword.

Recently we have had to deal with the problem of my oldest girl being upset when her best male friend told her he'd seen Paul in a film. Although her friend was impressed, she felt embarrassed. Trying to console her, Paul and I felt terrible. Look at what she was going through because of us! I was sure of the love I felt for Paul, but I still didn't know whether I would marry this man.

People who avidly watched adult films weren't judgmental. Many of Paul's fans, who seemed aware of his true qualities—his humor, wit, and acting talent—made the decision to marry easier for me. Through their eyes, he wasn't just another guy fucking on film; he was different, special. They had seen a glimmer of what I have come to know.

As my three-year-old became better acquainted with him, Paul would tell her stories and sing a couple of songs for her at bedtime. Was this the same man who screwed Ginger Lynn on the hood of a red Porsche? You'd never believe it. The thrill of my life was watching Paul get back on the ice at Abe Stark Rink in Brooklyn. With a wide smile on his face, he gracefully wove in and out of the other skaters, giving pointers to some of the young hockey players. *This* was the man I loved. Then someone swooped up behind him and broke the mood: "You're Jerry Butler," he said. But at that moment, Paul wasn't.

More than anything, Paul has wanted to write this book, to bare his soul, to cleanse himself, to come to terms with his life. And I made my decision to give him support in achieving this goal, to publicly reveal myself and stand by my man, no matter how it might affect my acting career. (The name "Lisa Loring" may not be a household word, but my face *is* known to many. As a child, I played "Little Wednesday" on "The Addams Family" for two years. I also played "Cricket" for four years on "As the World Turns.") I don't care what small-minded people might think of my marriage. If they don't want to hire me because of whom I chose to love, that's fine with me.

When we met Cathy Tavel and began working on Paul's tapes, my faith in Paul and my love for his total honesty grew even stronger. I was amazed at what I was hearing, even if I was also occasionally jealous. But that jealously prodded me into asking deeper questions, helping me to more fully carry out the job I committed myself to do.

The roughest part of the project was actually watching Paul's films. At that point, I'd seen only one or two and generally fast-forwarded through the sex scenes. But for the sake of the book, Paul needed to view them, and I wanted to be by his side. It wasn't all rough, though. I was really looking forward to seeing him in critically acclaimed films like Cecil Howard's *Star Angel* and Chuck Vincent's *In Love.* They didn't disappoint. Films like those made up for the poorer quality "quickies." Paul's talent, however, was clear in all of them.

At first, I couldn't watch the sex scenes. Parts of *She Comes In Colors* and *10½ Weeks* made me gasp. Knowing that people would be viewing the tapes made *me* feel naked, too. Anyone who saw us on the street or in the supermarket together could more or less picture what Paul did with me. But not really! No one can imagine the joy of our lovemaking. That intensity far surpasses anything you've seen on video or film.

I finally came to the conclusion that it doesn't really matter what anyone thinks about him or about us. The love, sensitivity, compassion, intelligence, and understanding of life that Paul's achieved is what is truly important and meaningful in a human being. And I have never found love so fully before.

After all has been said and done, "Jerry Butler," my Paulie, is a beautiful man and one hell of a person.

Afterthought

New Beginning

I would be lying to you if I didn't add this part to the book. In April of 1988 I told Lisa I had a still-photo shoot in New York. I lied. I really came East to do *Raw Talent 3*. I couldn't bear the thought of someone else taking my role. I know, it was a terrible thing to do. I hated myself for doing it, but I did it anyway.

On the last day of the shot, a crew member told Lisa's best friend the truth, and she quickly called Lisa in California. My wife was devastated. I couldn't explain why I had to do the movie. I really didn't even know the reason myself. *Raw Talent 3* almost destroyed our marriage, but Lisa decided to give me another chance.

You see, it has been very easy for me to be "Jerry Butler." Now I have to learn how to be Paul Siederman.

Paul Siederman
December 1988

Filmography

Most adult film stars don't keep a record of the films or videos in which they have appeared. In many cases, they don't even know the final *names* of a particular film or tape, especially if they weren't the featured performer. There are even cases where the director himself doesn't know the final name of his film, especially if it's a "one-day wonder" without much story line or even a script. Jerry Butler remembers most of the films he was featured in: But in order to compile a reasonably complete filmography, Catherine Tavel pieced together the following list using my *X-Rated Video Tape Guide,* Jim Holliday's *Only the Best,* and various adult film publications, like *Adam Film World* and *Adult Video News.* Information regarding the cast, release dates, and storylines are sometimes incomplete. We hope that some day someone with a computer will produce a "cast index directory," as well as a directory of all the adult films ever produced. The Kinsey Institute of Sex Research is attempting this with its vast collection of adult films, but its directory is far from complete.

The following filmography of Jerry's films and videos gives you the dates of their release (as closely as they can be established, because many directors, like Cecil Howard of Command

Video, release films as long as four years after they've been shot) and the names of Jerry's female costars. Wherever possible, Cathy also supplied a word or two explaining Jerry's role.

If you'd like more detailed information on particular films in which Jerry has appeared, I have reviewed practically all of them in much more detail in *The X-Rated Video Tape Guide,* published by Crown Publishers (New York). The guide has 1350 reviews and is available in some bookstores as well as by mail from Publishers Central Bureau, 1 Champion Avenue, Avenel, New Jersey 07001-2301. An 1989 update, with an additional 750 reviews (and 300 more to come), was published by Sundance Associates, 910 Dexter Street, Denver, Colorado 80222. Most of the films and videos in which Jerry has appeared are available, if not in your local video store, by mail-order from the actual producer/distributors.

—Robert Rimmer

Ali Boobie and the 40 D's (1988) With Keisha, who supplies the impressive measurements.

Amberella (1985) Plays a thoroughly mad scientist with Amber Lynn.

Amber's Desires (1985) With Amber Lynn, Diva Wolf, and Mai Lin.

The Amorous Adventures of Janette Littledove (1988) Produced and directed by Buck Adams, Jerry takes part in a scorching threesome with Kirian Minelli and Laurel Canyon and later on tumbles with the title lady.

Angel Buns (1980) One of his earlier films and the very first time he worked with many-time costar Veronica Hart.

Angel Gets Even (1988) With Angel Kelly.

Animal in Me (1985) Plays a doctor, as in M.D., and is featured with Karen Summer and Colleen Brennan.

Asses to Asses, Lust to Lust (1988) Guess what this one's about!

Baby Face 2 (1987) As Careena Collins's intended in this Alex deRenzy romp. The final orgy scene is legendary.

Babylon Pink 2 (1988) As Robert Bullock's campaign manager, Jerry manages to get into the panties of Ona Zee, Shanna McCullough, and Sharon Kane.

Babylon Pink 3 (1988) More of the same with much of the above cast.

Backdoor Lust (1988) A compilation tape of anal scenes—"safe-sex" for the viewer only.

Bad Girls III (1985) Jerry said that in drag he looked like his mother. Costarring were Traci Lords, Rachel Ashley, and Tina Marie.

Bad Girls IV (1986) With Laurie Smith and Rachel Ashley.

Beauty and the Beast (1988) Participates in a threesome with Nikki Knights and newcomer Alicia Monet in this Brothers Grimm takeoff.

Best Little Whorehouse in San Francisco (1984) Plays a "john" in a brothel threesome with two of Jerry's least-favorite ladies, Taija Rae and Lois Ayres (a.k.a. Sondra Stillman).

Beverly Hills Cox (1986) This has the breathtaking scene with Ginger Lynn and a sexy red Porsche.

Beverly Hills Exposed (1985) With costars Colleen Brennan, Bunny Bleu, and Mindy Rae.

Blazing Mattresses (1986) Second in the *Debbie Duz Dishes* series, Jerry reprises his role as Kirby the Wonder Vac salesman (a.k.a. Attachment #28). With Nina Hartley.

Blue Jeans (1983) You'll hardly recognize Jerry as Brooke Bennett's old boyfriend, a shy Preppie in tortoiseshell glasses.

Bootsie (1985) In drag again, with Amber Lynn and Taija Rae, in this *Tootsie* takeoff.

Bordello, House of the Rising Sun (1985) With Norris O'Neal, Taija Rae, and Amber Lynn.

Born to Run (1986) Plays a porno actor tenderly breaking

Careena Collins into the biz.

The Boss (1987) Costars Angel Kelly and Dana Dylan and features an especially hot scene with Krista Lane, who seems to know all his sensitive spots.

Both Ends Burning (1987) Unhappily married to Sharon Mitchell, he manages to get consolation from Amber Lynn and Bionca.

The Bottom Line (1986) Sounds like another backdoor bonanza.

The Brat (1986) The first in *The Brat* series. In later videos he is replaced by Tom Byron as Jamie Summers's husband. Note the threesome with Brittany Stryker and Siobhan Hunter. Jerry claimed he had trouble, but it earned them an XRCO (X-Rated Film Critics Organization) nomination for "Best Sex Scene of the Year."

Broadway Fanny Rose (1987) A desktop dalliance with stripper Lorrie Lovett, complete with black pasties.

Burlexxx (1984) In a burlesque-style schoolroom skit with "dunce" Rene Summers.

Can't Get Enough (1985) Plays horny Karen Summer's husband.

Cat Alley (1986) Flashbacks of a deceased businessman, with Candie Evens and Krista Lane.

Cheat American Style (1988) A non-sex role as a scared groom-to-be.

Confessions of a Middle-Aged Nympho (1986) With "middle-aged nympho" Charlie Latour.

Cummin' Alive (1984) Fun in the bathroom with Colleen Brennan.

Dangerous When Wet (1987) Another unhappy husband, this time married to Bionca. Pal Buck Adams and his wife Janette Littledove costar.

"Death of a Porn Queen" (1987) Segment on PBS television show "Frontline," which first aired in June 1987. Jerry comments on the suicide of Shauna Grant.

Debbie, Class of '88 (1988) Features a cut from *Debbie Goes* *to College,* with Barbara Dare and Jon Martino.

Debbie Does Dallas III (1985) With Kristara Barrington and Bambi Woods.

Debbie Duz Dishes (1986) Jerry introduces the role of Kirby, salesman of the Wonder Vac, a vacuum cleaner/sexual aid with twenty-seven different attachments, not including his own. With willing customer Nina Hartley.

Debbie Duz Dishes III (1987) Appears in outtakes from the previous "Debbie" film, *Blazing Mattresses.* Curiously, Joey Silvera takes over the role of Kirby.

Debbie Goes to College (1986) With Lois Ayres, Barbara Dare, and Little Oral Annie.

The Debutante (1986) Strained moments with Ali Moore in a red Ferrari.

Delicious (1981) Billed as "Arthur West," Jerry has a scorcher with Nicole Scent.

Deranged (1987) Plays Jane Hamilton's (a.k.a. Veronica Hart) husband-turned-zombie in this R-rated psychological thriller.

Despicable Dames (1987) Unhappily married to Siobhan Hunter (again). Also features an anal encounter with Buffy Davis and a threesome with a trisexual—a pretty Latin lady with a penis.

Dial-A-Dick (1985) As a hard-up guy whom Krista Lane, Stacey Donovan, and Sandy Summers do their best to soften. Jerry cracks up costar Steve Drake with his ad libs.

Dick of Death (1985) Actress/director Sharon Mitchell's effort, with Jerry playing secret agent James Blonde. With Marita Ekberg and Chelsea Blake.

Dirty Dreams (1986) Plays a judge of a write-in fantasy contest with co-judge Tracey Adams. Their initial mutual dislike evolves into a steamy encounter.

Divorce Court Exposé (1987) Seeking a divorce from Siobhan Hunter, Jerry makes an off-the-cuff reference to playing hockey as a kid. Also with Candie Evens.

Doctor Ginger (a.k.a. Pretty As You Feel) (1986) Munching on a carrot in a Bugs Bunny imitation, Jerry discovers Ginger Lynn and friend are just what the doctor ordered.

Doctor Lust (1986) With Vanessa Del Rio, Barbara Dare, and Lili Marlene.

Doctor Strange Sex (1985) Would you believe a nuclear physicist? Costarring Gina Carrera and Diva Wolf.

Don't Get Them Wet (1987) Just your average Joe presented with tattooed Viper as a birthday present.

Dynamic Vices (1986) Cops Alex Greco and Nina Hartley make it, uh, "hard" on Jerry as they try to (ahem) pull "vital information" out of him.

Electric Wet Dreams (1985) A hot sex scene with Samantha Fox and another woman who gets thrown out of the action by the director.

Erotic Zones #2 (1985) Plays a scriptwriter whose character (Tish Ambrose) comes to life.

Evils of the Night (1985) As a teen-zombie in a general-release film, which stars the likes of Tina Louise, Julie Newmar, and John Carradine.

Exposure (1988) As Studs Mackenzie, porn actor, he works with Taija Rae and Nina Hartley.

Famous Ta Tas Phase II (1986) An Essex compilation tape.

Femme (1984) Plays a photographer in actress Candida Royalle's directorial debut. Features a rare internal ejaculation with Rhonda Jo Petty.

The First of April (1988) As April West's confused hubby, Jerry gently breaks April into the jizz biz and has notable beauty-shop encounter with Stephanie Rage and her outrageous new hooters.

First Time at Cherry High (1984) With Tanya Lawson and Rene Summers.

Flashpants (1984) Plays a horny high school student in this takeoff of *Flashdance.* With Tanya Lawson.

The Four-X Feeling (1986) As himself. See "dueling egos" in the scenes with old-pro John Leslie. Also, a long, sweaty encounter with Amber Lynn.

Getting L.A.'D (1986) Plays a nutty guy Kristara Barrington picks up in a hotel lobby.

Getting Lucky (1985) Another high school student (at age twenty-six). With Janey Robbins and various female unknowns.

The Ginger Effect (1985) Dashes off with Cara Lott at a seance to show her his crystal balls.

Ginger Lynn's Hawaiian Scrapbook (1987) No evidence of Jerry and Ginger's bittersweet affair in this compilation tape of scenes from various Svetlana "Hawaii" flicks.

Girls on "F" Street (1986) As a punked-out and painted rock musician, he makes beautiful music with Amber Lynn and Pattie Petite.

Girl Toys (1986) With Nikki Randall, Erica Boyer, and Nina Hartley.

Glitter (1983) Plays a shy ad exec. Costars with Shauna Grant, Joanna Storm, and Kelly Nichols.

Good Enough to Eat (1988) As a crazy caretaker. With Ona Zee and German-bombshell Angela Baron's newly refurbished breasts.

Good Evening, Vietnam (1988) As a sensitive vet, with Alicia Monet.

Great Sexpectations (1984) A young stud trying to break into the business, Jerry proves his mettle with a porno producer's wife (Honey Wilder) as hubby R. Bolla looks on.

Honeymoon Harlots (1986) Plays a Jerry Lewis-type nerd—in a bow tie—newly married to randy Jessica Wylde.

Hostage Girls (1984) With members of the chain gang Danielle and Taija Rae.

Hotel California (1987) Jerry checks into Suite 69 to make a baby with wife Jamie Summers.

Hot Gun (1987) As a Marine pilot, he does some acrobatic flying with Sheena Horne in the front seat of a car.

Hot Nights and Hard Bodies (1986) With Carol Titian, Shanna McCullough, and Gina Carrera.

Hyapatia Lee's "Sexy" (1986) An encounter with Dr. Hyapatia's leg.

In and Out of Africa (1987) With Nina Hartley and Jeannie Pepper.

In and Out of Beverly Hills (1986) Plays a psychiatrist trying to cure Candie Evens's erotic dreams. Instead, he gives her a few new ones.

Initiation of Cynthia (1985) Costars with Colleen Brennan and Sharon Kane.

In Love (1983) The Chuck Vincent high-budget ($750,000) soap opera masterpiece. Costars with Kelly Nichols, Joanna Storm, Samantha Fox, Veronica Hart, and Sue Nero. Jerry's performance won him *Hustler's* Best Actor Award.

Inner Blues (1987) Acclaimed performance as a cocaine-addicted guitarist. With Taija Rae and Tami Lee Curtis.

Irresistible II (1986) Another carnal car consummation, this time with Janette Littledove in a 1950s convertible.

I Want to Be a Bad Girl (1986) An Anthony Spinelli venture with Colleen Brennan and Porsche Lynn. Ms. Lynn's adult film debut.

Jack & Jill 2 (1984) Simulated sex with Samantha Fox in this humorous look at spouse-swapping. The masturbation scene is a scorcher.

Jack Hammer (1987) As the he/she owner of an adult bookstore, Jerry's performance won him nominations for XRCO's "Best Supporting Actor" and "Best Group Scene" awards. With newcomer Sunny Daye.

Joanna Storm on Fire (1986) Married to the smoldering Miss Storm in this one, and trying to make it work.

Karate Girls (1986) A real connoisseur will be able to tell it's Jerry in the first scene with Danielle even *before* his mask comes off!

Kinky Business (1984) With the help of Laurie Smith, he turns his parents' mansion into a brothel in this *Risky Business* takeoff.

Ladies' Room (1987) A toot of cocaine with two ladies in a trademark Henri Pachard bathroom threesome.

Lady Lust (1983) Costars Edy Williams, Kimberly Carson, and Sharon Mitchell.

Late After Dark (1985) Another "troubled husband" role. With Tracey Adams.

Legacy of Lust (1985) With Little Oral Annie and Tamara Longley.

Little American Maid (1985) An al fresco backrub from Diedre Hopkins leads to much more. But he never takes off his sneakers!

A Little Bit of Hanky Panky (1983) That hot Ginger Lynn "rape scene" on the beach. Although he spouts all sorts of sexual promises/threats, he doesn't do half of them.

Little Darlings (1981) An early film with Lysa Thatcher and Lori Palmer.

Living in a Wet Dream (1988) Bring your raincoats!

The Long Ranger (1987) Features an extended doggie-style encounter with Sheri St. Claire. Cowboy Jerry comes complete with ten gallon hat. *Yee-haw!*

Looking for Mr. Goodsex (1985) With Joanna Storm, Taija Rae, Amber Lynn, and Tess Ferre.

Lover's Lane (1986) With Barbara Dare and Melissa Melendez in a torrid threesome.

Lucky Charm (1986) This compilation tape includes a scene from *Cat Alley.*

Lucky in Love II (1986) Sequel to *Sex Life of a Nerd.*

Lust at Sea (1986) On a sex cruise, Jerry explores Penny Morgan's posterior.

Lust in Space II (a.k.a. Whore of the Worlds) (1985) You'll have to try hard to spot him in the orgy scene toward the end of this sci-fi sexvid.

Lust Tango in Paris (1987) With sweet Honey Wilder and

Jeanna Fine.

Mad About You (1987) Playing a transvestite named Ralph/Rita turned head nurse, Jerry beds down with Porsche Lynn while he wears high heels.

Manhattan Mistress (1980) Listed under his real name in the credits, Jerry costars with Juliet Anderson, Erica Boyer, and Merle Michaels.

Mardi Gras (1986) Airline pilot Jerry takes Barbara Dare and Melissa Melendez for a ride.

Marilyn Chambers' Private Fantasies #5 (1985) Miss C., Traci Lords, and Tantala costar.

Marilyn Chambers' Private Fantasies #6 (1985) In "The Picnic" segment, there's Jerry's uneventful one-time match with Marilyn on top of a table.

Material Girl (1985) Plays a wealthy movie producer tussling with Jane Tussle.

Momma's Boy (1984) In this one, you'll see Jerry's sensitive portrayal of an autistic boy. Costars Sheri St. Claire, Tantala, and Shannon.

Moonlusting (1987) As private detective David Madison, Jerry prods the private parts of Siobhan Hunter, Tracey Adams, and Taija Rae in this wild takeoff of TV's "Moonlighting."

Moonlusting 2 (1988) Not as good as the original but worth seeing for his bathtub romp with Jeanna Fine. Also starring Rachel Ryan (a.k.a. Penny Morgan).

More Than a Handful (1988) With mountainous misses like Honey Wilder and Candy Samples.

"The Morton Downey, Jr., Show" (1988) Originally aired in September 1988. As a "male sex addict," Jerry speaks about his career and AIDS, actually silencing "the mouth that roared."

My Wife Is a Callgirl (1988) But it helps pay the rent. With Faryn Heights and Nikki Pink.

Naked Scents (1985) Plays a tennis pro and takes on Tish Ambrose, Taija Rae, and Sharon Kane in back-to-back marathon sessions.

Night Hunger (1983) On Bob Rimmer's "Top 50" list. Jerry plays a weary traveler entertained by a bartender's sexy stories.

No One to Love (1987) Complete with a screamer from Ona Zee and a threesome with Shanna McCullough, this one earned him a nomination for "Best Supporting Actor" from the XRCO.

No Way In (1988) Courtesy of a chastity belt. With Barbie Dahl and Amanda Tyler.

Nudes at II (1986) Jerry offers a hilarious parody of Andy Rooney. With Jeannie Pepper.

Nymphette (1986) In a threesome with Paula Harlow and Careena Collins, which was shot immediately following a scene in which Careena was left hurt and bleeding after an anal encounter with Ron Jeremy.

Once Upon a Secretary (1982) An early film shot in New York with Samatha Fox, Veronica Hart, and Kelly Nichols.

One Night in Bancock (1985) A steamy sauna threesome with Marine M.P.s Tish Ambrose and Tess Ferre.

Only The Best (1986) Compilation tape featuring an excerpt from *Peeping Tom.*

Pandora's Mirror (1981) Another early film with Veronica Hart, Kandi Barbour, and Merle Michaels.

Panty Raid (1983) Plays a lovelorn young man vacationing in Hawaii. Raven, Ashley Britton, and Lois Ayres help ease the pain, among other things.

Passionate Lee (1985) As a teenager cooking with Sharon Mitchell in the kitchen.

Passion Chain (1987) Married to Brazilian Elle Rio, throughout the tape he translates her Portuguese into English. Jerry also reduced Nina Hartley to Jello in their sofa scene.

Peeping Tom (1986) Plays the voyeuristic president of a multi-million-dollar investment firm. Costars Kimberly Carson, Tracey Adams, Nina Hartley, and Sheri St. Claire.

Piggy's (1983) In this takeoff of *Porky's*, Jerry plays yet another horny high schooler.

Pink Lagoon (1984) Sequel to *Surrender in Paradise.* As Lucky Arthur, he's rescued by five lovelies, including Raven, Lois Ayres, and Ginger Lynn.

Play Me Again, Vanessa (1986) A compliation tape with Vanessa Del Rio, Jerry's favorite Thanksgiving Day float.

Playpen (1987) His scene with Sheri St. Claire in a prison's visiting room earned him another XRCO nomination, this time for "Best Sex Scene."

Pleasure Channel (1984) With Brooke Fields, Laurie Smith, and Long Jeanne Silver.

Pleasure Maze (1986) Along with Joey Silvera, he has the hard job of testing out android hookers in this sci-fi flick. With Stacey Donovan and Amber Lynn.

Port Holes (1988) *Thar she blows!* A nautical Buck Adams directorial effort with the spurtingly lovely Fallon (a.k.a. Lori Peacock), Kathleen Jentry, and Cherry Hill.

Preppies (1983) Another R-rated Chuck Vincent effort. No explicit sex in this one, but Jerry gets to drive an Excalibur. Listed as "Paul Stuart" in the credits.

Pussycat Galore (1984) As a cowboy to Anette Heinz's hooker, she seems delighted with what she finds in his briefs.

Rambo-Ohh (1988) With Tracey Adams.

Rated Sex (1986) Fun with Kari Fox in a threesome and with Alex Greco in an elevator groupie.

Raw Talent (1984) In this closely autobiographical tale, Jerry is Eddie, an aspiring actor from Brooklyn who starts making pornos when he can't get other acting jobs. His costars: the infamous turkey carcass!, Lisa DeLeeuw, Cassandra Leigh, Tish Ambrose, and Rhonda Jo Petty.

Raw Talent II (1986) This follow-up to the original still has Eddie struggling to be a "legit" actor and earned him a "Best Actor" nomination from *Adult Video News.* With Cassandra Leigh, Sheena Horne, Aida, and an eye-popping scene with Tasha Voux.

Raw Talent III (1988) Jerry snuck off to shoot this in New York *after* he and Lisa were married. It almost ended their marriage . . . yet Eddie lives on. With Siobhan Hunter, Ona Zee, and three black women on the IRT.

Rears (1986) As Bernie the barfly, he shares a threesome with Eric Edwards and Brittany Stryker.

Red Hot Pepper (1986) With red hot Jeannie Pepper.

Return to Alpha Blue (1984) With Chelsea Blake,Taija Rae, and Sharon Kane.

Rockey X (1986) This *Rocky* takeoff pits Jerry, as Rockey, against bad guy Buck Adams. Melissa Melendez is Rockey's adoring wife.

Rockey X: The Final Round (1988) Another Buck Adams fight-to-the-finish, with his sister Amber Lynn and wife Janette Littledove. There's a surprising antidrug message at the end by Jerry and Buck.

Rock Hard (1985) Plays an amorous agent to Tajia Rae's singing and schtupping Adonna.

Romeo and Juliet (1987) Jerry steals the show with his madcap portrayal of a narcissistic actor. It earned him a "Best Sex Scene" nomination with Megan Leigh, Keisha, and Alicia Monet from *Adult Video News.*

Roommates (1982) Another Chuck Vincent masterpiece. As a gay aspiring actor, Jerry has only one romantic love scene, with Veronica Hart, but it's a substantial role and an impressive acting job.

Rub Down (1985) With Amber Lynn and Bunny Bleu.

Ruthless Women (1988) As a ruthless rogue with Brandiwine and Brittany Morgan, also in drag and in bed with a shocked Billy Dee.

Satin Dolls (a.k.a. Supermodels Do L.A.) (1985) Jerry's the head of a cosmetics firm in this one. Costarring Cyndee Summers and Bunny Bleu.

Scenes They Wouldn't Let Me Shoot (1983) Jerry participates in a groupie with Honey Wilder.

Sex F/X (1986) With Danielle, Summer Rose, and Robin Cannes.

Sex in Dangerous Places (1988) Some risky locales include an elevator, a beauty shop, and a public restroom. With Barbara Dare and the gorgeous subway shuffle with newcomer Lynn LeMay. Look for Cathy Tavel as a non-sex patron of the beauty shop.

Sex Life of a Nerd (a.k.a. Lucky In Love) (1986) Shows "nerdy" Harry Reems the ropes on how to pick up Nina Hartley and Tracey Adams. Two-fisted fun in a cock-tail lounge.

Sex Life of a Porn Star (1985) As a porno booking agent, he tests out Lili Marlene. There's a realistic gem of a scene with Nina Hartley as a bruised, coked-up actress with a bad reputation, begging her former agent for work.

Sex Spa U.S.A. (1984) Shot in New York City, Jerry takes on Brooke Fields in her office and shares Honey Wilder with Joey Silvera in a sex-spa threesome.

Sexual Odyssey (1985) With Amber Lynn (in a hideous blonde wig), Rachel Ashley, Karen Summer, and a strained three-some with Nikki Charm and Mai Lin.

Sexy Delights II (1987) Interrupting a bi-fling between Krista Lane and Stacey de Lavana, they all join forces. Also in a group scene.

Shack Up (1985) Another bout with Amber Lynn, Rachel Ashley, and Karen Summer.

She Comes in Colors (1986) F. J. Lincoln's impressive effort with Sharon Mitchell, Elle Rio, and the not-to-be-missed body painting scene.

She's So Fine (1985) To date, this is director Henri Pachard's personal favorite. Not only does it have wall-to-wall sex, but plenty of heart. With Sharon Mitchell (in a bizarre screamer), Sharon Kane, and Taija Rae.

Silk, Satin and Sex (1983) His scene with Vanessa Del Rio won the "Best Sex Scene" award from CAFA (an East Coast critics organization).

Sinners, Three-Part Series (1988) Shot in 1984, this three-part Cecil Howard epic was released in 1988. As a member of the nastiest clan the porn side of "Dynasty," Jerry takes part in a slick, professional production. With Sharon Mitchell, Laurie Smith, Tasha Voux, Kim Carson, and others.

Sinset Boulevard (1987) A clip from a previous Western Visuals release with Rachel Ryan.

Sleazy Rider (1988) A suburban couple versus the bikers next door. With Taija Rae, Fallon, and Gina B.

Snake Eyes (1985) A Cecil Howard masterpiece with Jerry playing Laurie Smith's troubled, philandering husband. Among his real and fantasy conquests are Rikki Harte, Sharon Mitchell on a motorcycle, and Cassandra Leigh. Look for that "double shot" with Laurie.

Snake Eyes 2 (1987) Separated from Laurie in the sequel, Jerry tries to sort out his feelings with psychiatrist Sharon Mitchell. Among his fantasies: an upside-down encounter with double-jointed Tasha Voux.

Space Virgins (1984) As a hillbilly, he shares a schtup with "sister" Kimberly Carson and tangles with sexy outer space aliens Sharon Mitchell and Amber Lynn.

The Sperminator (1985) With Rachel Ashley, Honey Wilder, and Crystal Breeze.

Spoiled (1987) In this one he plays Taija's confused and broke suitor. Also, hot telphone sex with Shanna McCullough.

Star Angel (1986) Another superb Cecil Howard/Anne Randall effort. Jerry plays a murderous rock promoter. With Tigr, Angel, and Colleen Brennan.

Star Gazers (1986) A pleasant little flick with Mikki Davidson, Lorrie Lovett, and Bambi Allen.

Starved of Affection (1985) With Joanna Storm and Nikki Charm.

Strange Bedfellows (1986) As "Genius," a scientist who acts like Jerry Lewis and talks like Liberace, Jerry finds Sahara's G-spot. Wearing thick glasses and with his hair combed straight up, he looks and acts bizarre. He disrupts an orgy attended by Kimberly Carson, Ami Rogers, and the others.

St. X-Where (1986) In this takeoff of TV's "St. Elsewhere," he proves to be very handy with rubber gloves. With Danielle, Porsche Lynn, and Nikki Randall.

Surf, Sand and Sex (1986) With Barbara Dare, Nina Hartley, and Sharon Mitchell.

Superstars of Porno (1988) Nothing new in yet another compilation tape, boasting scenes with Amber Lynn, Kay Parker, and Taija Rae.

Surrender in Paradise (1984) In this prelude to *Pink Lagoon,* Jerry plays Arthur, who's hiding out on a deserted island but is discovered by Ginger, Crystal Holland, Rene Tiffany, and others.

Sweat (1986) In the opening scene with Amber Lynn, Jerry lives up to the title of this Anthony Spinelli work.

Swedish Erotica #61 (1985) Hilarious as a man who ships himself cross-country. With Sheri St. Claire, Mindy Rae, and Tess Ferre.

Swedish Erotica #62 (1986) With Little Oral Annie, Ami Rogers, and Patti Petite.

Sweet Spurt of Youth (1988) Another Paul Thomas directorial effort.

T & A Team (1984) With Carol Cross, Rene Summers, and Joanna Storm.

Taboo III (1985) He embarks on an incestuous relationship with "mom" Kay Parker.

Taste of Cherry (1985) With Tish Ambrose and Beverly Glenn.

10½ Weeks (1986) Inspired by the film and book *9½ Weeks.* Barbara Dare is the object of Jerry's obsession. Also with Nikki Knights, Siobhan Hunter, and a simulated "cornholing."

Three Men and a Barbie (1988) An outdoor fling atop a

grounded sailboat with a pretty Sophia Loren look-alike newcomer.

"330" (1984) Jerry appears on a Los Angeles talk show hosted by Chuck Henry. With Seka and Kay Parker.

The Thrill of It (1986) Taking liberties with *The Big Chill* plot, Jerry heats things up with screen-wife Patti Petite and Danielle.

Throat 12 Years After (1984) Costars with Sharon Kane, Sharon Mitchell, and Joanna Storm in this Damiano flick.

Tight and Tender (1985) With Gina Carrera and Sheri St. Claire.

Traci's Big Trick (1986) The movie set where Lisa and Jerry met.

Traci Who? (1986) AVC compilation tape.

Twentysomething 1: Alicia Monet Reporting (1988) As an ace TV reporter. With Alicia Monet and Siobhan Hunter.

Twentysomething 2: The Art Lovers (1988) The sexsaga continues.

Unnatural Act II (1986) With Nina Hartley, Keli Richards, and Erica Boyer.

Unnatural Phenomenon I (1986) With Danielle, Careena Collins, and Gayle Sterling.

Up, Up and Away (1985) With the "All American Girls," Cody Nicole, Laurie Smith, Ginger Lynn, etc.

Vanessa, Maid in Manhattan (1985) Plays another shy guy behind tortoise-shell glasses, but he conquers his bashfulness with the family maid (Vanessa Del Rio) and Brooke Fields.

Visions of Jeannie (1986) With Nikki Charm, Tracey Adams, and Nina Hartley in a smoking encounter where he literally snips the clothes from Nina's body.

Vixana's Revenge (1985) With Lana Burner, Ali Moore, and Jessica Longe.

Vixens in Heat (1985) As a photographer, he snaps away at Rene Tiffany. Later, at a party, Amber Lynn leads him around like a doggie, with a belt around his neck.

Viva Vanessa (1985) The scene with Jerry, David Scott, and Vanessa Del Rio brings to mind Jerry's recollection about the off-set threesome he arranged with his friend and the lovely Latin.

Wet Dreams 2001 (1987) As a twenty-first century sex outlaw, with Sharon Mitchell and Danielle.

Wet, Wild and Wicked (1985) Clad in plumber's togs, Jerry reluctantly unclogs Tantala's pipes.

Wet, Wild and Wonderful (1979) Jerry's first porno movie. With Kandi Barbour.

What Are Friends For? (1985) In this wife-swapping story, Jerry trades Tamara Longley for Sheri St. Claire and has a difficult time on a staircase with Jeannie Pepper.

Whose Fantasy Is This Anyway? (1984) With Sharon Kane, Honey Wilder, and Annette Heinz.

Wild Brat (1988) As a rough and tough motorcycle gang leader with lace-pantied Jamie Summers.

Wild in the Streets (1986) At a Copperwear Party with Shanna McCullough and Gina Carrera.

Wild Nurses in Lust (1986) This madcap story of interns and nurses at a boarding house sets Jerry up with buxom older lady Helga, Bunny Bleu, and Kimberly Carson. Jerry makes a sexy woman when he attends the Halloween party in drag.

With Love, Littledove (1988) Because of the similar cast, this was probably shot at the same time as *The Amorous Adventures of Janette Littledove.*

Women at Play (1984) Danielle, Tigr, Cara Lott, and Sharon Mitchell take a break to play with Jerry.

WPINK TV, PART 2 (1985) Another nutty role played with much abandon, when, as a TV show host, Jerry is blown on the air by Bunny Bleu as she hums "Old MacDonald."

Xstasy (1985) Married to Shanna McCullough in this one, Jerry proposes a threesome with Nina Hartley and eventually loses his once-innocent wife. All alone at the end, his character remarks, "Some fantasies are better kept to yourself. . . . Now I don't have any hopes."

Special Acknowledgments

Raw Talent wouldn't be possible without the help of many people. During the course of the creative process, we contacted a number of individuals, magazines, and video companies we thought could assist us by supplying photos. Some helped, and some didn't. The ones who didn't know who they are. The ones who did took time out of their hectic schedules, fished through piles of chromes, and offered us invaluable advice. Their only compensation is the knowledge that they're good souls and pitched in to enhance the visual aspect of this book.

Many thanks to:

Al Bloom and Liza Skeeter of Caballero Control Corporation
Tim Connelly of *Adam Film World*
Erica Eaton of *Exposed Magazines*
Cecil Howard and Anne Randall of Command Video
Tony Lovett of VCA Pictures
Bill Margold
Richard Pacheco (despite his reservations)

Ann Rhine and Cheryl Leigh of Cal Vista Directs
Candida Royalle and Viv Forlander of Femme Productions
Solomon and Shirley Siederman (for sharing family photos)
Allen Tavel (for sharing in the madness)
Paul Thomas
Chuck Vincent and Marco Nero of Platinum Pictures Inc.
Steven Vlottes of Dreamland Entertainment

Jerry Butler
Bob Rimmer
Cathy Tavel
and Prometheus Books